The Human Side of Homicide

THE HUMAN SIDE OF HOMICIDE

*Bruce L. Danto, John Bruhns,
and Austin H. Kutscher
Editors*

WITH THE EDITORIAL ASSISTANCE OF
Lillian G. Kutscher

NEW YORK
COLUMBIA UNIVERSITY PRESS
1982

Library of Congress Cataloging in Publication Data

Main entry under title:

The Human side of homicide.

Includes bibliographies and index.
1. Homicide—United States—Addresses, essays, lectures. I. Danto, Bruce L.
II. Bruhns, John. III. Kutscher, Austin H.
[DNLM: 1. Homicide. HV 6499 H918]
HV6529.H85   364.1′523   81-21617
ISBN 0-231-04964-1   AACR2

Columbia University Press
New York   Guildford, Surrey

CONTENTS

◇

PART III. LAW AND JUSTICE

PREFACE
A Thanatologic Overview of Homicide

Austin H. Kutscher

<>

Thanatology is a discipline whose focus is on the art of enhancing humanitarian caregiving for patients who are critically ill or dying, with equal concern exhibited for the wellbeing of their family members. From a base in thanatology, interdisciplinary professionals are dedicated to promoting vastly improved psychosocial and medical care for these patients and assistance for their families. Proposed is a philosophy of caregiving that reinforces alternative ways of supporting positive qualities in the dying patient's life and that introduces methods of intervention on behalf of the emotional support of his family members and bereaved survivors.

In the course of reasonable expectations, the experiences of chronic or life-threatening illnesses are common ones shared by most people. But this pattern disintegrates when an act of homicide produces a dead victim, as distinguished from a patient with a negative clinical prognosis. Whereas therapeutic measures can be utilized to extend a patient's life, nothing can be done for the victim.

The capacity of humans to destroy each other has been documented over and over again since Cain commited his act of fratricide. Although man views the fatal gesture with abhorrence, still it persists. Brother kills brother; spouse kills spouse; neighbor kills neighbor; stranger kills stranger; the assaultive hand is turned even against the self. Homicide is sometimes justified as an act of defense yet condemned as an act of offense. To examine its every dimension, as the physician examines a disease state—from its symptoms, the pathology of tissues, to the therapeutic modalities for cure, palliation, or caregiving—challenges our humanistic sensibilities and the totality of our intellectual sophistication. The discrete categorization of individuals in our society according to age, sex or economic status does not provide immunity for the victims of homicide or restraint for the perpetrators.

Two basic questions beg to be answered in analyzing homicide: Why does one individual strike out against another or against himself—to kill with or without a cause, with or without control? How does society respond to this kind of ending to a life?

Definitive answers are elusive. Homicide victims, homicide perpetrators, and those who suicide are characters in true dramas that demonstrate the destructive capacity of man. If we could turn the research techniques of science to a thanatologic probing of homicide, perhaps the findings would offer mutually illuminating revelations. It becomes evident that the dimensions of the homicidal act must be measured by many instruments—the psychotherapeutic techniques of medicine and psychology, the pragmatic guidelines of police action, the thoughtful speculations of a legal system where guilt must be established beyond any reasonable doubt, the decisive scales that weigh justice, and the moral and ethical evaluations of what it really means to take a life and whether any circumstances (including capital punishment, war, or incurable illness) make such an act justifiable, condonable, and humanitarian.

Thus, it appears appropriate to establish an interdisciplinary base for exploring the phenomena of homicidal behavior. The results of data-supported investigations and the sharing of anecdotal experiences offer insights into the etiology of homicidal pathology. Inherent in the challenge to society is the demand for control of the destructive and support of the positive and nurturing aspects of human behavior. Beyond the task of preventing a homicide is the further task of intervening on behalf of all survivors. While enduring the emotional loss, they seek guidelines for living in a violent world. Where can they find such help?

In the past, thanatology's impact has been on improving the care given terminally ill patients and their family members. If individuals under these circumstances are denied their sense of personhood, humane caregivers can attempt to restore it. This concept has gained acceptance during the past two decades. Critically ill patients and bereaved survivors are offered support by many of the disciplines involved in our health care systems. Ex post facto, there can be no care for the homicide victim. Preventive care—an understanding of the behavioral patterns that lead to murder— may be one resource for the preservation of physical and emotional wellbeing among the survivors. When our laws fail to institute adequate preventive measures, other systems active within a free society must take over. Advancing our perceptions of man's inhumanity to man should bring us one step further toward protecting the dignity of the individual and preserving the fabric and wholeness of our civilization.

ACKNOWLEDGMENT

◇

The editors wish to acknowledge the support and encouragement of the Foundation of Thanatology in the preparation of this volume. All royalties from the sale of this book are assigned to the Foundation of Thanatology, a tax exempt, not for profit, public scientific and educational foundation.

Thanatology, a new subspecialty of medicine, is involved in scientific and humanistic inquiries and the application of the knowledge derived therefrom to the subjects of the psychological aspects of dying; reactions to loss, death, and grief; and recovery from bereavement.

The Foundation of Thanatology is dedicated to advancing the cause of enlightened health care for the terminally ill patient and his family. The Foundation's orientation is a positive one based on the philosophy of fostering a more mature acceptance and understanding of death and the problems of grief and the more effective and humane management and treatment of the dying patient and his bereaved family members.

The Human Side of Homicide

PART ONE

THE HUMAN SIDE OF HOMICIDE

1

A PSYCHIATRIC VIEW
OF THOSE WHO KILL

Bruce L. Danto

◇

This article reviews some of the known facts about homicide and killers and some of the research on the psychological aspects of murderers. However, before this material is presented, note should be taken of the fact that victims may also play a role in their homicide. Studies in Baltimore (Van Keuren 1977) and other places point out that in about 55 percent of all homicide cases the victim and killer knew one another, and the homicide often arose out of conflicts in their relationship. Lester and Lester (1975) point out that victims may be as strongly motivated to be killed as their killers are to kill. Viewed in this light a homicide may not be an isolated event; it may be an expression of an integral pattern of a relationship. An additional feature of the victim-precipitated homicide is the fact that in this type of homicide one can see a close relationship between suicide and murder. Certainly, if the victim seeks his own death, then his behavior toward the killer is provocative and clearly self-destructive.

In our efforts to understand the behavior of murderers, it is important to relate this behavior to aggression. Aggression, an expression or act of attack or hostility, may be defensive or offensive. The former serves the function of enhancing survival; the latter is destructive, unprovoked, and rooted in a person's character.

Aggression serves other purposes as well. For some, it relieves boredom, represents a mode of verbal communication, and can also provide a means for the nonverbal motor discharge of hostile feeling. Aggression develops last in the order of feelings, with love feelings developing first, fear of the world next at about three months of age and finally aggression at age one. For most people, when aggression assumes the form of violence, it provides the final solution to events connected with a conflictual relationship, imagined or real.

Violence and murder have always been prominent in people's minds, while today the news media, toymakers, television, and moviemakers exploit it. Classic tragedy established a tradition for the theater and literature. Even, or expecially, in opera, homicide provides excitement and suspense for the entertainment of the audience.

All societies and cultures seem to hold homicide as a value and preserve its various functions by attaching it to cultural practices. Some people do not accept homicide as a part of our life. They protest its existence and try to end its prevalance by moving to ban firearms, capital punishment, life imprisonment, hunting, and the eating of meat. Although common in all societies, these efforts represent ineffective approaches to control a type of behavior and social problem which has deeply rooted origins and feelings, and has not resulted from access to gadgets. An attempt is being made to stop a type of coping behavior which has been time-honored as a way for people to resolve conflicts, yet until we have a better grasp on what causes it and why some people chose to handle their problems and impulses by killing people, we shall find ourselves forever involved in an exercise of futility.

Surprisingly little has been written about the characteristics of murderers and their victims. Wille (1974), Lunde (1976), and Wolfgang (1958) have collected and analyzed some data. A summary of their information follows.

Characteristics of Murder

Murder occurs more frequently in the heavy business districts of large cities and in the low-grade residential areas around those business centers. The rate is higher during times of prosperity (except for lynchings, which occurred more commonly during the Depression). Henry and Short (1954) held this view and felt that this relationship to economic conditions supported the notion that suicide and homicide are ways people have of coping with frustration.

In his study of about 500 murderers Wolfgang (1958) observed that most murders occurred within a small population subgroup. A subculture of violence existed in this group; members reacted with violence to insults or slurs (even so-called trivial slights) and carried weapons in anticipation of violence or attacks. They were more likely to interpret daily neutral situations and challenges as threatening. Because weapons were carried, the use of force had the potential for producing serious injury or death. Those deviating from this value system were either ostracized from the subculture or became its victims.

Alcohol plays an important role in homicide whether it occurs in the subculture or the general murderer group. However, this does *not* mean that murderers are necessarily alcoholics. It *does* mean that judgment and control of aggression might be compromised when a person is drinking. Studies have revealed that persons arrested for most violent crimes, generally have, if they were drinking, a urine level of alcohol between .2 and .29 percent—about twice the level required to prove a drunk driving charge.

Results of Research About Murderers

1. Estimates report that from 25 to 67 percent of murderers have a childhood history of violence, that is, they either witnessed it or were victims of it.

2. Results of psychological tests, such as the Thematic Apperception Tests (TAT), show that murderers have less anger, less fear, less aggression, less awareness of the outcome of an event, and they are less inclined to see control as being due to chance, and more due to power. Surprisingly, there is no difference in the responses of psychotic and nonpsychotic murderers in these tests.

3. Murderers fantasize less about anger, fear, and aggression. It shows in their behavior. They do not express or show much feeling. It might be said that many murderers are emotionally inhibited.

4. Murderers have two distinct methods of coping with emotional tension: they either push back into the unconscious all elements of

intense thought or feeling (repression), or they display a behavioral set or expectancy in which they are ready to fight whenever they feel an inner sense of danger arising from their contact with others.

5. Murderers rarely verbalize feelings and, in general, maintain shallow or superficial interpersonal relationships.

6. Many male murderers struggle with deep, inner guilt feelings about sex; they see women as being dangerously seductive. Some attempt to deal with or relieve such sexual guilt feelings by killing a woman. Once she is dead, the killer does not have to feel guilty, have fear of her, or worry about being less powerful than she.

7. Most murderers are between 20 and 40 years of age; today, most are closer to 20.

8. A quarter of all murderers today are women; their victims are usually someone close. In order of greatest frequency, the victims are a husband, a lover, or an older child of the woman.

9. From a racial standpoint, a murderer is more likely to be black; ten times more black men than black women are murderers. The black female murder rate is five times higher than the murder rate of white females.

10. It has been observed that fewer than 30 percent of the victims are strangers to the murderer.

11. About 30 percent of all homicides are committed during the process of a felony.

12. Firearms are the chosen murder weapon of either the very young or old. In other cases, 20 percent use knives; for black murderers, the use of knives jumps to about 50 percent.

13. At least 50 percent of the time, the provocative incident which causes the murder is a quarrel, which has occurred within three days of the death.

14. The presence of a classic mental illness is rare among murderers at the time they kill. When present, psychosis occurs in about 7 percent of the cases. Dissociative reaction, a type of anxiety state in which the mind becomes explosively overwhelmed or flooded by anxiety, occurs in about 10 percent of the cases in which mental illness exists.

15. About 50 percent of all murders are premeditated. The killer is provoked by a disturbing event which causes him to lose self-esteem or feel less of a man: his wife has sex with another partner, a boss fires him from a job, a neighbor puts him down, and so forth.

16. About 70 percent of the murderers have defective super egos, that is, they have defective consciences. They are insensitive to the wrongness of violence, the importance of another person's life, and the importance of maintaining control and finding the right channels for expressing aggression. These factors are related to the murderer's lack of love and caring experiences.

17. About 13 percent of all murderers become psychotic after killing.

18. Most murderers kill on weekends. July and December are peak months for murders, which commonly occur between 8:00 P.M. and 2:00 A.M.

19. Murderers have higher rates of killing in certain parts of the United States. The South accounts for 31 percent of the population but 44 percent of all the murders committed in this country. The South is followed by the West, then the North Central States, with the lowest rate being in the Northeastern states.

20. Murderers chose men as their victims three times more often than they chose women. Of the men killed by their wives or girlfriends, alcohol has been imbibed by the killer in about 50 percent of the cases.

21. Of the victims, about 25 percent resemble the murderer in that they have a criminal record and are from the lower socioeconomic areas.

22. In terms of what happens after the murder, about two-thirds (66 percent) are in custody within 24 hours; if the murder is not solved within 48 hours, the chance of solving the crime and apprehending the murderer drops remarkably.

23. Following court trial and disposition, 60 percent of the murderers are convicted; the median time served by those convicted of first degree murder is 10.5 years, and for second degree murder, five years.

◇

Wille (1974) classified murderers into 10 different types. The first type he called the *depressive killer*. This murderer seldom has a criminal record and does not display antisocial behavior. He may commit suicide, murder, or murder-suicide. He feels that life is hopeless, and he wants to end the suffering of others. In this class of murderer, murder followed by suicide is very common.

The next type of murder has a psychotic disease, such as schizo-phrenic reaction, paranoid type. In this disorder, the murderer may be hearing voices that threaten to kill him or that tell him to kill in order to protect himself. He may feel he is aiding the Lord in a mission to rid the world of sin. He feels others are against him and may be following or plotting against him. He kills to prove some type of world or global idea—ridding the world of sin, or protecting himself from imagined enemies.

The third kind of murderer has some type of organic brain damage or condition that may be the result of head trauma caused by an auto accident, epilepsy, brain deterioration from senile brain disease, or from some type of hereditary organic disease which destroys normal brain function.

The fourth type of murderer has a psychopathic personality and displays a history of social maladjustment. He is nonfeeling and in-sensitive about the needs and rights of others, has a defective con-science and a callous and cynical outlook on the world. Despite his defective conscience, his behavior is confessional; he often leaves tell-tale evidence and clues to his homicidal act. From the standpoint of ego structure, he has a defective integrative function and does not seem to profit from experience, repeating the same basic mistakes in judgment and control.

The fifth type of murderer has a passive aggressive personality. His life history reveals countless instances in which he expressed great violence when a victim threatened to cut off or reject his dependency needs. A common example of this is seen when a murderer's wife cannot tolerate her marriage to this demanding and violent person and either files for divorce or threatens to do so. Instead of trying to get help to change his way of handling the relationship, he kills the person whom he drove away.

The alcoholic character makes up the sixth type of murderer. In this person, inner aggression is unleashed when the expression-en-hancing effect of alcohol is combined with its intoxicating effects (which act on the brain itself). Furthermore, brain damage from chronic alcoholism may occur and produce a rage which is seen with organic brain disease.

The seventh type of murderer has a hysterical personality—and is more likely to be a woman. She is more likely to threaten murder than actually commit it, yet such threats should not be taken lightly. Such persons do not bind anxiety well and may become flooded and overwhelmed by it; they may even appear to be psychotic. The usual diagnosis for such a mental state is *dissociative reaction*, a neurotic disorder which is frequently associated with amnesia about the murder.

The eighth type of murderer in Wille's classification is the child who is a killer. In New York, a two-year-old child killed another child by cutting, and in Finestere, France, a two-year old killed another child by bashing in his skull with a statue. Such child murderers use methods such as cutting, beating, pushing the victim from a height, drowning, and shooting. When a child is the murderer, his act may be precipitated by an intensification of rivalry in the family, feelings of rejection (resulting, for instance, from being placed in a foster home), some organic or medical problem that may make a child feel intensely inferior (such as growth problems, congenital anomalies, or low IQ), the existence of a learning disorder, or exposure to parental violence with an unconscious identification with it.

On the other hand, Bender (1959) found that children who kill are very impulsive, and all but 3 out of 33 children studied were suffering from schizophrenia, brain disease, or epilepsy. In their background, antecedent events like contact with violent death within the family or close neighborhood residents, pyromania, unfavorable home conditions, learning disorders, or retardation existed.

Suggesting a different factor was Sargent (1962), who found that the child who kills is a person who acts as an agent for an adult, almost as if he acts out the lethal wish of that adult. He may have felt hostility toward the victim but would not have acted on it in a lethal manner without unconscious prompting by the involved adult. When this happens, the murdering child is surprised that the victim is dead, as he really did not mean to kill him.

The ninth type of murderer might be a mentally retarded person. Murder by such persons is rare; but when they do kill, often it is to cover up some abnormal sexual contact they have had with a child. Mass murder by this type of killer is unheard of.

Finally, the tenth type of killer is known as a sex killer. He gains some type of sexual excitement from the act of killing, which may involve mutilation of the body before or after death of the victim.

Intercourse as well as acts of cannibalism may be involved—i.e., eating the flesh of the victim or drinking his blood. This type of person is usually psychotic and is not usually a rapist. Sometimes he kills a woman in order to relieve sexual jealousy or to deprive another man; the murder can be also a vehicle to reach the man. He may express latent homosexual impulses by being more concerned about the man's action than the woman's.

Murder by minor sexual offenders, such as window peepers and exhibitionists, is rare. Rare also is murder by one suffering from necrophilia. The necrophilic person is sexually attracted by the putrefactive stench and the coldness of the cadaver.

The adult who kills a child has become a more common type of murderer and constitutes a special area of interest for the Oakland County Child Murders Task Force. What is known about such killers merits examination. Kaplund and Reich (1976) studied 112 cases of child homicide in New York in 1968–69. They found that the victims were predominantly boys and were under five years of age. Two-thirds of the victims were born out of wedlock. The assailants were primarily the mothers. Paramours rarely murdered their own children but did kill the children of their predecessors. The assailants displayed histories of prehomicidal deviant behavior in terms of alcoholism, drug abuse, and criminal behavior. Severe mental illness and suicide attempts were rare. They murdered by means of kicking and beating, primarily, and such behavior was consistent with impulsive and explosive rage rather than with premeditation.

Resnick (1969) studied parents who kill their children. About 30 percent of the victims were under six months of age, which led him to conclude that the homicidal parents were women who suffered either a post partum depression or psychosis after delivery. If the children were older, it was found that their parental killers perceived them as being defective for some reason, real or imagined. Although the victims were evenly divided between the sexes, there were twice as many mothers who killed as fathers, a wider range in age, from 20–50 years, in contrast to men who fell between 25–35 years, and about 60 percent of all murdering parents were psychotic by psychiatric diagnosis. As a method of murder, fathers used striking, squeezing, and stabbing; mothers used drowning, suffocation, and gassing.

He felt they killed for specific reasons. *Altruistic Filicide* occurred when the parent wanted to spare the child from suffering from a real or imagined condition or from abandonment when the parent committed suicide. This was consistent with observations made by D. J. West (1966). The next type of filicide was *Unwanted Child*. In this type, the parent wanted to eliminate a child who was either illegitimate, a product of an extramarital affair, or was viewed by the parent as being in the way of some future aspiration. In *Spouse Revenge Filicide* the child was killed to deprive the spouse and cause suffering through the loss of a favorite child. *Accidental Filicide* is an inevitable consequence of a battered child syndrome. Frequently, it occurs as a result of intense rage when physical discipline is being administered. The final type he classified was *Acutely Psychotic Filicide*, one in which the parent is severely mentally disturbed. Running throughout all of these parent murders of children is a common denominator— anger and rage directed toward a child who is an object upon which anger felt toward the murderer's parents, spouse, or sibling has been displaced.

Among murderers who kill children none seem to be more feared than sexual molesters of children who are strangers to them. In my experience, child molesters rarely kill. In fact, they show violence toward their child victims in less than 3 percent of all reported molestings. However, the murder of a molested child generates tremendous anxiety in the community. The molester who kills is a person whose homicidal direction involves some interesting background. Many who become psychotic and subsequently kill are individuals who have been reared in a home atmosphere in which they have been a victim of homosexual assault by their fathers. Frequently, they commit a burglary before they abduct, molest, and kill a child. Not infrequently, they harbor deep resentment toward children because of sibling rivalry and competitive resentment they felt toward a sister or brother. In other cases, they kill a child as a way of striking back at the adult world. In this way, they deprive another parent, who represents a transference object, of a child to satisfy resentment they felt for being deprived of parents. Thus, the unconscious target is one or more parents who are survivor victims of homicide.

Guttmacher (1973) studied 175 murderers and classified them in terms of psychiatric diagnoses. Forty percent of his group suffered from a psychosis involving a number of serious conditions or illnesses that impaired mental functioning to the degree that the person could not handle the ordinary demands of daily living. Although paranoid schizophrenia is the most common of these diagnoses, mental patients, on the whole, have no greater incidence of homicidal behavior than the general population. Guttmacher's classification was not based on sane vs. insane. Rather, he attempted to classify murderers by psychiatric diagnosis so that he could apply psychological theory to explain their murderous behavior and see if treatment was possible. One-third of his group of psychotic patients had been hospitalized in the past because of their psychoses.

Guttmacher utilized psychoanalytic theory to develop a classification system based on psychodynamic concepts rather than the traditional descriptive psychiatric diagnoses with which he had initiated his studies. He concluded that the average murderer was free of any prominent psychopathology or mental illness, but has not identified with parental social values and conscience, and for that reason has a defective conscience. He comes from a socially disadvantaged family and, as a child, experienced emotional deprivation or inadequate nurturing. Such experiences cause the killer to fail to appreciate the deprivation caused when he kills. His own experience of deprivation causes him extreme frustration, and this can lead to murder.

Guttmacher's second type of murderer is sociopathic. His background involves a physically abusive father who was rejecting to a seductive, hysterical mother. Parental marital disharmony is usually found. The experience of childhood cruelty from his father makes the murderer behave cruelly toward others as an adult in order to achieve the feeling of revenge. His childhood cruelty to animals points to his future unconscionable violent aggression toward others as an adult. His adolescent history reveals delinquency, truancy, and running away from home. As he grows into adulthood, he will have a history of criminal offenses.

The alcoholic murderer according to Guttmacher is one who, when sober, is able to control his aggressive feelings. However, alcohol unleashes his violent aggression as controls are either removed or dangerously compromised. Prior to his act of murder, he has lost sexual potency, employment, or chances for advancement because of his drinking; and he imagines that he is losing his wife or love interest to another, worthier, man. Convinced of his woman's infidelity, his jealousy becomes pathological. While intoxicated, he kills her.

Guttmacher's next type is called the avenging murderer. This person kills in response to the sudden withdrawal of sexual interest by a spouse or lover. The relationship with the victim has been ambivalent. When sex is withdrawn, the hatred grows to the point that the killer directs his aggression to the destruction of the love object.

Guttmacher described the schizophrenic murder and the sadistic murderer. The schizophrenic murderer kills his victims in accordance with his paranoid delusions and hallucinations. The sadistic murderer kills to achieve sexual pleasure and chooses victims with specific occupations or qualities (prostitutes, teachers, elderly women, children, or those who are chronically ill). He sees his victims as being objects for his pleasure—not as fellow human beings. His pleasure may come from abusing, mutilating, or killing his victims. He has been a loner and unable to break strong emotional ties to his mother. His daydreams and fantasies are rich and ever-flowing; usually, there have been no normal sexual experiences. For the sadistic murderer, there is no history of identified mental illness.

According to Lunde, (1976) there is a difference between a mass murderer and a serial murderer. The mass murderer is almost always psychotic from a legal standpoint (legally insane). He kills a number of victims in a single episode and chooses victims he does not know well. However, they may have symbolic significance to him.

The serial murderer, on the other hand, kills one person at a time over a long period of time. He may know the victim quite well, or at least know a particular type of victim he is seeking (spouse, child, certain type of worker, blonde-haired person, etc.). Lunde considered the serial murderer to be one who might know his victim and does not have a history of diagnosed mental illness.

I would add to this discussion that the serial murderer usually has an obsessive-compulsive pattern to his killing; he needs to repeat the style and pattern of killing, as well as his choice of victim. His homicidal behavior is repetitive and frequently tells a story of his conflicts. For example, in the Oakland County (Michigan) child killings, the murderer selected children in the same age range, sodomized the boys and forced the girls into oral sexual acts, was gentle in his method of killing, washed the bodies and dressed the victims, and always left the body where it was sure to be found. He acted out a story in which he replaced the natural parents of the child he abducted, committed a sexually perverse act on the child, then murdered him or her; in so doing, he showed the parents how poorly they protected their child and how great their loss could be. The parents are his victims. He kills children to avenge some childhood hurt induced by his own parents toward whom he is now venting angry feelings. He checks on the parental loss by attending the child's funeral or following it on television. We know this because he dropped a funeral visitor's card where the body of the first murdered child was found.

Tanay (1976) offers other observations about murderers, and sees three types. When a person kills against his conscious wishes and the murder is carried out during an altered state of consciousness, it is *ego dystonic* murder. When this occurs, part of the psychic structure is split off from the rest of the personality. This process, called dissociation, may be induced by psychological, physiological, or pharmacological factors. A second type of murderer, one remarkably less common, he calls *ego syntonic*. In this type of murder, the killer deliberately chooses homicide as his method of coping with the important psychological issue. He accepts violence as a method of resolving conflict. Finally, the third type of murderer Tanay calls *psychotic*; his description is consistent with what Guttmacher and Lunde described as murder by a schizophrenic person.

Tanay's approach to murder focuses on ego states or impairment of the rational part of the mind and on the act itself, and does not deal with other personality features of either the murderer, the significance of his victim, or the social forces which might produce the murder.

Abrahamsen (1973) observed that murderers have certain psychological characteristics. They cannot spell correctly and do so by the way the word sounds. They display deep feelings of revenge and fantasize grandiose accomplishments. They feel extreme loneliness, withdrawal, distress, helplessness, fears, loss of self-esteem, and feelings of insignificance. As children, they were sexually overstimulated because they witnessed parental intercourse or slept with parents. They reflect a blurred self-image and are suggestible and impressionable. They cannot handle frustration or withstand it; this causes a need to release hostility. They are powerless to change their self-centeredness into healthy ideals and conscience. Because of this impairment, they fall into dependency states and develop a contempt for authority. They display suicidal tendencies with depression and see the victim as a composite image of themselves. There is also a history of antisocial behavior and threats of violence.

Both Tanay and Abrahamsen feel that the murderer is a particular type of person, with each type having certain well-defined character-istics; neither examines the role of the victim or the social forces that have acted on the killer. There is no room for interaction between killer and victim in such theories, and no vehicle for explaining the different motives and needs of murderers, as well as the dramas their murderous behavior reveals. Furthermore, Dr. Abrahamsen sees mis-spelling as being important, whereas most observers of criminals in general would agree that factors such as sound educational achieve-ment is sorely lacking in their backgrounds, and would not set mur-derers apart from other criminals.

There have been efforts to correlate electroencephalogram (e.e.g.) findings and psychiatric conditions or criminal activities like homicide. The most widely discussed finding on e.e.g. has been the 6–14 per second positive spike pattern in the temporal area. Gibbs feels this is a correlate of thalamic and hypothalamic epilepsy, one found in ad-olescents during sleep. When such cases have been reviewed it has been shown that psychodyanamic factors were responsible for the crimes, not organic factors. Any other than coincidental factor rela-tionship between e.e.g. finding and psychiatric condition as it relates to criminal behavior or homicide is either purely statistical or infer-ential and is not consistent with a real causal relationship (Lester and Lester, 1975).

Kutash et al. (1978) discussed results of psychological tests and con-cluded that information from them has been less than significant, as the results have not been correlated with clinical data. This has been especially true for studies of Rorschach responses by murderers. The latter test had been used to study movement responses, color shading responses, external restraints, body, family murder, murderers in com-parison to suicides, and prediction of murder.

Kahn (1967) studied Rorschach responses by murderers in terms of reality testing. These responses correlated to findings of legal insanity as determined by forensic specialists. However, it threw no more light on the murderer as a person or phenomenon than did studies on intelligence factors (Deiker, 1973).

Some studies have linked clinical material along with raw data from the protocols (Resnick, 1969). In this way better insight is available regarding the psychodynamics of the murderer. In the study by Satten et al. (1960) ten murderers displayed impairment in dealing with color. This means that patients studied expressed their trouble in making clearcut boundaries between fantasy and reality. In their responses to the TAT, there was striking evidence of primitive and murderous hostility even though their stories were brief and constricted. Tested murderers rationalized murder in their themes on the basis that the killer had been provoked into it. As they related their stories and responses, there was little accompanying affect. Significantly, although those patients tested denied conscious fantasy of homicide or ideas of murder, such material was clearly seen on their responses to test items and stimuli.

In a similar study, Miller and Looney (1974) studied murderers who seem to dehumanize others. Their findings indicate that such killers fail to see people as humans. They had trouble seeing if the figure was alive or dead in the TAT drawings. They failed to demonstrate an awareness of either life or death or that people are seen as being immortal and godlike and incapable of being dead.

Kutash et al. (1978) revealed that for the catathymic type killer, one who suddenly experiences an overwhelming intense type of emotional reaction like rage, the F column is tall and brittle on Rorschach responses. This result means that there is little intrapsychic or emotional stimulation. For this person there is a rigid ego which is prone to sudden disintegration under meaningful or significant stress. This sudden breakdown is seen in many murders where there is psychosis or significant psychopathology, schizophrenic reaction, or a schizo-affective or paranoid type.

These writers (Kutash et al., 1978) feel secure in the knowledge that the Rorschach test offers the psychological investigator the opportunity to record such responses of aggressive feeling as killing, explosions, blood, death, or fighting. "Integration of specific content with the specific stimulus pull of the various cards further clarifies the in-depth conflicts. Both the ability to empathize and the press of primitive impulses are extremely relevant findings brought out with clarity by the Rorschach." Despite the absolute merit of this test, it does not reveal the significant surface factors or psychodynamics. The latter information can be obtained from the TAT or Blackie Test. Among tests they found to be of little value were the MMPI and other personality inventory type tests. However, they felt figure drawings tests were often helpful. Kutash and his group cautioned that all psychological tests are beneficial to throw light on why people kill providing that the test results are integrated with the psychopathology of the crime.

Another way of classifying murderers was provided by Miller and Looney (1974). As a base for their system, they focused on the degree to which the killer dehumanizes his victim. They divided homicides into (1) high risk with total and permanent victim dehumanization, (2) high risk with partial and transient dehumanization, and (3) low risk with transient and partial dehumanization. Although this system could not be applied to forensic diagnostic problems, it could offer a judge psychological factors and issues in regard to pre-sentence psychiatric evaluations. It does offer a view of the killer in terms of how he sees his victim and how he relates to that victim. Over the years as a police officer and psychiatrist who regularly faces dangerous and violent persons, I can attest to the importance of looking for clinical signs in a person who gives me the feeling I am being dehumanized. I look for blank expressions, gazes which pass through or at me as if I were a lamp or wall or clear glass window pane. If that appearance is accompanied by little or no affect and an ice-cold emotional remoteness, then I know I am either in trouble or must exercise great caution and care not to act provocatively or in any threatening manner.

Revitch (1975, 1977) has developed a classification system which is easy to follow and quite helpful. He saw *Environmentally Stimulated Homicides* as resulting from social pressures and a weakening of authority and social controls. Examples of these in terms of military events like the massacres in Vietnam and strife in Iran and other Middle Eastern countries appear daily in the newspapers. Under social disintegration of this order, violence flourishes on a broad social basis.

Similarly, when violence constantly occurs on the streets, values about the importance of a life diminish and the aged and others who are otherwise helpless become targets on a broad scale.

Revitch defines as *Situational Homicides* those which occur in a stressful situation or relationship. They may occur impulsively or with premeditation and may be adaptive or maladaptive. They may even serve a logical purpose. Usually, interactional conflicts are involved in this type of homicide.

Impulsive Homicides are defined by Revitch as those which involve poor impulse control, possibly a multiplicity of antisocial acts; they can also involve homicides that are diffuse, poorly structured, and are either premeditated or unpremeditated. The offenders display a life-style which is unstructured and lacking in direction and predictability. Psychologically, they show looseness of personality integration. Certainly Richard Speck, who murdered several nurses in Chicago, is an excellent example of this type of killer.

Under *Catathymic Homicides* Revitch and others included those killers who kill under the influence or stimulation of ideas that are charged with intense feelings based on a strong wish, fear, or ambivalent striving. One example of this type of psychiatric state is schizophrenic reaction, schizoaffective type. Some hysterical personalities would fall into this category as well.

Another interesting feature associated with killers, according to psychiatrist Irwin Finkelstein (in a personal conversation) is that many of them act out a rescuer fantasy before the homicide. A girl who knew a boy who killed a rabbi right after morning Sabbath services reported that the killer had been firing into a couch in her apartment the night before. At that time he told her and others of his plan to kill the rabbi. No one stopped him or heard his pleas for control to be brought in from some outside resource. In another case in which I was involved a very disturbed man, when angry, would blow up appliances in his home with a military rifle. It had been taken away from him by his father, but he found where it was hidden and brought it back home. When violent at work he would become involved in fights. As a draftsman he had held 12 jobs in seven years and had been involved in 27 fights in that period of time. One night after his wife failed to serve him dinner first, he began shooting up his home. She left with the children, and the police were called. He saw this as sport and began firing at them. He killed two officers, wounded two others, an innocent bystander, and a boy who was watching television in his own home nearby. He surrendered, was acquitted subsequently due to insanity, and committed suicide in the Forensic Center.

This material clearly illustrates the fact that many violent and homicidal persons give early warning signs through their behavior. In my experience, these individuals are psychotic and usually suffering from either a schizophrenic reaction or paranoid type of personality trait disturbance. They are asking for help from others and communicating their need for control. When a homicide occurs, it is because that help and control has not been forthcoming and their cry for help has been unheard and unmet.

From my discussion, it is apparent that there have been many approaches to studying the psychological and psychodynamic factors in those who kill. Among those of us who deal with killers, study them, and treat them there has been a considerable move away from classical and traditional medical, psychiatric, and sociological models. Despite many insights that have developed from such research, there has been precious little money, talent or time devoted to this growing problem concerning the killer in our society. The incidence keeps rising and the number of victims are countless, yet there has been little governmental interest to turn to the places where killers can be found for volunteer studies, namely, the prisons. Our country has the greatest number available but the least amount of interest in turning to them for answers as to cause and solution.

REFERENCES

Abrahamsen, D. 1973. *The Murdering Mind.* New York: Harper.

Bender, L. 1959. "Children and Adolescents who Kill." *American Journal of Psychiatry* 116:510–13.

Deiker, T. E. 1973. "Wais Characteristics of Indicted Male Murderers." *Psychological Reports* 32:1066.

Guttmacher, M. 1973. *The Mind of the Murderer.* Selected Libraries Reprint Series. New York: Arno Press.

Henry, A. and J. Short. 1954. *Suicide and Homicide.* Glencoe, Illinois: The Free Press.

Kahn, M. W. 1967. "Correlates of Rorschach Reality Adherence in the Assessment of Murderers who Plead Insanity." *Journal of Protective Techniques and Personality Assessment* 31:44–47.

Kaplund, D. and R. Reich. 1976. "The Murdered Child and his Killers." *American Journal of Psychiatry* 133(7):809–813.

Kutash, I. L., B. Samuel, and L. S. Schlesinger & Associates. 1978. *Violence: Perspectives on Murder and Aggression.* San Francisco: Jossey-Bass Publishers.

Lester, D. and G. Lester. 1975. *Crimes of Passion: Murder and the Murderer.* Chicago: Nelson Hall.

Lunde, D. T. 1976. *Murder and Madness.* San Francisco: San Francisco Book Co.

Miller, D. and J. Looney. 1974. "The Prediction of Adolescent Homicide; Episodic Dyscontrol and Dehumanization." *American Journal of Psychoanalysis* 34(3):187–98.

Resnick, P. 1969. "Child Murder by Parents." *American Journal of Psychiatry* 126:325–34.

Revitch, E. 1975. "Psychiatric Evaluation and Classification of Antisocial Activities." *Disturbance of Nervous System* 36:419–21.

Revitch, E. 1977. "Classification of Offenders for Prognostic and Dispositional Evaluation." *Bulletin of Academy Law & Psychiatry* 8:1–11.

Sargent, D. 1962. "Children Who Kill." *Social Work* 7(1):35–42.

Satten, J., K. A. Menninger, and M. Mayman. 1960. "Murder Without Apparent Motive: A Study in Personality Disorganization." *American Journal of Psychiatry* 117:48–53.

Tanay, E. 1976. *The Murderers.* Indianapolis: Bobbs-Merrill.

Van Keuren, R. T. 1977. "Victim-Precipitated Homicide." *Vita* 4(2):19–21.

West, D. J. 1966. *Murder Followed by Suicide.* Cambridge: Harvard University Press.

Wille, W. 1974. *Citizens Who Commit Murder.* St. Louis: Warren Greene.

Wolfgang, M. E. 1958. *Patterns in Criminal Homicide.* Philadelphia: University of Pennsylvania Press.

2

REFLECTIONS ON HOMICIDE
A Public Health Perspective

Nancy H. Allen

<>

*Homicide is a major public health problem, yet very few public health
or mental health workers address themselves systematically to this issue.
The victim of the homicide becomes the concern of the police and
coroner. In 80 percent of the cases, the perpetrator of the homicide is
known to the criminal justice system—police, district attorney, judges,
juries, prisons, parole boards, and probation officers. But the health
system does not seem to play the significant role in prevention; it ought
to.*

Introduction

The first part of my article is a statistical-demographic study of homicides in California for the period 1960–1970. Changing patterns of
homicide will be discussed. State and national statistics will be compared whenever possible. The differences in reporting systems will be
touched on. The United States homicide crude death rates will also
be compared with other countries for the same period. When possible,
a statistical update will be given.

The second part is the more important: the prevention of homicide.
The literature on the subject of murder is vast. A great amount of
attention has been given to causes and treatment, but there has been
relatively little attention given to the *prevention* of the homicidal event

and the practical ways of how to avoid becoming a victim. I shall borrow concepts directly from suicidology and translate them into homicide-prevention terms. Just as there are critical points of prevention in some suicide scenarios, so too are there possible critical points of intervention in some homicides.

The third part of my presentation will consist of two case histories. I shall describe the homicide trajectory and points where intervention might have taken place. Finally, I shall propose suggestions for possible action for better homicide prevention.

Epidemiology

SOURCES OF DATA

The tabular data for homicide in this paper were obtained from all death certificates that indicated homicide as the mode of death, as submitted to the State Department of Public Health by the 58 California counties. This includes the full range of homicidal acts from first degree murder to accidental or justifiable homicide.

The years 1960 and 1970 were selected because, as two census years, they provide better population data points with which to measure change. Also, homicide death certificate information was available from the California State Department of Health for the periods studied. There have, of course, been changes since 1970. However, these statistics give us a broad picture of California's homicide problem and enable us to compare these data with some national and international data.

Homicidal deaths are, by law, medico-legal cases, and have to be certified by a coroner or medical examiner. These death certifications are classified for statistical purposes using the International Classification of Diseases and Death in accordance with the World Health Organization rules for the selection of causes of death. Although the classification of causes of death have undergone nine successive revisions since 1900, homicide is one of the several types of death for which classifications have remained essentially comparable.

The ninth revision became effective with the National Center for Health Statistics on January 1, 1979. This latest revision will help the epidemiologist to examine an improved indexing of causes (and methods) of homicide. This, in turn, has implications for better identification of high risk groups. Through this new knowledge, there may be a greater potential for the prevention of some specific homicidal events. The ninth revision of the International Classification of Diseases and Death isolates, for the first time, such causes as rape and child abuse. Guns are classified into five groups: handgun, shotgun, hunting rifle, military firearms, and other unspecified firearms. (It should be noted that there is a variety of sources reporting homicide—statewide as well as federal public health reports are higher in most instances.)

The statistics on homicide from the National Center for Health Statistics are based on information recorded on the official certificate of death filed in vital statistics offices in each state. Data on homicide from the criminal justice system are based on different collection procedures and definitions. Perhaps most significant is the fact that Health Department data include as homicides those deaths resulting from *legal intervention* whereas the criminal justice reporting system usually does not. Also, the uniform crime reports are obtained from only 94 percent of police and sheriff's departments (see table 2.1).

Between 1960 and 1970, the *number* of homicides in California has more than doubled (from 714 to 1,506) and the *rate* of homicides has increased over 60 percent—from 4.7 per 100,000 population in 1960 to 7.6 per 100,000 population in 1970. The number and rate have

Table 2.1
Homicides in the United States and California for 1960 and 1970 per 100,000 Population.

	CALIFORNIA				UNITED STATES			
	State Department of Health		*California Bureau of Criminal Statistics*		*National Center for Health Statistics*		*Uniform Crime Reports*	
	Number	*Rate*	*Number*	*Rate*	*Number*	*Rate*	*Number*	*Rate*
1960	714	4.5	620	3.9	8,464	5.2	9,030	5.1
1970	1,506	7.5	1,395	6.8	16,848	8.3	15,860	7.8

SOURCE: California State Department of Health Vital Statistics; California Bureau of Criminal Statistics; National Center for Health Statistics and Uniform Crime Reports.

increased since then in California and nationally. In 1976, the death rate from homicides was 10.5 per 100,000 population; the number of homicide deaths being 2,261. The national homicide death rate for 1976 was 9.1 per 100,000 population; the total number of homicide deaths were reported to be 19,554.

METHODS OF HOMICIDE

The methods (or means) of homicide remained relatively stable from 1960 to 1970, with death by firearms and explosives accounting for about 50 percent of the total.

Firearms, particularly handguns, play a major role in the commission of homicide. Firearms appear to be the instrument of choice in the United States as well as in California. The number of homicides in California caused by firearms and explosives more than doubled between 1960 and 1970, from 351 deaths to 818, while the rates in which firearms played a part in homicide remained about the same. Nationally, those rates increased from 60 percent to 66 percent in 1975.

What is to be noted is that the very *possession* of firearms exposes the owner to the risk of involuntarily committing a homicide. Many homicides could have been prevented if such an awareness had existed in the mind of the victim as well as of the perpetrator.

It is evident that the choice of lethal instruments varies according to the capacity of the victim to defend himself. Thus, firearms play a minor role in assaults on children, while hands, feet and other modes of assault predominate. From age 10 through 59, firearms are used in over 50 percent of all homicides. Male victims are killed more frequently by firearms or knives. Beatings and kicking account for a high percentage of women victims, perhaps because women are less able to defend themselves against this type of attack.

HOMICIDE DEATH RATES BY SEX, RACE, AND AGE

Death rates due to homicide increased from 1960 to 1970 for sex and race groups. Generally speaking, rates for males were about three times higher than those for females. The rates for blacks were about three times higher than those for whites. Rates for males increased noticeably more than did those for females. The major homicide trend during the 1960–1970 decade is clearly upward for sex, race, and age.

For males, the *peak* homicide rate for the decade studied occurred in the 25–34 year old group, an increase of almost 100 percent from 1960 to 1970. For females, death rates due to homicide are markedly lower than those for males, except in the 0–14 and over 74-year-old age groups. The peak occurs consistently in the 25–34 age group, but is much less marked than for males (see table 2.3).

For the 0–14 age group, the increase in death rate due to homicide appears to be largely attributable to an increase in the 0–4 year age group. There are more female infants and young children murdered than male. The percentage increase of the past 10 years in the 0–4 age group has reached an alarming proportion. For females, the homicide death rate has increased 128 percent and for males 116 percent. Of course, this touches on the topic of child abuse.

Those 75 years and older both males and females appear to be the targets for homicide. There has been an over 100 percent increase from 1960 to 1970 in this age group. The greatest increase in homicide death rate has been 200 percent in whites over 75 years of age.

The rate for black homicide victims per 100,000 population is higher than their white counterpart in every age group, with the exception of over 74, although the actual number (not the rate) of deaths from homicide are higher in whites than in blacks in every age category (see table 2.2).

OTHER COUNTRIES

Many countries have experienced an increase in homicide rates during the past decade, but the change in the United States has been perhaps the most dramatic: an increase of over 100 percent from 1960 to 1970. The homicide rate in the United States is more than five times higher than that for most European countries (see table 2.4).

THE MEANING OF THE STATISTICAL FINDINGS

The purpose of this statistical survey is to substantiate the fact that death from homicide is an increasing public health problem and to pinpoint epidemiologically where prevention efforts could be started. To summarize the data given above:

Nancy H. Allen

Table 2.2
*California Homicide Death Rates and Numbers by Age
and Race[a] 1960 and 1970 (by place of residence).*

	1960		1970	
	Rate	Number	Rate	Number
Whites				
0–14	0.8	34	1.1	55
15–24	5.1	98	8.1	254
25–34	5.6	108	9.2	217
35–44	4.7	98	6.8	142
45–54	3.7	61	5.5	116
55–64	3.9	47	5.4	84
65–74	3.1	27	4.3	44
75 +	1.8	8	5.5	36
Total	3.8	481	5.3	948
Blacks				
0–14	2.5[a]	8	5.5	27
15–24	38.3	47	59.6	155
25–34	44.1	59	83.0	164
35–44	45.1	59	47.9	77
45–54	31.3	28	45.9	62
55–64	17.8	9	27.1	24
65–74	3.9	1	17.0	8
75 +	19.6	2	—[b]	1
Total	24.1	213	37.0	518

[a] Does not include "other non-white" homicide
population.
[b] Fewer than 5 deaths in category.

1. Between 1960 and 1970, homicide in California increased 66 percent.
2. Between 1960 and 1976, homicides in California as well as the United States have more than doubled—in rates and in number.
3. Guns are the method of murder most frequently used.
4. The *rate* of homicide is highest in black men; the *number* of homicides is highest in white men.
5. The highest increase in homicides is over 200 percent from 1960 to 1970 in whites 75 years of age and older.
6. Homicide in children has increased at alarming proportions. For females, 0–4, the increase was 128 percent between 1960 and

1970. For males, 0–4, the increase was 116 percent for the same period.

Prevention

Many homicides can be prevented. By recognizing the causes of the homicidal event and correcting them through changes in attitudes,

Table 2.3

California Homicide Death Rates by Age and Sex per 100,000 Population for 1960, 1965, and 1970 (by place of residence)

	1960	1965	1970	Ten Year Percentage Increase
Males				
0–4	1.8	2.5	3.9	116
5–14	1.1	1.2	1.7	55
15–24	9.8	12.0	17.8	82
25–34	11.6	15.2	23.1	99
35–44	10.9	11.6	15.0	37
45–54	6.7	11.1	12.5	86
55–64	5.8	8.5	11.2	93
65–74	3.9	5.0	7.7	97
75+	3.1	8.0	7.2	132
Total	6.4	8.1	11.6	81
Female				
0–4	1.4	2.2	3.2	128
5–14	0.8	1.3	1.4	87
15–24	4.0	3.2	5.5	36
25–34	4.2	5.0	5.9	40
35–44	3.3	3.2	3.8	15
45–54	3.8	2.8	3.2	−18
55–64	3.3	2.9	2.4	−37
65–74	2.4	2.3	2.7	12
75+	a	3.1	4.2	b
Total	2.7	2.7	3.5	29

a Fewer than 5 in category.
b Not available.
SOURCE: State of California, Department of Health, Vital Statistics, Death Records.

Table 2.4
Homicide and Suicide Death Rates for Selected Countries 1960
and 1970 (Per 100,000 Population)

Country	HOMICIDE RATE		SUICIDE RATE	
	1960	1970	1960	1970
Australia	1.5	1.5	10.6	12.4
Austria	1.2	1.5	23.1	24.2
Bulgaria	n.a.	2.2	n.a.	11.9
Canada	1.4	2.0	7.6	11.3
Costa Rica	3.2	3.7	2.1	2.3
Czechoslovakia	n.a.	1.4	n.a.	23.2
Denmark	0.5	0.7	20.3	21.5
El Salvador	30.3	31.2	11.4	7.0
England & Wales	0.6	0.7	11.2	8.0
Finland	2.9	2.0	20.4	21.3
France	1.7	0.7	15.9	15.4
Germany (Federal Republic)	1.0	1.4	18.8	21.3
Greece	1.5	0.6	3.8	3.2
Hungary	1.6	2.0	24.9	34.8
Ireland	n.a.	0.4	8.0	1.8
Israel	0.7	0.6[b]	6.4	6.4[b]
Italy	1.4	1.0	6.1	5.8
Mexico	n.a.	17.5	n.a.	1.1
Netherlands	0.3	0.5	6.6	8.1
New Zealand	1.1	1.2	9.7	9.6
Northern Ireland	0.9	1.2	4.4	3.9
Norway	0.4	0.6	6.4	8.4
Poland	1.4	1.1	8.0	11.2
Portugal	0.9	0.7	8.5	7.5
Scotland	0.7	0.9	7.8	7.6
Spain	0.3	0.2	5.5	4.4
Sweden	0.6	0.8	17.4	22.3
Switzerland	0.6	0.7	19.0	18.6
United States[a]	4.7	8.3	10.6	11.1

SOURCE: *World Health Organization Epidemiological and Vital Statistics Report*, vol. 16, 1963 (for 1960 statistics).
World Health Statistics Annual vol. 1, "Vital Statistics and Causes of Death," 1976 (for 1970 statistics).
[a] National Center for Health Statistics Reports 5.2
[b] 1973.

behavior, and environment, it seems reasonable to feel that the occurrence of homicide can be reduced.

When discussing something as complex as the homicidal event, not even the statistics for a given period can be viewed as absolute. Just as there is no one simple cause of murder, pathways to prevention are complex—some are applicable to some persons and not to others. As with suicide, cancer, or communicable diseases not all can be prevented; but some can.

Attitudes toward homicide have influenced how we deal with the problem. Society may be outraged at the fact that the number of murders has been increasing, but they have been reluctant to take advantage of existing knowledge of causes, and thus prevent the homicidal event from taking place.

PREVENTION IN THE YOUNG

Prevention efforts must be directed toward the young. Early counseling is needed for preschoolers and elementary school children—especially those in high-crime areas. Special counseling should be provided for those young persons who manifest poor social adjustment. Assistance must be given before negative behavior patterns become fixed. We need to find ways that people can achieve significance and recognition so that destructive violence will not be necessary. The young person should develop reading and writing skills. If he fails, tutoring should be given. The ability to communicate is needed for meaningful employment. To have a good job is one way to have self-esteem and hope for the future.

COMMUNITY ORGANIZATION AND EDUCATION

Another model for the prevention of homicide is through community organization and education. Homicide prevention involves social problem solving, prison reform, improved police–community relations, better coordination between concerned agencies, and educating politicians to take a more active role and assume greater responsibility. There is a pressing need for more collaborative work between medicine, law, psychology, criminology, sociology, and political science.

The public needs to understand the nature and extent of the homicide problem and to be involved in the program planning and the decision-making process that will ultimately reduce the number of victims of homicide. Potential victims can be educated about the importance their attributes, attitudes, and behavior play in their being selected as targets. Besides an educated community, there is a need for more trained personnel in other than law enforcement agencies. Health workers need to be educated to see that homicide is their problem, too, and they must share responsibility in the prevention of homicide.

Education needs to be directed toward not only the health professionals, but also potential victims and perpetrators. What are the clues and changes of behavior that give warning? Once we have been alerted, what should we do? Where are the helping resources within the community? Specifically, the needed resources are those that can help potentially violent persons in a nonthreatening environment and that can give support to a person who fears for his life, or has already been victimized.

Potential perpetrators, perpetrators, potential victims and victims of violence must be involved—along with mental health, public health, schools, citizen groups, and law enforcement personnel—in program planning and program operations. The goal is the reduction of homicide.

Behavioral science can offer techniques that will reduce our murder rate. Research in suicidology has implications and correlations to further the understanding of homicide prevention. Perhaps the most clearly translatable concepts are:

1. Prevention, intervention, and postvention.
2. Clues to homicide (verbal, behavioral, and situational).
3. Lethality and the identification of high-risk groups.
4. The use of the psychological autopsy with victims and psychological biopsy with the perpetrator of a homicide.

These concepts are interrelated and should be interlaced in order to achieve an effective homicide prevention program.

PREVENTION, INTERVENTION, AND POSTVENTION

Primary *prevention* of homicide is the most complex and costly of any of the methods of stopping a murder from taking place. It means improving the human condition, in which infants will come into this world as a wanted person, into a decent living environment, and with the assurance of health, education, and meaningful employment. The solutions to poor housing, poor education, racism, unemployment, and crime itself are in part economic. We must make an economic commitment to end them. Primary prevention involves a reduction of the incidence of the homicidal act itself.

Statistical evidence and clinical studies show a correlation between the incidence of homicide and the availability of weapons. The nature of the weapon immediately available determines outcome. The fatality rate of firearm attacks is about five times higher than that of attacks with knives. This suggests the need for gun control legislation. Action in the field of gun control is long overdue.

Potential victims must be educated regarding techniques on how to avoid becoming a victim of homicide (see table 2.5).

Intervention relates to the treatment or care of the homicidal crisis or stress events that may give clues that help is needed. There is need for violence intervention centers, a place where people with a tremendous buildup of tension can go any time to talk to someone, to let off steam, and to defuse. The services of already existing suicide prevention centers could be extended to provide help to the angry potential perpetrator and the frightened potential victim—both may have constricted vision to the point they feel helpless in knowing what to do. Suicide prevention centers are already receiving telephone calls from homicidal persons. A sample of suicide prevention centers revealed approximately 12 to 18 percent of the telephone calls received are homicide related. Professional staff and volunteers from all suicide prevention–crisis intervention centers should have additional training in handling the homicide related phone calls, for example, training regarding assessment of homicidal risk, clues to homicide, and methods to reduce perturbation and constriction. Some of the callers can be helped through talking to someone who cares, other callers may need therapeutic counseling, some may need immediate attention from the emergency treatment units of mental health centers. There needs to be an expansion of all of these resources and services.

The public must be educated regarding the need for a homicide prevention service. The potential consumer must be educated regarding the availability of the service. The correctional future of the perpetrator lies in local responsibility and service. Rehabilitation methods must be changed and provided at the local level. Legislation has

Table 2.5
Techniques on How to Avoid Becoming a Victim of Homicide

The following techniques for prevention of victimization are based on case histories. Some methods are more publicized than others. They all have application.

1. Keep away from firearms when possible.
2. Avoid areas with high crime rate when possible.
3. Stay away from potentially dangerous persons or situations.
4. Do not hitchhike and do not pick up hitchhikers.
5. Walk in groups of two or more. Do not walk alone at night.
6. Carry a whistle.
7. Don't provoke. Consider the other person may become angry easily and be carrying a weapon.
8. When provoked, don't respond.
9. Don't leave valuables in sight, and carry only as much money as necessary.
10. Keep all doors of home, apartment, or car locked.
11. Know location of nearest police station.
12. Keep emergency police telephone number posted by or on each phone.
13. Use extreme caution when placing ads in the paper or on bulletin boards.

If Attacked:
1. Try to stay calm. The assailant will be less likely to attack you if you appear controlled and confident.
2. Run and scream or blow whistle if possible.
3. Don't resist robbery.
4. Get a description of the perpetrator (see below acronyms), report, and prosecute.
5. Defend yourself only as a last resort.

If Others are Attacked:
1. Shout and blow whistle to get help.
2. Gather others to help.
3. Call police.
4. Cooperate in prosecution.
5. Get a description of perpetrator and vehicle (if involved).

Recall Acronyms:
1. The acronym "ARREST HIM" is suggested for use in identifying the personal characteristics of the perpetrator:
   A— Age, as close as possible
   R— Race.
   R— Rags. Term used in clothing business, how dressed.
   E— Eyes, color, size, glasses, eyebrows.

S— Sex.
T— Tattoos.
H— Height, Hair.
I— Impediments, scars, limp, etc.
M— Movements (ran, drove away, in what direction), Mannerisms.
2. The acronym CYMBOL is a term developed by the Attorney General
   Younger's (1977) Office that may help one to be a good witness when a
   car is involved:
   C— Color of car
   Y— Year (as close as you can get).
   M— Make of the car.
   B— Body style.
   O— Occupants (how many? description if possible).
   L— License.

a role. For example, California law requires that dangerous mental patients be reassessed at certain periods during their hospitalization so that those patients who are incarcerated may be released only when appropriate. There are cases where the mental hospital is not advised of the murder committed prior to the patient's hospitalization, and the law enforcement agency is not informed when the "patient" is released. This communication gap is unfortunate and should be bridged.

Intervention needs to focus on the lessening of tensions, enabling the potentially homicidal individual to endure and withstand painful experiences so that he does not act out his aggressive antisocial impulses.

Postvention, a term introduced by Shneidman (1973b), refers to therapeutic assistance given after the dire event has occurred. What is different from postvention in suicide is that with homicide, the task is doubled. The survivors of the homicide victim experience a different kind of bereavement. The homicide death is stigmatizing, unnatural, especially burdensome, unexpected, and usually unwarranted. The survivor cannot grieve in a usual way because of the rage that is directed toward the perpetrator, who sometimes is not brought to justice. This prolongs the anger and frustration of the survivor, who lives with the murder stigma forever. A sense of loss is also felt by the families of the persons who have murdered. They too need counseling in understanding why the homicide occurred. Help is needed for both families in giving them some insights, when possible, regarding causes; plus bereavement counseling for better mental health, and future prevention. It is essential that public and mental health workers recognize the need for postvention help to the survivor-victim of a homicide and to the families of the perpetrator.

CLUES TO HOMICIDE

A person who murders, just as with the person who commits suicide, in many cases gives clues—verbal, behavioral, and situational, both conscious and unconscious. There are many methods of expressing a homicidal threat. None should be dismissed lightly. Threat can be expressed by gestures, facial expressions, overt aggressions, in writing, and in speech. Many murderers have conveyed their fears of losing control to legal officials, psychiatrists, social workers, behavioral scientists, and friends before the event takes place. This must be considered as a cry for help and intervention must be offered.

Verbal warnings range from the direct approach, "I am going to kill you," to an indirect signal like "I hate you so much it frightens me and you should be frightened, too." For example, a suicidal patient wrote a letter to our center. She was asking for help because of her suicidal state—but she was also thinking of homicide. She had not been assisted (to her satisfaction) by a worker at the crisis center she had telephoned in her community. She related in her letter, "now I keep thinking of getting a gun and shooting that center up. Every night I lay awake thinking of what I can shoot, sometimes who." The patient's letter was answered and I also spoke with the center and with the therapist who was involved. The California Supreme Court has passed a decision mandating psychotherapists "to warn the intended victim or others of the possibility of danger or violence"—a positive step.

Behavioral clues include planning in advance the person who will be the target of the homicide(s). Clues usually appear a few weeks to a few days before the homicide, although it may be seconds as with impulsive murders. The perpetrator's behavior changes. His mood shifts to restlessness, agitation, hostility, and isolation; he finds himself less able to conform to social strictures. Perturbation is noticeably heightened. Impulse control lessens and the perpetrator becomes unable to seek acceptable options to violence. He may increase his use of drugs (usually alcohol); this exacerbates the degree of perturbation and lowers the degree of control and ability to cope.

Situational clues have a wide range. Murderers frequently come from a broken home, if they have any home at all. They will usually have done poorly in school, and will have a history of juvenile delinquency and previous criminal behavior. This contributes to their low degree of self-esteem and self-knowledge and also leads to their inability to cope with their environment in a socially acceptable manner. Perpetrators may have a history of aggressive behavior, homicide-threatening parents, child abuse, firesetting, and cruelty to animals and to other children.

Many individuals involved with domestic homicides have previously been arrested for disturbance in related matters. When repetitive violent behavior persists, a permanent separation of the conflicting parties should be considered to avoid an untimely and unnecessary death.

The point is, the sooner the clues are noted and the sooner assistance given, the more likely the potential perpetrator will be able to defuse his perturbation, change his attitudes and behavior, and express his emotions in an acceptable way.

LETHALITY AND IDENTIFICATION OF HIGH RISK GROUPS

Shneidman suggests lethality to be "roughly synonymous with the deathfulness of the act and is an important dimension in understanding any potentially suicidal [homicidal] person." The homicidal crisis or the period of dangerousness is usually of short duration, but because of the deep-seated roots of the homicidal person, another aggravation may bring him to the crisis point again, so that murder reappears as the only solution.

When high risk factors are present, early intervention with the lethal person and his family must be initiated. Trained persons should be readily available to provide social, environmental, physical, and therapeutic options.

The high risk groups can be identified in part by looking at statistics, but case histories appear to be the best source for identifying the potential victim. Homicide victims come from all age populations, from all ethnic groups, from all economic groups, and from all educational levels; but within these groups there are some persons at greater risk than the average person. Specific high risk groups are as follows:

1. Unwanted pregnancies.
2. Infants whose parents experienced a traumatic childhood.
3. Juvenile gang members.
4. The hitchhiker, especially female traveling alone.
5. The sexually promiscuous and the lonely.
6. The elderly.
7. Persons connected with law enforcement (prison guards and police).
8. Criminals and prisoners.
9. Persons resisting a criminal act.
10. Hard drug users.
11. People with high-risk occupations: political leaders, physicians, liquor store workers, druggists, bank tellers, lawyers, and prostitutes—all are exposed to danger by virtue of where they are and what they are doing.

Knowing high risk groups has implications for prevention. There needs to be an increased focus on educating persons at risk regarding techniques on how to avoid becoming a victim (see table 2.6).

THE PSYCHOLOGICAL AUTOPSY AND THE PSYCHOLOGICAL BIOPSY

The concept of the psychological autopsy and the psychological biopsy has implications for the future, as the application of this method of gaining keener insights regarding the victim and perpetrator has not been used in homicide investigation.

The psychological autopsy is a procedure originally designed by Shneidman as a means for clarifying the appropriate mode of death in equivocal cases (usually deaths that are possibly suicidal, but also possibly accidental). The procedure is to talk to survivors and knowledgeable acquaintances of the decedent and to reconstruct the victim's lifestyle, thoughts, fantasies, and behaviors relating to his own death. The psychological biopsy is a procedure that should be used on the perpetrator of a murder to better understand the dynamics of the homicide trajectory, not only from the murderer's viewpoint but from the significant others in his life.

Table 2.6
Assessing the Risk of Committing a Homicide

Clinical Characteristics	Low	Medium	High
INIMICALITY (Past History)			
Family Life	Wanted child, good, loving family	Some family disruption, loss of a parent or one-parent family	Early violence, battered child, poor parent model
Significant Others	Several reliable family or friends available	Few or one available	None available
Daily Functioning	Good in most activities	Moderately good in some activities	Not good in any activities
Lifestyle Socioeconomic Employment	Stable Upper Employed	Moderately stable Middle Employment history fairly stable	Unstable Lower Unemployed
Education	High school graduate or more (university/technical training)	High school dropout, can read and write	School dropout, semi-literate to illiterate
Housing	Lives in adequate housing, clean environment and space	Fair housing, some overcrowding	Poor housing, crowded, slums
Isolation/Withdrawn	Able to relate well to others, outgoing	Mild, some withdrawal and feelings of hopelessness	Long history of being a loner, anti-social, withdrawn, hopeless, helpless feelings
Alcohol/Drug Use	Non-drinker/occasional social use	Social drinker/user to occasional abuse	Chronic abuse

Table 2.6
(Continued)

Clinical Characteristics	Low	Medium	High
Psychological Help	No history of need for or use of psychiatric hospitalization	Some outpatient help, moderately satisfied with self	History of psychiatric hospitalization, negative view of help
PERTURBATION (Negative emotional states)			
Anxiety	Low, good emotional control	Occasional feelings of anxiety	Easily aroused to anxiety, high or panic state
Depression	Low	Occasional depression	Severe, Chronically moody
Self-Esteem	Good, has reinforcements from others	Usually good, has times of being put down and not being able to handle	Chronically poor self image
Hostility	Low	Some	Marked, aggressive
Impulse Control	Controlled	Some impulsive acting out. Not physically violent	Feels need for violence
CONSTRICTION (Narrowing of vision)			
Coping Strategies/Devices being Utilized	Able to cope with stress and outside aggravating influences; well developed defense mechanisms	Usually can cope under most pressures; sometimes becomes constrictive in thinking and acts out	Becomes constrictive under most stress; acts out in destructive, socially unacceptable ways

Disorientation/ Disorganization	None, is in good contact with what is happening	Little to moderate	Marked, losing contact with reality
Resources	Able to make good use of resources available	Some use, aware of most resources	Either unable to use resources available or recognize that there is help
CESSATION (Stop the person causing the problem)			
Previous Arrests	None	Has been arrested, has not served time	Multiple arrest history. Served time in prison, would murder to avoid going back to prison
Previous Homicide Attempt	None	Has exhibited aggressive behavior; been in fights but no attempt to kill another	Yes. Looks at the killing of another as a feasible act
Homicide Plan	None	Has held fleeting thoughts of killing another, no definite plan	Frequent or constant thoughts with a specific plan
Weapon Available	None that person thinks of	Yes. Person aware of weapons in immediate environment, but not seriously considering use	Yes, and planning on use. A loaded gun should be considered as highly lethal

This procedure will yield information about the murderer and his victim(s). There has been a noticeable increase of motiveless homicide. A careful history-taking and psychological evaluation will reveal factors that may explain the reason for the homicide. The role the victim and the perpetrator played in the homicide event will be better understood. By understanding homicide at a more thorough level, perhaps our efforts at prevention can be more lasting (see table 2.7).

Case Histories

Aspects on prevention and intervention can perhaps be better understood by looking at specific case histories. Two such follow.

HELEN'S HOMICIDE

Phillip had been retired for a year. He was doing very little with this new free time. His feelings of jealousy toward his wife became increasingly noticeable. This was Phillip's second marriage. He had been widowed at 55 and married Helen a year later. Helen was twenty years younger than Phillip and after their marriage, she continued her job at a local restaurant. Phillip "knew" that Helen had another gentleman friend at work and continually would check up on her. The week before killing Helen, he went to the restaurant with a gun and told Helen he was checking up and that she was "all he had to live for."

Frank, Helen's son by a former marriage, who was temporarily living with them, was also aware of the gun. One evening a week later, Helen came home from work and sat down for a drink with her husband. At approximately 6:00 P.M., neighbors heard a scream followed by one gunshot; ten seconds later, another shot rang out. Four hours later, Frank found Helen and Phillip dead in the living room.

Discussion: Helen might have prevented this homicide: Helen should have stopped seeing "the other man" and, if this was an innocent flirtation on her part, she should have communicated this to Phillip with assurance that it would stop.

Helen or Frank should have removed the gun and discussed the matter with Phillip. Phillip needed reassurance and a sense of hope.

This "retirement time on my hands" syndrome brings out the point that people should plan for their retirement. There are many mean-

Table 2.7
The Psychological Autopsy/Biopsy

The following types of questions asked during a psychological autopsy have been adopted for homicide investigation of victim and perpetrator.
Data to be included in the Psychological Autopsy/Biopsy:

1. Identifying information on the victim and the perpetrator (name, age, address, marital status, religious practices, occupation, and other details).
2. Details of the death (including the cause or method and other pertinent details).
3. Brief outline of victim's and perpetrator's history (siblings, marriage, education, employment, medical illnesses, medical treatment, psychotherapy, previous suicide or homicide attempts).
4. Death history of family (homicides, suicides, cancer, other fatal illnesses, ages at death, and other details).
5. Description of the personality and lifestyle of the victim and perpetrator.
6. Victim's and perpetrator's typical patterns of reaction to stress, emotional upsets, periods of disequilibrium, and coping mechanism.
7. Any recent—from last few days to last 12 months—upsets, pressures, tensions, or anticipations of trouble.
8. Role of alcohol and drugs in (a) overall lifestyle, and (b) his death.
9. Nature of victim's and perpetrator's interpersonal relationships (including relationships with physicians).
10. Fantasies, dreams, thoughts, premonitions, or fears of victim and perpetrator relating to death, homicide, accident, or suicide.
11. Changes in the victim and the perpetrator before death (of habits, hobbies, eating, sexual patterns, and other life routines).
12. Information relating to the lifestyle of victim and perpetrator (upswings, successes, plans).
13. Assessment of intention, i.e., role of victim in his own demise, and intention for murder on the part of the perpetrator.
14. Previous arrest history, convictions, serving time, and for what reason.
15. Rating of lethality.
16. Reactions of informants to victim's and preperator's death (surprise, expected, grief, etc.).
17. Comments, special features, etc.
18. What happened immediately before homicide event took place (envy, robbery, humiliation, etc.).

It is suggested that the psychological autopsy be used on the victims of homicide and psychological biopsy be used on the perpetrator of murder.

ingful activities for the retired that will contribute to a sense of achievement and self-esteem. Phillip had neither.

Phillip committed suicide probably because of despair rather than hostility. His attitude toward Helen was marked by ambivalence—jealous rage and affection so strong Phillip removed himself from the murder through suicide.

Behavior changes and clues: Behavior changes were noted at the time of Phillip's retirement—an increase in perturbation; increased feelings of hopelessness; increased loss of self-esteem; increased jealousy; purchase of gun; communication to wife and son about gun; communication to wife that he "can't live without her."

How to defuse the situation: Remove gun; give reassurances of love; better communication between the two partners.

PATRICK'S HOMICIDE

Patrick, 66, owned a neighborhood bar which he tended on a regular basis until he had to be hospitalized, due to a heart condition. This illness naturally took some of the zest out of his life. The day of his murder, Patrick had been working at his bar for a few hours. He again started bragging to his customers about his valuable stamp collection. On several occasions, Pete, Nick, and Jeff had listened to Patrick's comments about his stamp collection and failing health. They decided he would be an easy person to rob, but because they were regular customers, they felt they would be recognized.

They brought in Bob, who they knew had served "hardtime" in prison, was on parole, and needed money. Bob was told that Patrick would be an easy person to rob, that he had a "valuable stamp collection," was an "invalid," and lived with an aging wife. The three men had followed Patrick home before. They drove Bob to Patrick's residence. Patrick arrived home around 7:00 P.M. and after changing to some comfortable clothes, was sitting in the living room with his wife. The door bell rang. The wife went to the door and asked who was there. She received a response asking if Patrick were home; Bob was then asked to come inside. Bob drew a gun (he later admitted to purchasing the gun "over the counter") and said, "I want the collection. This is a hold-up. You behave or I'll kill you."

Much to Bob's surprise, Patrick responded by stating, "I don't have any." Bob then took the telephone off the receiver, ushered the wife into the den, and returned to the living room. Patrick was gone. Bob went outside to look for Patrick and was struck by Patrick on the side of his head. Bob fired the gun "just trying to scare him off." Later, during Bob's testimony, he stated, "Then the next thing I remember is hearing the gun go off, I panicked. I don't know how many times I fired. I didn't know he was dead 'til I heard it on the radio this morning." Patrick's wife heard the shots and ran to the front of the house to see the car with out-of-state license plates full of men drive off.

Patrick had been shot five times. He died of gunshot wounds to the chest. Before the crime actually took place, one of the conspirators called the police. This made it easier to put the intricate plan together since all of the participants' names were given. Each went to court separately. Bob was convicted of second degree murder and sent back to prison. It is sad to note that Patrick did not have a stamp collection— or any collection. It was something that he had talked about and this fantasy simply got out of control.

Discussion: Patrick should not have bragged about a "valuable stamp collection," whether he had one or not. An old, sick man talking to bar patrons about valuables is an invitation to robbery. That was his first mistake. The second mistake was allowing Bob entry to the house. Patrick should have determined if he knew Bob and told him to leave as he had just called the police. The third and fatal mistake was not remaining cool. Patrick should have calmly showed Bob around the house, told him he was lying about the stamp collection and given him what cash he had available. If Bob had not been attacked by Patrick, chances are he would have left without shooting. Why was it so easy for Bob, a parolee, to purchase a gun "over the counter?" There are laws that presumably prevent easy accessibility of legal purchase of guns. Perhaps more needs to be done to enforce this law.

Suggestions for Possible Action

1. Education is needed at many levels.
   A. The victims must be made aware of their own character flaws and gaps in knowledge which make them susceptible to the perpetrator. There are numerous case histories noting that victims were given clues regarding their possible

murder yet failed to take the warning seriously. High risk groups need special education and awareness training.

B. Perpetrators must have community resources available to help them. There must be places they can telephone or go to—in a nonthreatening environment. The network of suicide prevention centers throughout the United States has staff trained to work with people in crisis. With some additional training, the staff of these suicide prevention–crisis intervention centers could be ideal resources for assisting the potentially homicidal individual.

Better methods are needed to help the perpetrator handle his aggression. The perpetrator must be educated not only to know about community resources available, but to use them. Violence must be viewed as an unacceptable way to resolve interpersonal conflict.

C. Health care providers need to recognize homicide as one of the nation's major public health problems. There is a need to have more comprehensive education regarding the problem and to enable the health care worker to take action toward prevention. For example, homicide prevention techniques should be developed and taught in medical schools, nursing schools, and schools of social work.

D. The general public must support needed changes. To accomplish this, they must be better informed. Information is needed on the what, how, and why of homicide and steps that can be taken toward prevention. This can be done in part through community awareness teams, team speakers, bureaus (from mental health and law enforcement), and continuing education in schools and through the media.

E. Curriculum

1) Schools need to revise their curriculae to provide more relevant education for those students developing crime patterns. Better counseling is also needed.

2) Crime prevention should be introduced into schools at all levels, from kindergarten through graduate programs. For example, the five year old should be taught not to talk to or accept rides or candy from strangers.

3) Just as some Schools of Public Health are now beginning to recognize suicide as a major public health problem and offer some instruction in suicidology, so should they recognize homicide as a major public health problem

and offer education on homicide (statistics, demography, epidemiology, role of health department, health care workers such as public health nurses, physicians, social workers and health educators).

2. The Psychological Autopsy and Biopsy should be used to gain new insights on the victim, perpetrator, causes, motives and prevention. The following is suggested for consideration by each state crime commission. Dual responsibilities should be given to each state's department of health and each attorney general's office to launch and expedite this program. There are several ways this could be accomplished:
   A. A trained behavioral scientist should be employed on the staff of every major metropolitan police department. This person, most probably a psychiatrist or clinical psychologist, could train, deputize, and supervise a core of volunteers who would conduct most of the psychological autopsies and biopsies.
   B. A trained behavioral scientist from the local community mental health services or suicide prevention services could train and supervise well-screened volunteers to man a crisis line or suicide-homicide prevention service.
   C. Trained teams from metropolitan areas could be loaned to small rural areas to train others or assist with the psychological investigations.

3. Greater Use of Volunteer Workers
   A. Volunteer tutors are needed in the schools. Far too many young persons cannot read or write. This leads to unemployment or employment in low paying, meaningless jobs. Repetitive caring help is greatly needed.
   B. Big brother or big sister volunteers are needed to take deprived children out to see part of the city or county they have not seen. By befriending the young person, the volunteer gives him opportunities to develop a sense of self-esteem, usefulness, and hope.
   C. A core of well-trained volunteers should be developed to counsel youth and help young people find jobs.
   D. Volunteers should be used on a homicide prevention telephone service hotline.

4. Use of Postvention for the Family Survivors of a Homicide. Postvention, as previously discussed, refers to the help that is given after the homicide has occurred.
   A. Counseling should be available for survivors of victim and also of the perpetrator.
   B. Professional counseling of the survivors of the victim and the perpetrator and his family can benefit two very special groups. These survivors are better able to cope with the horrendousness of the act, the hate, fear, hopeless feelings, and the grief that takes on different proportions and meaning. The mental health of these individuals ranges from being bruised to shattered. The professional, through postvention, can help put these pieces together.
5. Criminal laws that are obsolete should be repealed, current laws evaluated, and new laws and techniques of control advanced; relevancy to today's needs must take place.

6. More caution should be exercised when releasing prisoners and mental patients who have murdered.
   A. There is a need for more careful, thoughtful parole and follow-up.
   B. The parole board should be able to accurately distinguish between normality and degeneracy, corrigibility and incorrigibility and know when they are being "conned." There should be a former inmate on the parole board.
   C. There should be improved coordination of parole officers with community resources—like special employment groups, community mental health, and other community service agencies.

7. Consider Alternatives to Prison
   A. Community-based agencies where people can go on a voluntary basis (those in trouble because of drug use, alcoholism, child abuse, rape, wife beating, etc.).
   B. Probation houses.
   C. Improved community resources. For example, the proliferation of parents anonymous groups throughout the country where parents can meet and talk about the child they have neglected or are afraid of beating, rape counseling centers, suicide prevention centers and hotlines.

Early and clearly identifiable resources are needed for the potential perpetrator and victim.

8. Gun Control

   United States citizens are the most heavily armed in the world. Typically, the gun owner has never shot a gun, is unfamiliar with guns, has not received training in the use of guns, and is most likely to be the parent of the victim.

   Although only 25 percent of all firearms in this country are hand guns, they are used in 75 percent of the homicides involving firearms. The possession of firearms by civilians is a dangerous and ineffective means of self-protection. The public has to be convinced that handguns do not provide the kind of safety and security their owners hope for. The gun becomes an instrument of family tragedy, not protection from the intruder.

   Year after year, police records show that people who keep guns around for protection hardly ever use them to shoot down burglars or other intruders. They are much more likely to use them to kill themselves or friends or members of their own families—and not always accidentally.

9. Establishment of a state and national homicide registry (with built-in safeguards) to record and analyze facts about each homicide recorded (as suggested in psychological autopsy–biopsy).
   A. Use of consistent coordinated records—standardized reporting methods and records.
   B. Establishment of a national crime information center.
   C. More scientific epidemiologic research on the full range of homicidal events—from justifiable to first degree murder.
   D. Development of an international felony registry system so that no foreigner will be admitted to the U.S. with a previous history of murder or other major crimes.

10. There is an increasing need to decrease the number of gang-related murders. Gang leaders can effect change in younger members.
    A. One method that is being tried in Los Angeles is facilitating the meeting of rival gangs. This gives them a chance to

talk and work out problems in constructive ways. As one
gang member stated, "It's up to ourselves to stop all this
and we're going to do it ourselves."

B. The mothers of gang members have started meeting to
help each other.

C. A special center is needed to help juveniles find jobs.

11. Establish a national center for the study and prevention of
violence. Assistance could be given to communities in inte-
grating homicide prevention into suicide prevention services,
initiating new services, training, and continued research.

These suggestions barely scratch the surface of the many layers of
activities that are needed to reduce the number of preventable homicides. But it is a beginning.

Summary

Homicide is a major public health problem. Since 1960, the rate and
number have more than doubled.

Some homicides can be prevented. Suicide prevention techniques
have applicability to homicide prevention—specifically, clues, identification of high risk groups (victim as well as perpetrators), and lethality rating regarding these risk factors. It is important to take the
homicide threat seriously and know that *intervention* in many cases
is possible. More research is needed. I would like to see the use of the
psychological autopsy and the psychological biopsy on victims and
perpetrators. Surely, some of the 51 billion dollars spent on fighting
crime in America could be spent on more extensive homicide prevention efforts. When intervention is not possible, the skillful use of
postvention not only will help the bereaved, but will perhaps prevent
future homicide as well.

REFERENCES

Crime in the United States, Uniform Crime Reports. Washington, D.C.: Su-
perintendent of Documents, 1972, 1973, 1974, 1975.
Homicide in California, 1973. State of California: Department of Justice,
Division of law Enforcement, Bureau of Criminal Statistics, 1974.
Monthly Vital Statistics Report Provisional Statistics Annual Summary for

the United States. Rockville, Md.: National Center for Health Statistics, 1974, 1975, 1976.

Shneidman, E. S. 1973a "Suicide." *Encyclopedia Britannica*.

Shneidman, E. S. 1973b *Deaths of Man*. New York: Quadrangle.

Vital Statistics of California. State of California Department of Public Health, Bureau of Health Intelligence and Research Review, 1965, 1970.

World Health Organization Epidemiological and Vital Statistics Report, vol. 16, 1963.

World Health Statistics Annual, Vol. 1, 1976. "Vital Statistics and Causes of Death."

Younger, E. J. 1976. *Child Abuse*. Sacramento: California Department of Justice, Information Pamphlet No. 8.

Younger, E. J. 1977. Message from the Attorney General. "Senior Crime Preventers' Bulletin" 5(1):6. Sacramento: Department of Justice.

ADDITIONAL BIBLIOGRAPHY

Hatton, D. L., S. Valente, and A. Rink. 1977. *Suicide Assessment and Intervention*. New York: Appleton Century Crofts.

Kastenbaum, R. and R. Aisenberg. 1972. *The Psychology of Death*. New York: Springer Publishing Co., Inc.

Lunde, D. T. 1975. *Murder and Madness*. Stanford, Calif.: The Portable Stanford.

MacDonald, J. H. 1961. *The Murderer and His Victim*. Springfield, Ill.: Charles C. Thomas.

Newman, J. ed. 1972. *Crime in America*. Washington, D.C.: U.S. News and World Report, Inc.

Shneidman, E. S. and P. Mandelkorn. 1967. *How to Prevent Suicide*. New York: Public Affairs Pamphlet no. 406.

Shneidman, E. S. 1976. "Psychologic Theory of Suicide." *Psychiatric Annals*, 6:9–121.

Wilson, J. W. 1975. *Thinking About Crime*. New York: Basic Books.

Wolfgang, M. E. 1958. *Patterns in Criminal Homicide*. New York, Wiley.

3

THE PSYCHOANALYTIC (SELF-CONSCIOUS) APPROACH TO AGGRESSION
Affect and Act

Henry Krystal

◇

Certain commonly used concepts and ideas have become incorporated in psychoanalytic thinking, along with the prevalent attitudes about them. These attitudes, however, often include meanings derived from childhood and infancy that could bear further examination from the analytic point of view. One such concept is that of passivity. A scrutiny of that feelingful characteristic shows that it often requires tremendous activity for an individual to remain "passive." The most conspicuously and noisily "passive" people—drug dependent individuals—have been shown to have the need to deny their activity while creating in their minds all their world, including their love objects. Thus, they need to experience their self-helping resources as inaccessible to them though present in their very own mind's endopsychic object representations. They use their drug to get around their inner, self-created, repressive barriers in order to gain access to their ability to help and comfort themselves by "introjecting" an object "transubstantiation," i.e., their drug (Krystal and Raskin 1970). I shall discuss the affectivity of aggression to see whether it is subject to similar vicissitudes. For this purpose I shall use the satisfying power of self-consciousness (self-insight) honored in my life orientation as it is in the life-work of my colleague, Dr. John M. Dorsey. This point of view represents an emphasis of psychic reality as the key psychoanalytic concept. Reconsidering aggression from the point of view of psychic reality, I have become aware that it is difficult to study it without some isolation. In order to deal with its totality one has to identify and reconstruct mental events such as the nature of aggression as an affect which includes its cognitive, physiological, dynamic, genetic, and adaptational aspects. In addition, I have become aware of the tendency to handle affects in terms of object and self-representations, and thus to ward off experiencing affects as "feelings" by acting out. These concepts and observations I shall elaborate later.

Freud (1920) has identified aggression with the death instinct and dying, the opposite of the life force, the libidinal energy invested in the survival of the individual and the species. Hartmann et al. (1949) worked out the details of this aggressive drive as it relates to the death instinct.

In our day we are also confronted with one of mankind's biological and psychological puzzles: the survival of the human species may become endangered by a manifestation of libidinal force—the population explosion. The fate of individual man may hinge on a number of paradoxes:

• The poorer, the more miserable the people, the more driven they are to enjoy their child-bearing (not child-raising) function. In a manner of speaking, their aggression toward their world (or oppressors) may seem to be passed on to their children (made unhappy by their "inherited" living conditions).

• The joyous libidinal indulgence in the act of "consumption" can be seen to represent an aggressive act when the United States population, representing 6 percent of the world's population, "devours" 40 percent of the earth's natural resources. As Arthur Miller's (1968) wise Mr. Solomon put it: "the main thing today is—shopping. Years ago a person, he was unhappy didn't know what to do with himself—he'd go to church, start a revolution—something. Today you're unhappy? Can't figure it out? What is the salvation? Go shopping. . . . If they would close the stores for six months in this country there would be from coast-to-coast a regular massacre."

• Our life-prolonging technology has produced thousands of abandoned, inhumanely treated old people who must cope with their capacity to commit suicide.

• Our reaction formations against aggression, especially cannibalism, prevent us from disposing of our corpses by grinding them up and using them for fertilizer. Instead, we use up available ground for cemeteries or create air pollution with cremations. Then the drive to proliferate the funeral preservatory rituals (embalming, cement vaults, etc.) for our "dear departed" in a world currently experiencing genocide and mass fire bombings poses life and death issues worthy of sober inquiry.

Limitations to Aggressive Acts

One aspect of the conditions that make murder possible is, thanks to the mass media, so well-known that it can be considered commonplace: the objects must be dehumanized and made to represent an amorphous evil force. Thus, Lieutenant Calley (1971), when questioned as to whether he shot and killed unarmed women and children in the Mylai Massacre, kept answering to all the questions pertaining to it, "I shot at the *enemy.*" I would like to reexamine my stories involving such depersonalized murder with deepening concern for the vicissitudes of the perpetrators' aggression as a drive, and as an affect.

For example, it appears that in contrast to the "crimes of passion," some mass murderers did not experience any anger. The 6 million dead estimated to have been produced by the 150 years of slave trade were apparently not, for the most part, killed in a rage, but died as a result of destructive transportation methods, which were designated for "efficiency" and cheapness (Mannix and Conley, 1962).

Rudolf Hoess the commandant at Auschwitz considered that his finest achievement was the development of a procedure in which "the whole business of arriving and undressing" took place "in an atmosphere of the greatest calm." Hoess wrote his memoirs in 1959, while in a Polish jail, coolly awaiting his execution. Still, he marveled about the members of the *Sonderkommando*, who knew that they had exactly four months to live, yet carried out their task of emptying the gas chambers and burning the bodies—smoking and eating and behaving as if nothing happened. What impressed him most of all was that the members of the *Sonderkommando* helped to unload the transports, get them undressed, "selected" and into the gas chamber with kindness and consideration, although they were also ready to subdue and remove for shooting any "troublesome" prisoner. Hoess even wrote that he had some "inner anxieties" and was "no longer happy in Auschwitz once mass exterminations had begun," yet he had attended every killing.

In his historical studies of the Nazi genocide policy Hilberg has also found that the Nazis forbade and punished sadistic acts in their entire operation and especially their SS structure; most of it was "built in, in the camp nature" such as "hunger, exposure to freezing weather, overwork, filth and utter lack of privacy" (Hilberg 1961: 577). On at least one occasion when "SS men and German political prisoners tossed 90 Jewish women from a third floor window into a courtyard below, the SS men were transferred to another unit" (*ibid.*: 518). The disciplinary action for the above orgy was not a severe one, because, despite the policies of the upper echelon, the sadism of the camp guards did get "out of hand." For instance, they tried to investigate Hoess, but could not carry the prosecution to completion and as Hilberg (580) notes, Hoess won (*ibid.*: 580).

It appears that the tacticians of genocide knew that mass murder had to be carried out as an unpleasant task (something like fumigating a house) in which each killer had to feel that he was doing it unwillingly, without enjoyment, and as Hoess put it, with "intense self control," "iron determination" necessary to prevent his "innermost doubts" and feelings of aggression from becoming apparent. It might be said that Hoess was the perfect mass murderer, and in fact he has been recognized as such by his Nazi superiors. His background is described by Hilberg as follows: "He was brought up in a very strict Catholic home, and his father intended him to be a priest." Hoess recalled, "I had to pray and go to church endlessly and do penance for every misdeed." While French occupation forces were in the Ruhr, a German terrorist, Leo Schlachter, was betrayed by a school teacher, Walter Kadow. Hoess murdered the school teacher. As a consequence, he was sentenced to ten years in prison (he served five). "While commanding an enterprise in which a million people were killed, Hoess did not personally commit another murder" (Hilberg 1961: pp. 515–16).

He felt that he was performing a chore which was necessary for the German people. Hoess saw himself as a long-suffering victim of his own genocidal activity. Historians have not adequately appreciated the fact that this feeling was shared consciously or unconsciously by

every German, by every human being for whom it had meaning, for
that matter. It was this feeling that they had been victimized that
helped the Germans make possible the period of guilt-free expansion
of the economy and consumption in Germany after World War II
(Krystal 1966).

In order to promote the dehumanization and diabolization of the
object of aggression, it helps if he seems conspicuously different from
oneself. A different uniform will do to identify the enemy, who will
then rapidly be given evil, conspiratorial, ghost, or vermin-like characteristics. The Nazis made a special point of reducing the Jews to
abject poverty and degradation in the ghettos, thus equating them
with vermin to be "squashed" without compunction. Hilberg (1961)
points out that the Nazis had much more difficulty in killing the
"Western Jews" than those of Eastern Europe who were "preprocessed"
through ghettoization to fit the vermin stereotype. Following are examples of illustrations of the failure of such projective defenses.

1) THE "EUTHANASIA" PROGRAM

The antecedent to the Final Solution was the German program of
"euthanasia" originally related to severely retarded and other institu-
tionalized "mental incurables." The program had many similarities to
genocide, beginning with its original rationalization. On July 14, 1933,
the Nazis passed a law "for the prevention of progeny with hereditary
disease." However, as later in the killing of the Jews, the laws did not
tell the truth, but used the words *"Special treatment"* as a euphemism
for the murders. As with the Jews, Hitler expressed the hope that "if
war came" it would be easier for him to carry out the mass murder of
the mental patients (Mitscherlich 1949: 91, quoting the testimony of
Brandt). Hitler ordered that with the best available human judgment,
"after critical evaluation of their state of health, [they] may be granted
a merciful death" (*ibid.:* 92).

Hitler even bragged about the nobility of his enterprise: "I free mankind from the yoke of reason which weighs upon it, from the obscene
and humiliating intoxication derived from chimeras of so-called conscience and morality and from the exigencies of personal liberty and
independence of which only a few can serve. After centuries of croc-
odile tears shed over the defense of the poor and the humiliated, the
moment has come when we must decide to defend the strong against
the weak" (Delarue 1964).

The program against Germans themselves was designed with more care for secrecy and efficiency than the Nazi plan for the extermination of the Jews. Only five centers with volunteer staff were used for the killings; two special organizations were formed for transporting the selectees in specially disguised SS buses and ambulances. However, even this "program" could not be carried out secretly.

A variety of "mistakes" were made by the personnel, such as getting drunk in the local beer halls and telling all about it while crying in their beer. Notifications of the "sudden death" of the mental patient were discovered to always follow the transfer to one of the killing camps. Fancy diagnoses such as "brain edema" were used, sprinkled with threats of "epidemics" to be avoided by immediate cremation. But the clerks notified the wrong people, or reported a patient's death more than once, or actually sent out notices about missing people living and even discharged home (Mitscherlich 1943: 104).

The "careful selection" of the victims also deteriorated allegedly as a result of overwork and indifference, most of the doctors leaving the selection of victims to the nurses and hospital orderlies. Anyone who appeared ill or who in the eyes of the nurses and orderlies appeared to be a "case" was put on a list and dispatched to the place of destruction. "The worst feature of this affair was the brutality exercised by the staff, they simply chose whom they did not like and entered them on the list" (Delarue 1964: 287).

It is interesting to note that some doctors reacted to their guilt about the killing by letting the "thing happen," as it were, on its own. What they really did was to let mentally retarded children starve to death. A Dr. Pfanmueller boasted about his "natural method" to Ludwig Lehrer: "our method is more natural and simple [than poison, injection or such]. With these words he drew one of the children from its crib aided by a nurse evidently on regular duty on the ward. He showed around the child like a dead rabbit and with a knowing expression and cynical grin said, 'This one for example may take another 2 or 3 days'" (Mitscherlich 1949: 101).

The storm raised by the clergy and courts caused Hitler's order to stop this "euthanasia" program. It was claimed that Hitler never openly passed the killing orders, and that the murders were "illegal."

What really made the despotic program unbearable for the German people is best expressed in this statement by the Court of Appeals in Frankfurt: "the [people] are disquieted by the question of whether old folks who have worked hard all their lives and may merely have come to their dotage are also being liquidated. There is talk about homes for the aged being cleared out too" (Mitscherlich 1949: 105). Pastor Browne spoke for the welfare mission of the German Protestant Churches: "Even now it has probably become a matter of thousands of fellow Germans already eliminated without due process of any kind, or about to die in the immediate future." He demanded stopping this awful carnage and having "valid laws" for ordering killing. What he really worried about was "how far will it go?": "Six girls have been killed despite their impending discharge from the institution to become domestics in workhouses. Will the line be drawn at the tubercular? *How about soldiers who incur intractable diseases fighting for the fatherland?*" (Mitscherlich, 1949: 106—Emphasis mine).

2) THE NAZI MEDICAL EXPERIMENTS ON PRISONERS

Among the physicians who engaged in destructive experiments one man, Dr. Rascher, stands out as an individual who indulged in destruction of his "objects" in a most painful way and for no apparent benefit to anyone. Some of the other so-called experimenters had a personal (albeit dishonorable) reason for their experiments: for instance, "Professor Gebhard's sulfonilamide experiments were done to clear himself of the accusation that he contributed to the death of SS General Reinhard Heydrich ['The Hangman'] either negligently or deliberately by failing to treat his wound further with sulfonilamides." Of course, he rigged all the experiments so that the proper prisoners died (Alexander, in Mitscherlich 1949: 58).

But Rascher's infamous experiments proved nothing. His two groups of experiments were killing each human being in a vacuum (he was concerned with the effect of high altitudes on pilots bailing out) or freezing each person. The vacuum experiments produced no data except that the killing of a large number of prisoners was such an extremely gruesome spectacle that his vacuum chambers were later selected for particularly vengeful executions. The freezing and restoration of body heat produced no information beyond that already found in 1880 by the Russian doctor, Depcziwski. However, the orientation and views in the "experiments" reflected attitudes shared by many Nazi leaders. Their aggression was directed toward human beings, rather then animals.

One of the first edicts of Hitler was to prohibit animal experimentation (Ivy 1948). Goebbels entered in his diary in October 1925: "I have learned to despise the human being from the bottom of my heart" and in August 1926, "The more I know about the human species— the more I care for my dog."

Himmler shared many traits and elements of life history with Rascher (also with Hitler and Horst Wessel). Like Horst Wessel, Himmler had been a pimp. Until 1920 he lived with and was supported by a prostitute, Frieda Wagner, who was seven years his senior. They fought savagely. In 1920 she was found dead. Himmler was accused of the murder, but was acquitted. Later, he married Margo Comizarone, a nurse who had worked in a hospital. The doctors there sold drugs and performed "criminal" abortions. She had contempt for doctors, as did Himmler. Through her help Himmler started chicken farming. Later he treated his SS companies much like his chickens— both in dieting (ordering milk and porridge for breakfast, no coffee or mineral water) and in breeding. He established "stud farms" (*Lebensfond*) where fifty thousand children were born (Delarue 1964: 71).

There was an affinity between Himmler and Rascher. Rascher also married a woman older than himself (by 15 years), while she was pregnant for the second time. She was a friend of Himmler's. Himmler and Rascher seemed to be looking for each other. Himmler wrote to General Milch that he needed a man to conduct human experiments who would be a "non-Christian doctor of good scientific reputation, not prone to intellectual activity" (Delarue 1964). Rascher, on the other hand, volunteered for the human experiments and wrote to Himmler on May 15, 1941:

I have noticed with regret that no experiment on human material has yet been introduced here because the tests are very dangerous and no volunteers have offered their services. I ask in all seriousness is there any possibility of obtaining from you two or three professional criminals to be placed at our disposal. These tests, in the course of which the "guinea pigs" may die, would be carried out under my supervision. They are absolutely indispensible to research into high altitude flying and cannot be carried out, as has been previously attempted on monkeys whose reactions are completely different (Delarue 1964: 280).

When they got going, they caused some eighty persons literally to explode in a vacuum, after the subjects suffered pain which caused them to tear their hair out and tear their faces—and of course, nothing was contributed to medical knowledge.

The next project in which Rascher and Himmler were involved was freezing people. The idea was to learn how to save German pilots who were forced to bail out in the North Sea. Still, "for the sake of completeness," Rascher started his project by freezing to death many prisoners. The physiological and pathological findings were reported to the German Medical Societies, with no one objecting to the experimental methods.

Eventually, after killing more than 100 men that way, they stopped the freezing while the prisoners were still alive to try to rewarm them to normal temperature. Himmler (who "believed in magnetism, mesmerism, homeopathy, sorcery and clairvoyancy" [Delarue 1964]) came up with the idea that the frozen fliers could best be reheated by being sandwiched between two naked women trying to have sexual intercourse with them. He wrote in a letter to Rascher: "I am very curious about the experiments into animal heat. Personally, I believe these experiments may bring the best and most sustained results, but of course, I may be mistaken" (Mitscherlich 1949: 26). On one occasion, the following most revealing incident was described by Mitscherlich (p. 27): "For the warming tests with animal heat, four women from concentration camp Ravensbruck were 'marched' to Dachau."

On arrival of the four women in Dachau Dr. Rascher made a discovery which disquieted him, and on November 5, 1943, he wrote the following letter of protest to Himmler:

Four women were assigned to me from the women's concentration camp at Ravensbruck, for the purposes of testing the warming of chilled persons by animal heat as directed by Reichsleader SS (Himmler).

One of the women assigned showed impeccably Nordic racial characteristics: Fair hair, blue eyes, corresponding skull shape and physical build, age 21¾. I asked the girl why she volunteered for brothel service. This was her reply: "To get out of the concentration camp. All who volunteered for half a year's brothel service were promised that they would be discharged from the concentration camp in return." When I objected that it was shameful to volunteer as a brothel girl, I was advised: "Better half a year in the brothel then half a year in the concentration camp." There ensued an enumeration of very curious conditions in the Ravensbruck camp. The conditions described were for the most part confirmed by the three other brothel girls and the woman overseer who accompanied them from Ravensbruck.

My racial conscience is outraged by the prospect of exposing to racially inferior concentration camp elements a girl who is outwardly pure Nordic and might be led on the right path by proper deployment. For this reason, I decline to use this girl for my experimental purposes, and I have rendered an appropriate report to the Kommandant of the camp, and to the adjutant of the Reichsleader SS.

Dr. S. Rascher

Thus, Dr. Rascher, who arranged and watched the most cruel destruction of many men (and who denounced his own father—a physician—to the Gestapo [Delaru 1964: 286]) could not stand the idea of this young woman being exposed to the cold bodies of his victims.

I wish to reemphasize that Dr. Rascher's behavior involved here is the aggressive functioning of his own superego and the life-destroying effect of his ego disassociations. His reasoning about racial theories does not explain it. In fact, what led to the arrest of Rascher and his wife, and their eventual concentration-camp-style execution, was their attempt to deceive Himmler into believing that they had a third child—when the child was actually stolen and "racially impure" (Delarue 1964: 284). Both his destructive impulse and its inhibition were dictated by emotions that were related to the "breakthrough" of identification with the "victim" and the recognition of the victim as representing a child or parent. To generalize the observation—i.e., to give it an ethological frame of reference—an individual may not be free to indulge his aggression if he recognizes the object-representation of his "victim" as being like his self, or related to his child or parent images. If he is to fully indulge his aggressive impulse, he must create a "disidentification" between his self-representation and his object-representation. "Disidentification" is a term used by child psychiatrists to describe a disturbance of the mother–child relationship. It names a situation where the mother is not able to recognize her child as entirely her own mind's creation, and therefore is not able to understand and to fulfill her baby's needs. As a result, the infant is deprived in his own life of his mother's love and care. When that happens, as when a mother feels that it is good for a child to "cry himself to sleep," she acts as if she believes that the child does not experience painful feelings as she does herself. Thus disidentification represents lack of consciousness for experiencing one's object-representation as the creation and organic functioning of one's own mind. This disidentification is (like other defenses) actually based on an unconscious fantasy. In fact, the aggressor and his victim, the "active" doer and his "passive" sufferer or any other endopsychic operation *seemingly* involving two or more people necessitates, by the very nature of the individual mind, each individual's maintaining a view of single identity, and assuming responsibility for *all* of his living, or live in a state of repression.

The repression of this identification may be the most intense and intrapsychically motivated defense. By imagining the emotional reaction in a Nazi considering himself to be identical with the Jew he persecutes and kills, one can get an idea of the urgency for his repressing this identification. Still, the identification is acted out in various ways, and when it is, it shows that the identification is with the stereotype of the hate object which was created by and in the persecutor's mind. For instance, after the collapse of Germany, Julius Streicher donned a disguise of a stereotype of an "Eastern Jew" which he had created in his newspaper *Der Stürmer*—but he was very readily caught—because the Nazis had destroyed all possibility of a Jew's wearing a traditional ethnic garb. Similarly, the hate-dominated unconscious identification includes the most despised characteristics of the hated object.

The codifiers of the inquisition took up most of their manual (*Malleus Maleficarum*) to describe the evil and treacherous behavior of the witches and how the various accomplices of the devil cruelly hurt people in many ways (Springer and Krause 1968). However, when they proceeded to give instructions for the "judicial proceedings in both ecclesiatical and civil courts," they described how the combination of the torture chamber and deceptive promises should be used to entice the accused (assumed always to be a woman) to make confessions which would involve *additional* people.

They considered every accused person guilty and anticipated that she be killed. The instructions they gave, in fact, described not only how the judge should torture and execute the accused but in fact, that he should constantly trick, deceive, and betray her. A technique used has the judge promising to spare her life, but with the promise later rescinded, or another judge substituted. The pattern is the same as in the behavior of the Nazis who accused Jews of being dishonest Merchants and as a matter of official policy engaged in lying, deception, betrayal, thievery, and murder for profit.

Intense unconscious identification with the aggressor's dread of what has been repressed becoming conscious is equally consequential and possibly even more repressed in the victim than in the perpetrator.

Survivors of concentration camps greatly fear their awareness of their identification with their Nazi persecutors. Still, they could not have survived without doing all that they did to live. Since they act this identification out in many aspects of their lives, it would be helpful to become more aware of its force (Krystal 1968).

There is deep wisdom concealed in the fact that, in the period of the holocaust, only the madmen were conspicuously aware of their identification with their Nazis. The so-called madman has ready access to his unconscious identifications. Ringelblum, the chronicler of the Warsaw Ghetto, notes on May 9, 1940, that an eight-year-old child went mad, screaming, "I want to steal, I want to rob, I want to eat, I want to be German." On September 9, 1940, he reports that the psychotic patients in the ghetto asylum "praise Hitler and give the Nazi salute" (Sloan 1958). Among the most persistently disturbing memories of the survivors are abuses by Jewish policemen or Capos, or by "friends,"—e.g., rape by Russian liberators.

The playwright R. Shaw (1967) with profound insight in his play *Man in the Glass Booth* depicted the idea that if either the survivor or the aggressor tries to become fully conscious of his identification with his sadomasochistic object-representation, he is confronted with the threat of madness and death. Although the number of detailed psychoanalytic studies of Nazi mass murderers is virtually nil, we do know a great deal about them through work with people who have identified with them: namely their victims and family members.*

Niederland and I have repeatedly reported the fear experienced by concentration camp survivors when they became parents (especially mothers) that they would somehow destroy their children (1968, 1971). Thus we came to consider thoroughly the handling of aggression by people for whom it is ego-dystonic.

3) THE BREAKTHROUGH OF AGGRESSION

I have observed above that even people for whom extreme aggression and destruction are acceptable and ego-syntonic may run into "inner" psychological blocks—limits to their ability to act aggressively. The

---

* Incidentally, one occasionally sees eating disturbances in children who because of their dread of cannibalistic impulses cannot eat any animal products that are like a person, i.e., revealing skin or recognizable organs.

opposite phenomenon is destructive action in men dedicated to the avoidance of aggression, and to the pursuit of peace and love. We run into such startling observations periodically. An educator discovered that Pestalozzi, the father of kind, humane, and considerate views in education of children, was given to violent attacks upon his son, and almost killed him (E. Krystal 1970). Without making judgments, I shall examine such "lapses" to study the dynamisms involved when one lives one's aggressive feelings.

a) Mahatma Gandhi and Aggression   By his dedication to nonviolence and love for all men, Gandhi brought about the peaceful liberation of India, and tried (but failed) to obtain a resolution in the Indian's attitude toward the Untouchables. In his sincere devotion to love, Gandhi has become an inspiration to his countrymen and all men. There is little question that he represents a modern-day idea of a true saint.

Yet, despite his lifelong struggle against aggression and dedication to love and peace, there are some curious lapses in his life. Gandhi had a generally condemnatory attitude toward his wife, Kastrubai. He blamed her for his not having been present at his father's death because he had been in bed with her. As he attacked and condemned his own "lust" (genital sexuality), he increasingly considered her a threat and a burden until he prepared to separate permanently.

As Erikson (1969: p. 120) puts it: "His wife . . . came to personify a threat to his higher loyalties, even as all loss of semen was traditionally perceived as a drain on a higher vitality." Though he professed to love her, he was given to strangely cruel acts toward her. He was pleased and relieved by every separation from his wife he could arrange.

When Gandhi made his vow of sexual abstinence, it did not seem to occur to him that it was a decision which involved a deprivation for his wife, even though he had long castigated himself for using her merely as an object of his lust. Since the vow of poverty came along with it, he turned to Kastrubai and asked her to give up the few jewels which he had given her.

This little incident is illustrative of the Mahatma's relation with his wife, namely that he resented and criticized her not only for her own characteristics that he disliked (such as her truculent illiteracy) but also for the aspects of himself that he was "fighting" and displacing upon her. Simultaneously, but especially later in his life, he tried to usurp her power as a mother, thus depriving her of the one role he had left her previously. He even blamed her for his impulses to eat, linking her entreaties to eat with mortal danger:

although I had told Kastrubai: that I should have nothing for my midday meal, she tempted me and I succumbed. As I was under a vow to taking no milk or milk products, she had especially prepared for me a sweet wheaten porridge with oil added to it instead of ghi. She fixed too a bowlful of mung for me. I was very fond of these things, and I readily took them, hoping that without coming to grief I should eat just enough to please Kastrubai and satisfy my palate. But the devil has been waiting for an opportunity. Instead of eating very little, I had my fill of the meal. This was sufficient invitation to the angel of death. Within an hour dysentery appeared in acute form. (Gandhi 1927: 332)

Gandhi tended to be quite self-righteous about his actions, unaware of their aggressive implications. Erikson pointed this out (ever so gently) in connection with an incident at the Tolstoy Farm, which Gandhi established. As part of his interest in Satyagraha (passive resistance), he made the young people bathe together, having "fully explained the duty of self-restraint. . . . One day one of the young men made fun of two girls and the girls themselves, or some child, brought the information. The news made me tremble. I made inquiries and found the report was true [that the women had engaged in sex]. I remonstrated with the young men, but that was not enough. I wished the two girls to have some sign on their person, a warning to every young man that no evil eye shall be cast upon them, and as a lesson to every girl that no one dare to assail their purity" (Gandhi 1928: 244). What he did is what many men at many times did in attacking women for whoring (especially with the enemy): he cut off "their long fine hair."

However, the most persistent, and the least conscious expression of aggression persisted in Gandhi's relationship with his oldest son, Harilal, who became a derelict within a year of the Mahatma's death. Gandhi believed that his firstborn son was intrinsically bad, because he was conceived in a state of (the father's) lust, and was not the product of intercourse for conception alone, devoid of pleasure or "passion" (Gandhi 1927: 148). Even though the son did try to devote himself to Gandhi's causes, became a lawyer, and, in 1913, took part in an invasion of Transvaal which led to his spending three months in jail at hard labor (Erikson, 1969, 209), he could never live up to his father's expectations.

When Harilal wanted to get married, his father not only objected strenuously, but in fact started telling even relatives that he had ceased thinking of Harilal as a son (Erikson 1969: 234). Gradually, the situation deteriorated to the point that Harilal was driven to do "bad" things that he knew his father would disapprove of, while Gandhi alternated between protesting his devotion and love for the son (even taking his children to be raised) and expressing the "bad egg" feeling. For instance, when Gandhi learned that his son had become involved in a con game, he intimated that "everyone acts according to his nature"— indicating that the son was the equivalent of what in our society we call pejoratively and hatefully a "constitutional psychopath" (Erikson 1969: 364).

The most clear expression of the pathetic rebellion on the part of the son of this Hindu Saint, was when he abandoned his faith, became a Muslim, and finally perished on an Indian equivalent of our "Skid Row" (Erikson, 1969, 140).

b) Albert Schweitzer and Unconscious Aggression Like Gandhi, Schweitzer had dedicated his life to nonaggression, and his feeling extended beyond man to include all living creatures. After Schweitzer embraced the creed of "reverence for life" (in the summer of 1915), he extended it to plants, insects, and bacteria. During the years when he performed surgery, Schweitzer regretted being a "mass murderer of bacteria" and "once found himself pitying the bacilli of sleeping sickness exposed to a new drug." He did not allow insects, even mosquitoes, to be killed but "installed hinged latches in the screens of his main rooms in Lambaréné, so that a mosquito, if caught under a tumbler can be released gently" (McKnight 1964: 56). Still, Schweitzer was reported to have knocked "the brains out of a litter of kittens or puppies at the river edge rather then see the hospital overrun. He beats the backside of a rooster when he comes over to steal the corn he puts down for his pet hens" (McKnight 1964: 56).

I do not doubt that Schweitzer's devotion to the reverence and preservation of life was sincere and extraordinarily consistent. I believe that he did have difficulty though in the degree to which his aggression was acted out by him without his conscious awareness. One area pertained to his need to be the sole authority, virtually worshipped in his community. He seemed unable to delegate any authority to the people in his hospital. In fact, his behavior caused men to feel oppressed in a way that interfered with their masculine fulfillment. This characteristic caused male doctors to be unable to remain long with him (McKnight 1964: 98–108). It also appears that his attitude toward the natives of Gabon was characterized by a paternalistic devotion and love, similar to the colonialist view that they were childlike and incapable of attaining adult stature (in the European sense) or intellectual and emotional maturity. In other words, he was given to the typical imperialistic view of life.

Schweitzer's ability to live his life in terms of his dedication to love was most markedly limited in his relationship with his wife and daughter. He sent his daughter away to Switzerland and never got to know her. When she came to visit with him to celebrate his 83rd birthday, he said to her, at the end of a fairly long birthday speech:

I thank you for coming to celebrate this birthday with me on your own initiative. I do not know the story of your life well, and I am not much of a psychologist, so I cannot guess whether your life has fulfilled your wishes. However, I think that, having me for a father, and having good children and a good husband, one might feel rather contented.

McKnight wonders if the many admirers in Lambaréné and throughout the world "knew that the birthday they celebrated was also of his daughter Rhene [Eckert]? Who knew that le grand docteur of Lambaréné had a daughter then 39 years old? The coincidence of the birthday is striking enough, but it is even more astounding that the Doctor made no attempt in his speech to honor it with more than a passing reference—and one which would be missed altogether by anyone who did not know that it was Mrs. Eckert's birthday" (McKnight 1964: 166).

Both in relationship to his daughter and his wife, Schweitzer seems to have been unable to experience close affection and intimacy. He allowed them only to be among his most loyal admirers.

These comments are not intended to deprecate his greatness or his dedication and actual ability to live a life of love and helpfulness to his fellow man. On the contrary, perhaps the relationship with his daughter, and especially with his wife, illustrates the point that, if neglect is considered a form of aggression, then it appears that his intense dedication to many good deeds left him with no ability to see his wife except as a faithful (though mostly failing) assistant. It is as if he had to turn his back somewhere, and his family relations were the area of his life where he had to limit his investment. The reason that his relationships with his devoted and adoring wife may be discovered to be the locus of Schweitzer's unconscious aggressive impulses is elaborated in detail by McKnight (1964). Only a few of those will be discussed here, since no "proof" is intended, just an intimation of a man's struggles with his own powers.

Mme. Schweitzer was the daughter of a German-Jewish historian. Her young husband's research activities were the kind that she was familiar with, and apparently she was quite helpful in his scholarly pursuits. However, with her family background it can hardly be expected that she shared her husband's missionary zeal. Out of her adoring love for him, she became a trained nurse, left her family and country, and went with him to Lambaréné. In those harrowing days she labored in a way which made her, in advanced age, refer to herself as: "I was his oldest nurse." Still, Schweitzer never, even in his publications, thought of their travails in any other way except "*my* work" (McKnight 1964: 159).

Tuberculosis was virtually epidemic in Africa, and she contracted the disease. Thus, she spent most of her life away from her husband, coming to Lambaréné when her health permitted to perform her function as mother. As a result, Mme. Schweitzer seemed to feel that her value and self-respect depended solely on her ability to work with her husband; in other words, she found acceptance only in her function as her husband's assistant. Six months before her death and already quite ill and "struggling for breath" she said to Norman Cousins that she felt "foolish" about "this being so helpless. I ought to be working with the Doctor" (McKnight 1964: 162; quoting Norman Cousins). McKnight felt that her boundless adoration for Schweitzer protected her from becoming bitter about her husband's self-centeredness. They both shared a common cause: adoring him. The reality is that even if missionary work had been part of her traditional thinking, which is doubtful, there would still be the unresolved question whether *self-sacrifice* in general instead of self-devotion, is not contrary to the very idea of "reverence for life," since it is a form of human sacrifice.

If we were to make a generalization of the two groups we have considered, the modern saints and the sadistic aggressors, we can find one thing in common to them: *they are unable to be consciously aware of the affects, and motivations, that are contrary to their ideology.* The Nazis were not aware of their love for the "defective" Germans or Jews. Gandhi and Schweitzer were not aware of the areas in which they lived their hatred and aggression. For the reader who is jarred by the juxtaposition of saints and sinners in the same sentence, may I quote Pascal? "Man is neither angel nor brute, but unfortunately if we want to make him an angel, he is made a brute" (In Pivnicki 1970). John Dorsey (1970) has made a generalization concerning affects which is relevant to these considerations: "I have found that whenever I am unaware of the existence of any emotional potential in myself (such as envy, or suspicion, or shame, etc.) my living is then being excessively affected by this particular emotion that I am not even aware is operating in me. Thus my negated jealousy, shame, disgust, or whatever, becomes (unconsciously) hyperactive in guiding my behavior" (p. 90).

DISCUSSION

In the above studies of aggression I have observed that there were inner and unconscious factors that surfaced and greatly influenced the actual performance of the individuals and groups studied. In our survey of people who were dedicated to the indulgence of aggression and destruction on a grand scale we found that they ran into inner blocks, even though their activities were sanctioned by the significant segments of their society and their worshipped leader. Their actions seemed even consistent with their ethics. In point of fact, in the example of Dr. Rascher, the block he developed against using the "Aryan" prisoner-prostitute for his experiments seemed to indicate inner consistency of his moral principles. Still, the act which led to his and his wife's death, the stealing and "illegal" adoption of a "racially impure child," was an extraordinarily inconsistent one and so clearly self-destructive that it certainly must suggest that, despite all, Rascher was burdened with unconscious guilt about his killings.

The failure and discontinuation of the euthanasia program also shows that there are limitations to the capability of groups to indulge in overt, unbridled aggression. As I have already mentioned the SS leadership was especially fearful that sadistic orgies for pleasure might have a detrimental effect on the aggressor.

Both Himmler and Hitler repeatedly addressed themselves to the killer units of the SS, saying they were performing a most unpleasant and painful task to themselves, and one they were doing against great reluctance within themselves, under duress, and only because these acts were necessary for the German people. They acted as exterminators of vermin would for the inhabitants of an infested house. Still, the elite SS-guard, carefully indoctrinated for this task into cadaver-*Gehorsamkeit*, did not always carry out their task in this fashion. On the one hand they were troubled with the feeling of disgust against the people, who did not "fight back"; on the other hand, they showed many symptoms of guilt, and many suffered depression and chronic drunkenness (Hilberg 1961).

Nor is the outcome of the war itself to be totally separated from the Germans' feelings about their indulgence of sadism, as illustrated by Hitler's verbalized attitudes that if the Germans became a defeated people (like their previous victims), then they should be treated in the same way—that they did not deserve to live because they were weak, they were losers, and should be exterminated. This statement clearly shows the identification of the aggressor with the victim. In other words, unconscious guilt and self-punishing activities, as well as inhibitions of destructive activities, can be detected even in people who consciously considered their destructive activities as good, virtuous, even heroically self-sacrificial.

At the other extreme: in my survey of the lives of two of the saints of my age: Gandhi and Schweitzer, I found that these men were successful in developing their lives closer to their dedication to love and service than most of us might even aspire to. Yet, these great and profound men did, without being conscious of it, allow their aggression to get out of hand towards their wives and firstborn children. Even the most consistent and intense lifelong dedication and self-education by these extraordinary men was not successful in protecting them from acting upon destructive impulses toward their love objects.

If self-discipline and the devotion to a life of love and goodness failed to protect these extraordinary men, then possibly a new self-education, or upbringing, or moral and ethical identification can successfully control the aggressive needs of the "ordinary bread-eater."

Self-assertiveness generally is not a matter of choice or preference. Aggression and murderous impulses are within each one of us, and will become manifest toward those who matter to us. We might as well admit it to ourselves and build our educational efforts in the direction of conscious self-awareness for aggressive impulses as a fact of life and love. In fact, it may be useful and necessary for us to recognize and teach ourselves to recognize aggression as an inseparable concomitant of love, and as modality of love (Dorsey 1971).

We must choose between living and bringing up children in the atmosphere of innocence, or of discovery and confrontation with the murder and complicity with murder in ourselves. Psychoanalysts take it for granted that the conscious recognition and verbalization of an impulse makes possible its consideration and moderation on the highest level of mental function. The "highest level" involves not just the availability of judgment, discrimination, and anticipation, but in fact refers to the broadest possible sphere of self-conscious associations. Ideally, both the cognitive and affective aspects of an impulse would be confronted with all types of associations, which would also be fully conscious (self-conscious). In practice, the action will be influenced by a variety of influences that will remain unconscious. It will be no surprise to anyone that the impulses toward oneself, including one's object representations, will include aggressive tendencies. Aggression as hate is a fact of life, whether we think of it as primary or reactive. The difficulty arises when we try to simplify and insist on the "fairness" of aggressive impulses—e.g., that they should be experienced only specifically when "provoked."

Conclusion

The motivation for the current interest in aggression and war stems from two sources: the widespread occurrence of violence in our cities, and the belief that the next war would be destructive to humanity, and that therefore we have to do something about it. However, nothing that we know from archeology or paleontology indicates the possibility of any species surviving indefinitely. Knight has pointed out that the acceptance of the idea of the perpetual survival of the human species is a religious belief, the framework of which is that of a pre-oedipal child: "Judeo-Christian man has nurtured himself psychologically on the belief that his own existence was made meaningful as an expression of a God, who in turn has no significance other than that his children were the center of all His concern." Knight is talking about the infantile, "narcissistic" view of oneself when he adds: "This defining and explaining of all things, even first causes, in terms of oneself, is paranoid, and leads to a need to control last causes, that is eschatology" (Knight 1971: 20).

In other words, there is a residual of the infantile view that if one is "good," everything will go well. Conversely, bad things happen as a punishment. There follows the rest of the magical thinking on which fantasies of eternal survival of the human species are based. Since I do not have to feel only that humanity *must* survive, I do not have to expect only that we shall necessarily come up with the answer that helps us to control aggression and thus save us from self-destruction.

Fortunately, as we have learned through psychoanalysis, unconscious parental aggression may differ little from the Nazi attempts at genocide or from any other "nameless" war of killing. When Freud (1933) acknowledged that the ultimate source of war was to be traced to "a lust for aggression and destruction," he commented that the aggression becomes generally unconscious. "The satisfaction of the destructive impulses is of course facilitated by their admixture with others of erotic and idealistic kind. When we read of the atrocities of the past, it sometimes seems as though the idealistic motives served only as an excuse for the destructive appetites; and sometimes—in the case, for instance, of the cruelties of the Inquisition—it seems as though the idealistic motives had pushed themselves forward in consciousness, while the destructive ones lent their unconscious reinforcement" (p. 210).

Thus Freud indicates that the relegation of the aggressive impulse to unconsciousness, and its rationalization and camouflage behind "idealistic" motives, makes possible the indulgence of the destructive act. If that is so, then perhaps even the recognition of the possibility of a death instinct need not condemn us to pessimism. On the contrary, it appears that an enormously powerful influence upon the future of humanity could be exerted by changing our social attitudes towards the aggressive impulses and the feelings of hatred and anger. Judeo-Christian morality has acted as a repressive social force in regard to aggression, necessitating that it go underground and "break through" in an alienated, unrecognized way, not as self-conscious living.

Psychoanalysis has started the chain of events which has freed much of mankind from a degree of repressive attitudes toward sex. Psychoanalytic contributions have already led to a more comfortable acceptance, and more hygienic handling by many people of one form of aggression: sibling rivalry.

In reconsidering the above "case material" I feel that the way to peace will not be merely through the idealistic way of Ghandhi, Schweitzer, or our own "peaceniks." We can endeavor to help ourselves and thereby help our people to live their aggression consciously, to experience the unpleasant affects and their ideational components without fear of fear. Hate can be lived as a helpful painful emotion and need not be forever acted out in aggressive behavior of individuals (including each individual's society) unconsciously and under the cover of various ideologies.

I have, of course, not demonstrated how I make the jump from observation of certain individuals to the expectation of the effects on groups. However, the progress in psychoanalysis in the last 10 years has included the observation of the mutual interaction between the individual and his societal forces and effects. Still, within this framework, the unique psychoanalytic contribution will be in the area of the individual's understanding and self-appreciation, which will include his handling of his impulses and affects in a way that will enhance his self-respect and integration. Only fully conscious awareness of the aggressive and destructive impulse, and the painful feelings of anger, hate, etc., can avoid acting out an isolated, "chopped up" part of a chain of mental events. In the last resort, I have to go beyond the question of whether I shall "express" my aggression against my self-representation or my object representation to the consideration of how I can live it helpfully and lovingly—that is, self-consciously.

REFERENCES

Calley, L. W. 1971. "All the People Were Enemy, Calley Testifies." *Detroit News*, Feb. 26, p. 2a.

Delarue, J. 1964. *The Gestapo.* New York: Morrow.

Dorsey, J. 1970. *Psychology of Emotion, Self-Discipline by Conscious Emotional Continence.* Detroit: Center for Health Education.

—— 1971. *Psychology of Language,* Detroit: Center for Health Education.

Erikson, E. H. 1969. *Gandhi's Truth, On the Origins of Militant Nonviolence.* New York: W. W. Norton & Co., Inc.

Freud, S. 1915. "The Unconscious." *Standard Edition,* 14:159–209, 1953.

—— 1920. "Beyond the Pleasure Principle." *Standard Edition,* 18:7–64. London: Hogarth Press, 1955.

—— 1933. "Why War?" *Standard Edition,* 22:197–218. London: Hogarth Press, 1964.

—— 1937. "Analysis: And Interminable and Terminable." *Standard Edition,* 23. London: Hogarth Press, 1961.

Gandhi, M. K. 1927. *An Autobiography or the Story of my Experiments with the Truth.* Translated by M. Desai, Ahmadabad: Navajivan.

—— 1928. *Satyagraha in South Africa.* M. Desai. Ahmedabad: Navajivan.

Hartmann, H., et al. 1949. "Notes on the Theory of Aggression." *Psychoanalytic Study of the Child,* 3(4):9–36.

Hillberg, R. 1961. *The Destruction of the European Jews.* Chicago: Quadrangle Books.

Hoess, R. 1959. *Commandant of Auschwitz.* New York: World Publishing Co.

Ivy, A. C. 1948. "The History and Ethics of the Use of Human Subjects in Medical Experiments." *Science,* 108:1–5.

Knight, E. H. 1971. "Eschatology and Ecological Ethic." *Psychiatric Digest,* January, pp. 13–22.

Krystal, E. 1970. Personal Communication.

Krystal, H. 1966. "A Psychoanalytic Contribution to the Theory of Cyclicity of the Financial Economy." *Psychological Forum* 1:357–76.

Krystal, H., ed. 1968. *Massive Psychic Trauma.* New York: International Universities Press.

Krystal, H. and G. Niederland. 1968. "Clinical Observations on the Survivor Syndrome." In *Massive Psychic Trauma.* New York: International Universities Press, pp. 327–49.

Krystal, H. and H. A. Raskin. 1970. *Drug Dependence Aspect of Ego Function.* Detroit: Wayne State University Press.

McKnight, G. 1964. *Verdict on Schweitzer.* New York: John Day.

Mannix, D. P. and M. Conley. 1962. *Black Cargoes: A History of the Atlantic Slave Trade 1518–1865.* New York: Viking Press.

Miller, A. 1968. *The Price.* New York: Viking Press.

Mitscherlich, A. 1949. *Doctors of Infamy.* New York: H. Schuman.

Pivnicki, D. 1970. "Aggression Reconsidered." *Comprehensive Psychiatry* 11:235–40.

Shaw, R. 1967. *Man in the Glass Booth.* New York: Harcourt.

Sloan, J. 1958 ed., *Notes from the Warsaw Ghetto* by Emmanuel Ringelblum. New York: McGraw-Hill Press.

4

MURDER AND THE MEDIA

Stephen Cain

◇

The *Christian Science Monitor* and the *Wall Street Journal* are fine newspapers which rarely, if ever, send a reporter to cover a murder. But for the rest of us, homicide is a staple like the crossword puzzle, horoscope, race results, and "Dear Abby." When the physician-originator of the Scarsdale diet is shot and killed by a former lady friend, it rates a four-column headline in the august *New York Times*. Let even a handyman get murdered in a small-town barroom misunderstanding, and it's big news to the weekly paper.

Yet we're schizophrenic about homicide. When we write extensively about murder—particularly a sensational killing close at home—the local boosters and cheerleaders feel we are demeaning the community and accuse us of trying to sell papers. It is a curious charge. We sell papers to exist (or exist to sell papers). That means attracting readers by writing what they are interested in, and a "good" murder is a far surer bet than almost anything else.

A "good" murder, in the specialized lexicon of a journalist, is one with any quality which can be highlighted to attract readers. Some, like the Manson family rampage, simply command attention. Others depend on a reporter's insight into some aspect which strikes a harmonic chord in the reader.

And our fascination with the subject ranges from the profound to the trivial. *Oedipus Rex* and *Hamlet*, possibly the two greatest mas-

terpieces of western literature, deal with murder. Creation had barely
gotten started before Cain slew Abel. And what young man has come
of age in the last couple of decades without, in fantasy, notching his
guns along with Wyatt Earp, Mike Hammer, or Agent 007?

So for better or worse, we're hooked on homicide, and it would
seem to be a good idea to look at the kinds of murders journalists
choose to write about and some of the ways they approach the stories.
Here are the major, although sometimes overlapping, categories:

- The mass murder or rampage murder, such as the Tate-LaBianca
  killings of the Manson family, Charles Starkweather's five-day
  spree across Nebraska and Wyoming, or David "Son of Sam"
  Berkowitz's lovers lane slayings in New York.
- The assassination of national figures.
- A gangland or professional killing, particularly anything hinting
  at a gang war.
- A prominent victim like James R. Hoffa.
- Prominent perpetrators, such as the famous Leopold and Loeb
  case of the 1920s.
- Any murder that is bizarre, dramatic, unusual, particularly vicious, or particularly stupid. The latter brings to mind the case
  of a suburban homeowner who armed himself with a pellet gun
  to protect his van against vandals and was killed by the police who
  thought he was a burglar.
- Any slaying which triggers the political mind-set of the community
  at the time. A cop-killing always falls into this category, as would
  the shooting of a grocer in the midst of a law-and-order campaign.
  In the early 1970s Detroit had a police decoy unit (STRESS, for
  Stop the Robberies Enjoy Safe Streets) with such a high kill ratio
  that the community's adverse reaction became the story.
- Murder, as a test of how the system of justice functions. As in the
  film *Northside 777*, finding someone unjustly convicted of murder
  and searching for the evidence that will set him free is a journalistic
  version of the quest for the Holy Grail. Another kind of crusade
  is to rage against the judge or jury (or Supreme Court ruling)
  which set free some "obviously guilty" individual.

A major daily newspaper, such as *The Detroit News* (for which I
work), will devote an incredible amount of time, money, and news
space to a killing that falls within one of these categories. Yet they
probably represent no more than 5 percent of the homicides that

actually take place. The other 95 percent, the result of a falling out among family or friends, is generally regarded as mundane, banal, and usually lowlife. Its account is generally condemned to an inside page, where three or four paragraphs appear. Ultimately, the story gets an exceedingly modest form of immortality via the newspaper morgue. A clever or insightful writer like Truman Capote can sometimes create a masterpiece from such material (the book and movie *In Cold Blood* had far more impact on Holcomb, Kansas, than the slaying of the four members of the Clutter family, which is described in the work), but that is rare.

I got to wondering about the 5 percent and the nature of fame (or infamy) and bet several friends they could name five times as many killers as U.S. Senators, but got no takers. I named 54 killers in 20 minutes, giving up after being stumped on who shot Huey Long. Consider a partial list.

There are the assassins: Sirhan Sirhan, James Earl Ray, Lee Harvey Oswald, Jack Ruby, and John Wilkes Booth. Some of the mass killers of recent years: Starkweather, Berkowitz, Manson, Juan Corona, John Wayne Gacy, the Boston Strangler, Los Angeles' Hillside Strangler, San Francisco's Zodiac, nurse-killer Richard Speck, and Charles Whitman (who climbed the University of Texas Tower, produced a rifle, and killed 16 and wounded 31 in 90 minutes), and the Atlanta child-killer. The gangster days saw Al Capone, Baby Face Nelson, John Dillinger, Dutch Schultz, and many more. How about Billy the Kid, the Daltons, the Youngers and Frank and Jesse James as a start on the old west? Skipping through history gives us the likes of Cain, Pontius Pilate, Brutus and Cassius, the Borgias, Henry VIII, Nate Turner, Jack the Ripper, and Alfred E. Packer (the cannibal of Donner Pass). You can take it from there. The point is that, if we don't treasure our killers, at least we remember them.

Yet going through the newspaper clipping files containing the most famous murders of recent decades, one finds rather pedestrian writing. Indeed, a formula emerges.

First there is the breathless, almost incredulous unfolding of the event itself. . . . Starkweather on the run, Speck methodically killing the eight student nurses, or the digging up of Gacy's bodies.

Then there are the second-day stories, such as "Who is 'X' and how does a 'nice boy' turn monster?" They always ask the question, rarely attempt an answer. There are the imagery pieces—going into the student nurses' residence the day after Speck and writing under the headline: "In Terror House—12 Teddy Bears and a Rosary."

While the story is still page-one news, there will inevitably be a roundup story from the files on past mass murders and a syndicated column by Dr. Joyce Brothers failing to make sense out of what happened.

For the really "good" murders, there will be a five-year anniversary article and a 10-year anniversary piece. United Press International, on Aug. 9, 1979, had this to say of the Manson murders:

"LOS ANGELES—On a quiet night in Beverly Hills 10 years ago, a crime occurred that tore the fabric of American Society."

Hyperbole is another characteristic of the really good national murder. Another, if it is to survive in our long-term memories, is that the murder has to have a name or a tagline. Leopold and Loeb were "thrill killing." Berkowitz was the ".44 caliber killer" before he was caught and revealed to be "Son of Sam." "Sam" will live on long after "Berkowitz" is forgotten. Similarly, if California's Zodiac is ever identified, certainly his Christian name will slip our memories as have the four men who were the Zebra killers and the man known as the Hillside Strangler. When the otherwise unidentified "Beast of the Autobahn" claimed his 20th victim in seven years in 1954, German readers didn't need a proper name to once again feel that sense of terror.

Here's a test for your friends: the challenge is that three of the four situations will probably be familiar but the names will be obscure. Ask them to match the situations with the names. (They are listed in the correct order below.)

1. *In Cold Blood* (Perry Smith and Richard Hickock).
2. The "Texas Tower" (Charles Whitman).
3. The French Bluebeard (Desiré Landru).
4. The "Bible reading army veteran," as he was known in a hundred stories, who randomly killed 13 people on the streets of Camden, New Jersey, in 1949 with his Luger (Howard Unruh).

These are killings, remembered throughout the nation over the years, but I would guess that we do not primarily take our view of homicide from them. They scare us from their distance and seem alien to our personal experience.

But if we draw our understanding of homicide from local murders, the way the press elects to handle them is more idiosyncratic than patterned, depending in large measure on the character and personality of either the reporter or editor involved. And it can be almost a matter of chance whether the killer or victim becomes the focal point.

Therese Gallagher would have received three paragraphs had a friend not called one of my editors to say she deserved more or had I not been between assignments. The story, which ran in the October 28, 1970, editions of *The News*, began:

He called her "Tweedy"—not even her regular nickname—but then he didn't know the real name of the pretty girl who had stopped to buy gas at this station for more than a year.

Twenty-year-old Therese Gallagher—Terry to her close friends and family—"got along with everybody, kidded with everybody," in the words of her father.

Had Terry been cold or aloof, gas station manager Ronald G. Rogers, 42, wouldn't have paused at the store where she worked.

He wouldn't have tapped on the window to get her attention or gone into the store to tease this casual acquaintance behind the cash register.

He wouldn't have accidentally blown out her brains in one of those senseless tragedies in which people keep asking "Why?" but never get an answer.

People die every day in ways that are easier to accept or at least understand—at war, in a traffic mishap, during a family feud or even an armed robbery.

Often the victims are a party to their own deaths, but not Terry, not unless we're willing to say the type of outgoing friendliness that allows a person to smile rather than scowl is a defect, a dangerous flaw in character. . . .

Rogers was drunk and waving the gun as a showboating gesture for the benefit of the equally soused girlfriend on his arm. The gun fired.

Part of the story followed Rogers from the gas station through various bars to the chance encounter. The greater part of the article, though, told about Terry—her hopes, what she meant to friends and family, and the fact that she had lived her entire life in the central city of Detroit without guile or fear.

The article attempted with at best only partial success to avoid the major defect of victim-oriented stories—the overwhelming temptation to speak only well of the dead. Even if family and friends were willing to talk more fully about the victim, including the less attractive as well as the attractive aspects of her life, the conventions of our society are such that writing ill would certainly bring an angry reaction. So we write only the good. Since monochromatic good is dull, victim-oriented stories are only a minor part of general newspaper homicide coverage today.

It was not always so. There is a strong "sob sister" tradition in journalism—stories which always carried the same inner message that, no matter how bad things were for you, they were tougher for someone else. Homicide victims were a part of this tradition once. The ultimate limiting factor, however, is that murder victim stories are almost always single-shot affairs. A sob sister story about a family being evicted by an evil landlord can be kept alive for article after article until the problem is solved.

On the other hand, there was nothing sob sister or even remotely sympathetic to the victim-oriented stories that followed Nick Arvan's death on October 20, 1970. Arvan, a moderately successful 42-year-old Detroit area criminal lawyer, had been found in a rural wooded area, bound and blindfolded with tape, dead from a single shot behind the left ear—"gangland-style," as they say.

The stories in *The News* and *Detroit Free Press* at first followed a standard progression: "Lawyer missing," "Lawyer found dead," "Few Clues in lawyer slaying," and "Murder probe foul-up charged." Then nothing was written about it for four months. It was the kind of case that an editor puts on his calendar for a phone check every week or so to see if any progress is being made (but not big enough, as in the Jimmy Hoffa case, to write "no progress" stories).

What happened next was the kind of semi-random event that determines, in the final analysis, a lot of newspaper content. It was a slow news day and an editor, rather than ordering the routine phonecall, said: "Cain, find out what the hell they're doing on the Arvan case."

Several weeks later, the answer filled a bit of the front page and an entire inside page. Arvan, it turned out, had lived and worked too close for too long to too many petty hoodlums, many of them violent men or surrounded by violence, and had made too many enemies. Pulling together information from a half-dozen police agencies who had not been talking to each other revealed that three different criminal groups each had the motive, means, and opportunity to reduce the population of lawyers by one.

There was a gang of professional burglars, the leader of whom was also involved in a million-dollar counterfeiting ring and was mad at Arvan, who had extracted a large fee on the promise of being able to spring his girlfriend—and failed. One of the gang members was known to tape his robbery victims in the same way as Arvan had been taped.

Then there was a major drug ring which was also heavily into burglary, fencing stolen goods, double-cross and murder of its out-of-favor members. Arvan defended two of the principals on narcotics charges, but they were convicted and each sentenced to 20 years to life in prison. They were enraged. A third man, who had brought Arvan into the case and paid his fee, was apparently murdered at the same time as the lawyer, although his body wasn't discovered for three months.

The third possibility, tenuous but fascinating, involved a one-time member of Detroit's infamous Prohibition-era Purple Gang and a couple of other men involved in a Chicago "scam" to liquidate stocks and bonds originally stolen from mail sacks at New York's Kennedy Airport. When the scam collapsed, one of the men abandoned his partners, fled to Detroit, apparently with some of the mob's securities in his possession, and is believed to have visited Arvan. A tipster told police he gave the stocks and bonds to the lawyer as an insurance policy against any rash action by his confederates. But he was gunned down five days after Arvan's body was found.

What *The News* finally printed was a kind of journalistic "Lady or the Tiger." But unlike the famous short story, the reader was offered three doors, not two. The murder remains unsolved.

Nick Arvan, murder victim, became more of an abstraction than a flesh-and-blood human being, an excuse to delve into the netherworld of crime and the corpse any good mystery story needs. In stark contrast is the case of Mrs. Margaret Lynch, the portrait of a murderess as victim. In 1971, she had been convicted of first degree murder for starving her month-old baby daughter to death and sentenced to mandatory life in prison—hardly an obvious object of sympathy. Yet to discover her as a flesh-and-blood person and to view the tragedy through the tortured circumstances that made up her universe was to learn that there had been no murder. Dr. Bruce L. Danto became involved through myself, helped Mrs. Lynch earn her freedom, and established—for the first time in the State of Michigan—the defense of "diminished mental capacity."

The story of how Mrs. Lynch became a story illustrates that journalism professors, public relations specialists, and others who think they understand the media don't really appreciate the odd twists and turns that determine what ultimately appears in print.

This tale begins when a Detroit judge, who has his own view of justice sentenced a women to 10 years at the Detroit House of Correction for a minor larceny; he had intended to set her free after a year or so, but forgot. She escaped, was recaptured, and faced an additional term—even though she had already served two years.

I was curious to see how the judge would explain his negligence to the young woman and accompanied him to the prison, which at that time housed all the female felons in the state. He fell to talking about a new judge in Flint, Michigan, who had failed in previous tries for the bench but topped the incumbents when she ran on a strong law-and-order platform. That election, apparently turned the entire bench of that city into a nest of hanging judges. He boasted that he could identify Flint cases knowing only the crime and the resulting sentence. I challenged him, and we went to the prisoner files to check it out. He got four in a row before missing on Margaret Lynch, who was from Midland.

The file said Mrs. Lynch's baby had a cleft lip and palate. I forgot all about the uncomplimentary story I was going to write. My oldest son was a cleft-palate baby, which meant he hadn't been able to get enough suction on a bottle (or nipple) to eat. I had to feed my son with a turkey baster, yet Mrs. Lynch had been given instruction in bottle-feeding. Without that coincidence, together with the emotional tie and special knowledge it entailed, I would not have pursued the Lynch case. A second coincidence: The editor who gave me the freedom to follow the story also was the father of a cleft-palate son.

My own personal sense of justice was offended. In Detroit and Wayne County, for example, infanticide is prosecuted as manslaughter, a recognition that it is more a family tragedy than murder in the holdup-murder sense.

Moreover, Mrs. Lynch was listed as having a dull-normal IQ of 80. From my talks with her, I doubted that it was that high. Dr. Danto said it was 63. For example, even though she was convicted of deliberately withholding the bottle from her baby, Mrs. Lynch neglected to tell her lawyer that on the day the baby died, she had fed the infant in the presence of two social workers, and that the previous day, she had taken the baby to a meeting of Operation Head Start mothers and passed the baby to other women who had attempted bottle feeding. That the death was either accidental, negligent, or resulting from incompetence seemed more plausible than premeditated murder.

Why, then, had Mrs. Lynch signed a confession, after five hours of most skillful interrogation, stating in one damning sentence that she had deliberately withdrawn her baby's bottle?

Enter another coincidence and piece of incidental knowledge. Working for a small paper four years before, I had written a story based on a sheriff's department crime report about the homicide detectives investigating the "apparent smothering" of an infant. They labeled it a "death under mysterious circumstances," were interrogating the parents and had ordered an autopsy. I had never heard of Sudden Infant Death Syndrome (SIDS) which, of course, was what the autopsy revealed. With the help of some equally ignorant officers, I had compounded a family's tragedy.

I made what amends I could in print. I learned, for example, that even though "crib death" is entirely blameless, there is an informal subspecialty in psychiatry dealing with the needless but very real guilt feelings of SIDS parents. Moreover, there were instances in the literature both of parents being accused of murder and of mothers confessing to killing their children in instances later medically proven to be crib death. Since Mrs. Lynch was jailed immediately after her child's death, told repeatedly by both her stepmother and the authorities that she killed her baby, and had no one to turn to for support, it seemed logical she would confess whether or not it was true.

One significant question remained: Why were the authorities so damned sure she was a murderess even before the confession? The complete transcript of the interrogation made it clear that the detective sergeant who conducted the marathon questioning "knew" she was guilty and had set out to gain her admission from the outset. A veteran investigative reporter and editor I have respected for years insists that the police never frame someone out of whole cloth. He said there is usually some secret piece of inadmissible "evidence" which so convinces them of someone's guilt that they consciously or unconsciously bend the rules to build a case. I turned the tables on the sergeant.

With the help of a couple of six-packs of beer, I interrogated the sergeant for seven hours in the basement recreation room of his home before he told me about "Margaret's dog."

Mrs. Lynch's "best friend" and neighbor had told the authorities that Mrs. Lynch had starved the family dog as a dry run for her baby and that the local Humane Society had been called out to pick up the creature who was so far gone that it had to be put out of its misery. A simple telephone call to the Humane Society revealed that the dog had throat cancer—a large tumor which prevented it from swallowing. And it turned out that the "best friend" believed that Mrs. Lynch had been having an affair with her husband. So much for the secret "evidence."

Despite the new defense evidence from the social workers and Head Start mothers, despite demonstrable prejudice on the part of the trial judge, and despite a confession which never should have survived a "Walker hearing" test of admissibility, 28 months passed before Mrs. Lynch was released. It was Midland County's only first degree murder conviction in 10 years, a case which helped propel an assistant prosecutor to a judgeship, and the authorities fought her release all the way to the Michigan Supreme Court. In the end, she had to plead no contest to involuntary manslaughter to gain her freedom.

Once one concluded that she was NOT guilty of infanticide, Margaret Lynch—the victim of a double tragedy—became a fundamentally sympathetic figure. But there was nothing sympathetic about the "bikers."

Thomas V. Gladish ("Ten Speed"), Ronald B. Keine ("Grub"), Clarence Smith Jr. ("Sandman"), Arthur Ray Smith ("Monterey Flash"), and Richard Wayne Greer ("Doc") boozed too much, sold whatever pills they didn't pop, shot at stray dogs, beat up stray people and otherwise acted out the pridefully antisocial lives of outlaw motorcyclists.

They had the misfortune to pass through Albuquerque, New Mexico, on a Los Angeles-to-Detroit trip. All but Flash were framed for a particularly brutal emasculation murder, convicted of first degree murder, kidnaping, rape, and sodomy, and sentenced to die in the pale green gas chamber of the New Mexico State Prison in Santa Fe.

The Detroit News, which had never heard of Albuquerque's "crime of the decade," became involved when a friend of one of the bikers wrote a letter which began: "To who it may appeal to." She said her "ole man" and "brothers" were innocent. The editor who read the letter misunderstood the relationships, admitted feeling instant sympathy for this poor girl whose father and brothers were in such dire trouble, and assigned me and *News* Reporter Douglas Glazier to check out the case.

Four of the original five bikers had once been Michigan residents, as had the murder victim. Assistant Managing Editor Boyd Simmons (since retired) sent Glazier to New Mexico to reevaluate the evidence and me to California to backtrack the gang. The expectation was that we would come back and write one rather lurid murder story with a local angle.

It didn't work out that way. We made 13 trips to New Mexico, four to California, three to Minnesota, two to Arizona and one to Virginia, logged 3,000 hours on the investigation, cost the paper more than $50,000 in travel expenses and salary and wrote in excess of 100 stories. Thirteen months after we started, on December 15, 1975, the bikers walked free. During those months, we managed to:

- Provide the bikers with solid alibis for the time of the murder.
- Discredit every single piece of physical evidence and expert testimony that went into the conviction.
- Turn around the prosecution's "eye witness" to the murder, who would later return to New Mexico from hiding and testify that she had invented her story about the bikers after being bribed and blackmailed by the authorities.
- Unearth the existence of the murder weapon, which turned out to be the key physical evidence proving the identity of the actual killer.
- Convince the actual killer—whose out-of-state confession was discounted by the authorities—to return to Albuquerque to stand trial. (He was convicted of second degree murder two years after the bikers were freed.)
- Provide the District Attorney with a witness to solve and gain a conviction in a totally unrelated murder.

All this sounds too heroic. We succeeded only because it was a sloppy frame, the authorities were incredibly stupid when they tried to be clever, and every time they tried to tie up a loose end they gave us another tool to help unravel their case.

Glazier had reason to believe his Albuquerque motel room was being searched and many of his phone conversations monitored. The police once tailed me half way across New Mexico, and another time the District Attorney tried to get Glazier fired. With time and expenses mounting, leads turning sour and the case going nowhere, we might have dropped out.

But then we learned that investigators from the Bernalillo County (Albuquerque) DA's office were interviewing everyone we had talked to, even the people we encountered on our many false trails we followed. The pattern of their questioning was clear: they were attempting to build an obstruction of justice case against us. Later, the threat was made explicit.

It was another example of official stupidity. There is an iron rule of journalistic attitudes and behavior: Push a newspaper and it will push back harder (even when it's wrong). We were in the battle to the end no matter what, once we felt we'd been threatened.

During the many months, Glazier, Simmons, and I got a lot of static from a number of readers and even a few fellow staffers about why we were spending so much effort defending such God-awful bad people as the bikers. The answer, which we truly believe, is that justice is punishing individuals for their bad deeds, not for being bad people. The very badness of the bikers made it all the better a story—there was no sentiment to cloud up the principle. The joke on us, the final irony, was that the bikers turned out not to be nearly so bad as they had tried to be. One went back to the old ways. A second, the brightest and most introspective, couldn't face the mess he'd made of his life and committed suicide. The remaining pair have become reasonably upstanding family men and contributors to the community.

Beyond the nobility of principle and the less noble pushing back when pushed and even the fact that four lives were at stake, one other factor above all else gave us motivation: the exhilaration of the hunt.

Whenever you see a newspaper uncovering a corrupt public official, tracking a company which was secretly dumping toxic wastes, or exposing brutality in a child care facility, there will be a reporter behind the byline all tanked up on adrenalin. It is a phenomenon to which you can attribute many of journalism's successes and excesses.

And a good murder pumps a lot of adrenalin.

5

SURVIVORS OF HOMICIDE
The Unseen Victims

Bruce L. Danto

❖

In the 1960s, almost nothing was taught to psychiatry residents about homicide or survivors. My training was no exception. In January 1966, just six months after completing psychiatric residency, I learned how true this was.

On a Saturday morning, services were coming to a close in a large suburban synagogue. Without warning, a young man raced toward the pulpit, pointed a gun at the chief rabbi, and read a psychotic indictment of the congregation and the world in general. Then he fired one shot into the rabbi's head and another into his own. The killer lingered for about eight days before he died; the rabbi survived for about 3 weeks.

This event shocked everyone. The rabbi had been loved by his congregation and the community at large. The killer came from a well-respected family, had been loved by many of his peers, and had been a Woodrow Wilson scholar. The story touched a congregation, a community, and a country.

My relationship with the rabbi had been a long one; we had been neighbors and he had assisted in officiating at my wedding. Before going into military service, I had seen him serve as a chaplain in the Army where he had been in combat in the South Pacific. He was a heroic, wise, and well-loved man. However, notwithstanding my feelings about the rabbi, my attention was drawn to the killer and his family. I felt the need to visit them and offer support.

While their son still lived, my wife and I met and visited his parents in the hospital. They were grateful for the support we offered them. At one point during our visit, the father excused himself to see his son in the Intensive Care Unit. I sensed he was apprehensive about that visit and followed him. His son was connected to a respirator which was taped to his mouth. His head was swollen to the size of a pumpkin as a result of neurosurgery and cerebral edema. Physiologically, he was alive, but clinically, he was dead. On seeing him, his father bowed his head and wept. I reached out for his hand and squeezed it as a token of support. Although nothing was said, there was a touching of hearts between two humans—one who lost a loved one and another who sensed his tragedy. Our next visit was at his son's funeral. We would not meet again for another 12 years when, by chance, we met the father in a restaurant. He introduced himself and extended a warm greeting. Initially, I had not recognized him.

Another personal experience with violent death occurred in January 1976, when my family and I were huddled on a sandy beach on Marco Island, Florida, trying to feel some warmth from a rather elusive sun. As I was digging in the sand to find a religious medal my son had lost, a little girl was also digging for seashells in a nearby mound of sand. Unfortunately, she located something other than shells. She exposed the toes of a 16-year old girl who had been reported missing from a New Year's Eve party some 12 hours earlier. I walked over to investigate and saw the toes in a circle of sand which had been scooped out.

Someone called the sheriff's department. After introducing myself and showing my own police identification, I joined them in the investigation. The crime scene was protected, checked for clues, the sand was sifted for evidence, and the body was disinterred. It was apparent that the girl had been beaten, raped, and then strangled with her own pedal pusher shorts. After the body was removed, I accompanied the detectives to the nearby condominium and offered to break the news to the surviving parents.

When they saw us enter the room and saw me holding my medical bag, they knew their daughter had been found and was dead. They moaned, wailed, and expressed intense rage at the police. They accused them of spending time writing traffic violations rather than catching criminals and preventing girls from being murdered. The police left quickly.

I embraced the parents, held hands with them, cried with them, and listened to their cries and self-recriminations. The mother was guilt-ridden because she had permitted her daughter to attend New Year's eve festivities with other teenagers on the patio. Her brother, who was two years older, felt intense guilt because he had left her alone and agreed to let her walk down to a pitch-black sandy beach with a boy she had met only two weeks earlier. As it turned out, this boy was the killer. The father felt guilty for bringing his family to Florida and said that she would have been alive if he had made other plans. The parents snarled at one another, each blaming the other for faults such as the mother being overconcerned and too controlling of her daughter, and the father being too trusting and too interested in his business.

During the rest of the evening I stayed with them, confronted them with their distortions and unrealistic charges, guilt feelings, and recriminations. I pointed out that the reason their daughter was dead was not because they had brought her to Florida or permitted her to attend the party. The reason she was dead was because some man had killed her. I pointed out that the killer had made that decision and nothing they had done was responsible for his decision and action.

Particularly touching was the fact that the father had always been a peaceful man who worked hard, spent much time with his family, and was deeply committed to them as was the mother. He made a special point of the fact that he never went to violent films, never watched violent television programs, and never read stories about murder or violence.

As we drove out of town the next day, we learned that the police had arrested the girl's killer. Her death and my investigative role were topics of conversation with my children. This was their first real contact with violent death. The victim had been a little older than most of my children. They sensed the human tragedy of that event and the loss experienced by her parents.

After arriving home, I telephoned the parents several times. There were many discussions about the court procedures which awaited them, in terms of the preliminary hearing and trial. There was discussion about whether the mother would have to be present since she was not an actual witness of the crime. Although they were still depressed, their guilt feelings were lessening and becoming more manageable. They expressed concern about the killer's being successfully defended and walking away from jail. Daily living activities were encouraged and supported, such as the father's returning to work, initiating contact with friends and relatives, handling their questions and feelings, and proceeding with the business of rearing their two sons. Plans were made for further telephone calls to them. Some of the emotional upset was calmed when they saw the killer convicted and sentenced to prison for second-degree murder. At my last contact with this family they all seemed to be returning to a normal life.

Some years ago, a woman was referred to me for psychiatric evaluation regarding an injury she received while working as a nurse in a local hospital. While lifting a patient, she developed a chronic low back syndrome. She was unable to work and carry on normal activities, such as taking care of her home, working in her garden, and even engaging in sexual relations with her husband. Her pain was formidable, and she became very depressed; she could see no future, and her husband had found it necessary to take on a second job. Her depression was treated effectively in four months, and she dropped treatment without a word. She was functional and had made an adjustment to her new life style.

Some years later, she phoned again for an appointment. Her Workman's Compensation and Social Security cases had been successfully implemented and her depression had lifted until a new development occurred. Her oldest son had been charged with the murder of two young adults in a drug-world robbery he committed. The son steadily protested his innocence, but the weight of evidence was against him, including a deathbed statement by one of the victims. Money and jewelry, along with the murder weapon, had been recovered from his room in his home.

The woman was all but destroyed. She and her husband had been devout in their religion. They had both worked hard to support and rear their children. They loved one another deeply and had come from the South where they had been taught to be responsible, family-oriented persons. Missing was the stereotype of inner-city dweller, parental model of violence, family disruption by divorce or desertion or any sign of instability that might fit the usual sociopsychological explanation of why a young man might turn killer. She and her husband were crushed, hurt, humiliated, and oppressed by the unrelenting guilt feelings of having produced a moral monster. They became socially withdrawn and functioned like automatons, in a lifestyle based on fulfilling only routine chores. This woman could not visit her son in jail; any news of him came to her through her husband or letters from her son, which she did not answer.

Sensing her emotional turmoil, the prosecuting attorney informed her that she could not attend the trial; her son also requested that she not come. It was apparent to me that he wanted to ensure she would not have access to information about his crime so that he could continue to play the role of innocent victim of the police and court. That had been his style some years earlier when he was convicted of armed robbery and served in a local prison.

In her treatment, we focused on her anger toward her son for what he had done to the victims, one of whom she had known because the young man had been a friend of her son's. In therapy, pressure was brought to bear to support her in a decision to attend his trial and become involved in the process. Becoming active in dealing with her life and feeling capable of making decisions rather than being told what to do diminished her feeling of helplessness. Her depression began to lift as she watched her son, and made him watch her, as the people's case unfolded against him. He witnessed his mother's sense of strength; when he was convicted, she was prepared to hear the life sentence pronounced by the judge.

When last seen, she was less depressed, had written to her son in prison, was intending to visit him, and was able to confront his protestations of innocence. Of equal significance was the fact that she and her husband picked up the pieces of their life, and she agreed to take a vacation trip with him to visit their family in the South. She was prepared to face their curiosity and concern about the murders. That trip was made successfully, and their sexual relationship was resumed with pleasure. It became a source of great satisfaction to her that she and her husband had a happy marriage, a meaningful future together, and were not the killers or makers of their killer son. They realized that their son was the one who decided to kill and that he had been held responsible for his actions in the eyes of the community.

They knew they had not reared him to take a life. She felt she owed it to her husband to make a happy life for them. As happened the first time, she dropped out of treatment. It would appear that future contact with her will depend upon whether a crisis presents itself to her.

These stories establish the tone for a discussion about the persons who are the real survivors of homicide. The persons mentioned have lost a loved one or an important person in their lives has been killed; or else they are related to or are emotionally involved with the killer of someone else. I shall use the term "survivor" to describe all such persons. Each has his or her own type of victimhood.

It would be short-sighted to define such victimhood merely from the standpoint of loss of a loved one or from anger and hurt at being viewed as an extension of a killer. Other things happen to survivors of homicide. They become victimized by police, staff at the medical examiner's office, the media, officers of the court, or socially significant persons. It is necessary to explore these areas as well to gain a better understanding of the magnitude of this type of survivorship.

Police work, especially homicide investigation, can be very stressful for police officers as well as victims. Like the doctor who must also deal with death from unpleasant causes, the police officer finds it necessary to isolate his feelings about what he sees. After a while, like his medical colleague, he views the dead as if he were observing slabs of beef in a packing house. He may dehumanize the dead person and all persons associated with him or her. Anger toward society in general may occur if he feels he is being buried by an endless number of corpses and violent persons. He becomes surrounded by nothing but ugliness and diminution of life. Without realizing it, he may become emotionally dead.

Some doctors suffer the same consequences on account of their work. They may come to feel that they are dealing in terms of things rather than people. As Jack Webb used to say on *Dragnet*, "Just give me the facts, ma'am."

Compounding his reaction to the people he meets and deals with is his need to handle anger being directed toward him, the anger which survivors of homicide feel and direct toward the detective who has the task of breaking the news to them. They scream, cry, wail, moan, and spit out, "Why are you people spending our money chasing people to issue tickets instead of going after the *real* criminals, the people who killed our _____?" The experienced officer will wait painfully until their rage subsides. When the survivors' mood changes and they retreat into a passive-dependent type of surrender, the officer feels more inadequate because he has isolated all feelings about his work. How can he deal with the openness of such raw feelings in others when he has denied the quality and intensity of his own?

As a consequence of his own struggle with feelings, he may concentrate on sifting and listening to facts and diverting his feelings and those of the survivors; he may try to bow out of confronting such feelings by mumbling things about trying the best they can to catch the criminal, that progress is being made, that leads are being checked out, and that they don't have the information because that is handled by another police bureaucratic department such as the public information section.

If a particular homicide is followed by another or a series of them, then a new source of pressure on the homicide detective appears. The press and politicians raise public questions about the competency of the homicide division. Complementing this pressure is that which comes from his own feelings of impotence and demoralization. This type of pressure was graphically illustrated in the case of members of the Child Killer Task Force in Oakland County (Michigan), where the killer or killers of four children have not been caught, despite an intensive three-year manhunt.

Some homicide investigators, like other police officers, may feel that the only people who can understand the nature of their pressures and work are other policemen. Soon they may find themselves unable to communicate socially with nonpolice persons. This becomes significant in viewing the homicide survivor, as he too is a non-police person.

More feelings of isolation are seen in regard to the relationship between the homicide investigator and survivors of the killer, who frequently are viewed by the investigator as an extension of the killer. They are mistrusted because it is feared that they will try to aid the killer and help him obtain an acquittal. In reality, they may hide evidence or deny the killer's responsibility for his crime. Sometimes, however, they show great rage toward the killer.

Staff in the Medical Examiner's Office practice greater degrees of emotional isolation of feeling, more emotional remoteness from the survivors, and less concern about their psychological death survivorship. Showing concern might involve simply draping the body, or washing off bloody areas where wounds were inflicted. Contact can be limited by confining it to a simple identification of the body, and then taking leave of the survivor to return the body to its drawer. Questions about the case can be referred to the Medical Examiner or the homicide investigator. More than the police, the attendant in this office deals with *things* rather than people. This "thing" orientation spills over into their relationships with survivors. For many of them, everyone is a thing; in this way, they have dehumanized the living, who appear to them as if they were dead. From this group of persons, the homicide survivors will receive no support. Nothing has been done to change or educate them; those who apply for and work in this type of job are poorly educated, poorly paid, and poorly trained in terms of offering any degree of emotional support to the survivors.

Members of the media frequently become hardened, much like vultures who descend upon the remains of a decomposing corpse. The spectacle of Jonestown is still fresh enough to remind us of photographs and video reports of masses of bodies lying over a field of leveled jungle, arms about one another, adult bodies covering babies who had been poisoned, and closeup pictures of chief characters such as Reverend Jones decomposing in the heat. The dead and their survivors become objects to be exploited. The children who saw their teacher killed in a Detroit schoolroom were questioned by reporters who hounded them so that when an expression of fear appeared, hidden photographers could capture this and print their pictures on the front page of the daily newspaper.

The media may opt to investigate the character of the deceased or the killer after the crime details have been published. New angles and information are sought and published in the papers and aired in radio and television accounts. Survivors in a state of grief and survivors of killers who cover their faces or try to avoid an expression of humiliation over a crime they did not commit are caught by the snap of a shutter and impress of a ballpoint pen. In this way the list of victims grows and the battlefield of media activities and coverage turns a brighter shade of red; involved persons begin to bleed as their lives emerge in print.

Sensationalism is the name of the game in newspaper coverage of a homicide and in stories about killers, their families, and to a lesser degree, in regard to the family of the victim. However, little attention is actually paid to the survivors of the homicide. The eyes of most reporters are turned toward the police and their search for the killer. In radio and television, movies and plays, the survivors are scarcely touched. The television program *Roots* was a rare exception, as was the play *Shenandoah* (later made into a movie). Both presented some material concerning the event of homicide on families, a community, and in the case of the television series, the history of a people .

Usually, however, the entire focus is on "Dirty Harry" or Kojack— their roughness and toughness and idiosyncrasies. Nothing is mentioned about survivors of homicide (unless a policeman is killed, in which case you might see a 10-second scene depicting the grief of his widow or his buddies on the force).

The net effect of such media coverage of homicide is to deny the reality of loss to the survivors of the deceased as well as the killer, to glorify and exploit violence, and to cast people in the roles of good guy and bad guy. Although the media have been presented with a marvelous educational opportunity to educate people about problems encountered by the survivors of homicide, their cries go unheard; and the public remains ignorant and insensitive to their plight. For the media, homicide appears to remain a target area for exploitation and fascination rather than as a source for meaningful information.

Adding to the list of involved persons who have been insensitive to the needs of the survivors of homicide have been officers of the court. This may be due in part to the court's traditional focus. For centuries, the court has been concerned with facts of a crime as they relate to the law as it has been written and interpreted by local and appellate courts. The court's interest is to ensure that the law is followed, and that, if found guilty, the perpetrator is sentenced. Its only concern about people relates to the presentence report about the convicted defendant. Usually, scant attention is devoted in such reports to the characteristics and problems of the survivors of the killer, and nothing is ever mentioned about the survivors of the homicide victim. In light of such presentence information, the court appears interested only in, for example, whether the defendant has been so mentally ill that he will be sent to prison with recommendations for treatment.

In cases of murder, the sentence is usually determined by statute. In lesser charges of homicide, such as manslaughter, the judge has greater leeway about sentencing and the presentence report has more meaning and practical purpose. However, in spite of this, the court traditionally has shown little interest in survivors.

Court police officers' primary concern about survivors of the victim is to make certain they do not take their revenge for their loss in the court. Similarly, they also watch friends and relatives of the perpetrator, to make certain they do not attempt to aid in his escape. These security concerns are realistic and appropriate, but such limited focus offers no support for these people who do not pose such security risks.

The attorneys are officers of the court and primary figures in the murder trial. The defense attorney engages in contact with survivors of the killer only to ensure his fee if he is retained counsel and to use them, if possible, to show the good character of his client. They become actors in his strategy of defense. On the other hand, the prosecution might seek them out to show how bad the defendant's background, family, and lifestyle were so that a picture of an apple rotten to the core can be painted for the jury. He might want the family survivors of the victim in court so that the jury can see the loss brought about by the killer and for the killer to see them, so that he can squirm and possibly feel guilty. Once again, little effort is exerted by either court officer to offer assistance to the survivors of homicide.

When neighbors and relatives of survivors of homicide are involved, they can serve as an effective support system for survivors. They can offer sympathy, take over important responsibilities such as shopping and food preparation, and see that the little details of living are handled. However, on the killer's side, usually little support is forthcoming. Adding to what might be outright hostility toward them is the embarrassment, humiliation, and guilt they may feel about the act of the killer. They become victims of a collective sense of guilt. If the homicide has been well-publicized and family problems have been aired, their sense of embarrassment and need to retreat socially intensify.

A sensitive parent of the killer feels the guilt of having failed the sociological mandate to be an effective parent and to rear a socially identified child. Homicide challenges the achievement of a warm and confident feeling of accomplishment of this mandate. If neighbors and relatives shun the parents of the killer or victim, their feeling of having failed to properly rear the killer or protect the victim takes over and dominates the survivor to a point of relentless insecurity and doubt.

For example, the brother of the girl who was buried on the beach will have to live forever with the feeling that perhaps if he had accompanied his sister with the young stranger she had met two weeks earlier, she would still be alive. Their mother felt she had shown poor and fatal judgment by permitting her daughter to attend the New Year's eve party near the beach. Her father experienced the agonizing feeling that his daughter would still be alive if he had not brought his family to the condominium in Florida.

Of concern is the practice of some neighbors to seek contact with the survivors to satisfy curiosity and morbid needs or to view the survivors as "celebrities" of a kind if the homicide has been well publicized and captured the interest of the media and community. Like some members of the media, neighbors and relatives may indirectly exploit the survivors, whose suffering usually prevents them from either seeing what is going on or protesting the mistreatment they receive.

It should be apparent from this discussion that survivors of the victim and killer require skillful and open emotional support, which members of the institutions that come into contact with them usually fail to render. The police, staff of the Medical Examiner's Office, and media personnel usually fail to recognize their needs or develop any interest in correcting the problem and sponsoring efforts to provid. programs to make support available.

Each community should encourage existing social health and welfare agencies to develop programs to supply a support system for such survivors. Not only should these programs focus on the survivors themselves, but also they should develop contact with the police, medical examiner personnel, court personnel, and trial lawyer associations. The latter groups really need information and education about the problems of survivors. They need to hear about what their role and behavior toward them could mean in terms of lightening their burdens as victims.

Probably the first effort to start a program for survivors of homicide has begun at the Suicide Prevention and Drug Information Center at Detroit Psychiatric Institute. The program was formulated in 1978 and opened with initial publicity on February 21, 1979. This announcement led to the first group of survivors contacting the Center for group therapy assistance, and the program developed as a result of careful planning and contact with Deputy Chief Gerald Hale of the Detroit Police Department.

The program's aims were explained to volunteers of the Suicide Prevention and Drug Information Center. Those who were interested in being trained and oriented to work with the group therapist who was the social worker at the agency participated. Some who had been active as therapists for Survivors of Suicide were also interested in this project, one designed to offer help to survivors of those homicide victims or killers. One of the volunteers had been a survivor of homicide himself. He had regained custody of his son following the death of his former wife at the hands of her boyfriend, and he had gone through his son's adjustment to his mother's death.

Following the selection of a nuclear group of therapists, a meeting was scheduled with Deputy Chief Hale, who had been the chief of the Homicide section for the Detroit Police Department. He and his staff were interested in the project, but were not in a position to adopt or enter into a direct administrative relationship, because department policy prohibited endorsement of any specific community agency outside the police department. As the department had worked closely with suicide prevention, it was evident in view of a specific need for this type of mental health program that the department would support the program in a cooperative manner.

A press conference was called and local newspapers, radio, and television stations ran stories about the program and the need for help for survivors of homicide. The response was immediate. An initial group of 10 was formed and after the callers were screened, a location for evening therapy was obtained from a local church. One caller was screened out of the initial group of survivors of victims as she had killed her husband who had been a wife abuser for some years. Since a group of survivors of killers could not be formed, she was referred to a wife abuse agency which had a treatment program. It was felt that too many members of the group would either reject her because she had killed another person, no matter how justified, or would feel inhibited in front of her. Furthermore, it was feared that she would feel socially isolated in the group because there was no one with whom she could feel a common bond.

In 1977, a young woman, whose cousin was stabbed by an addict who robbed her of $7.00, was deeply depressed over the death and tried to develop this type of support system for survivors of homicide. However, because she was too involved in her own grief and emotional problems, the group never took hold. Her efforts were lost when she committed suicide.

I had considerable contact with her and tried to offer as much emotional and professional support as I could. I permitted her to telephone me collect. Efforts were made to assist her through psychiatric treatment in her own community. Although her program and life failed, I was convinced further of the need for supportive services for survivors of homicide. Certainly her own homicide survivorship tipped the scales and contributed to her decision to commit suicide.

In this discussion, there has been a focus of the needs of survivors of homicide from the standpoint of the victims and killers. What effect the reaction of medical examiner's personnel, police, court officers, the media, and neighbors and family have on the survivors was discussed in terms of additional weight added to shoulders already sagging from emotional loss. Some of the problems of survivors were presented and what factors arise from unconscious forces and sociological factors were viewed in light of how they determine or influence their reactions to the kind of survival they have.

What is glaringly apparent is that nothing has been done to help these persons. Occasionally, a survivor shows up for psychotherapy. It is hoped that this discussion and proposal will encourage the creation and support of programs for persons whose human needs have been ignored for centuries. Once such programs are developed, it should be possible to determine effective ways of helping the survivors and should also provide a way in which significant research data can be collected.

6

EUTHANASIA
A Clarification

Leah L. Curtin

◇

The issue of euthanasia is much in the public mind today as is evidenced by the introduction of no less than 37 proposed statutes in the various state legislatures in 1978. Health professionals are inevitably drawn into this controversy, not only by virtue of their role and function in society, but also because the proposed legislation specifically names the physician and the registered nurse as the "implementors" of euthanasia. While the debate rages, it has become increasingly clear that confusion is mounting in regard to what this term means and its potential implications for individuals, health professionals, and society at large.

The function of language is to facilitate communication—to clarify, to accurately convey meaning and thought. "To understand a word is to grasp how it is used in the language game" (Passmore 1968:427). The meaning of a word "does not consist in the objects it names, but rather in the way it is used in the English language" (*ibid*:428). My article considers the meaning of the word "euthanasia" and how it is used in the English language. I believe "euthanasia" has losts its utility; it no longer clarifies or promotes understanding.

Certainly, expressions do occur for which better substitutes could be found; in the case of euthanasia, one ought to be found. Many persons are unfamiliar with the term. Its meaning is equivocal and ambiguous; it is general where it should be specific, often allusive where the allusion is not known or obvious, and often a malapropism or a misnomer (Ryle 1966). The word's would-be defenders may well claim that euthanasia is a perfectly good word, which connotes a happy or painless death. It is from the Greek *eu* (well) and *thanatos* (death).

This is all very well, if one can assume that the meaning of a word is derived strictly from its etymological origins rather than from its use in the language. But in usage, euthanasia does not, in fact, always accurately reflect its etymological origins. A happy or good death has been defined by Daniel Callahan of the Institute of Society, Ethics, and the Life Sciences as one in which: (1) an individual has lived out his normal life span; (2) has fulfilled those goals in life which he set for himself; (3) has fulfilled all of his obligations and responsibilities; (4) has not experienced excessive or prolonged pain; (5) has died owing to natural means (he has not been shot or run over by a truck) (Callahan 1976). The dictionary definition of euthanasia, i.e. "the painless inducement of death for merciful reasons" (*Webster's New World Dictionary, 1966*) can hardly claim to meet these criteria. To "induce death" would imply that some artificial means were taken; otherwise, death would occur naturally and there would be no need to induce it. It may then be presumed that there is no reason to suppose that the individual had lived out his normal life span. Whether the individual has fulfilled his obligations and responsibilities or goals in life is a moot point, and certainly not addressed in the dictionary definition. The definition would imply that the intention must be merciful, but no mention is made of for whom the death is merciful (for an individual suffering pain? for the family or friends of that individual, who cannot bear to see his pain? for society, which must often bear the painful burden of the expense of his care?). Such a phrase is certainly ambiguous in its meaning.

Still, this ambiguity might have been tolerable, were the semantic waters not muddied further. Now it seems that euthanasia is used to denote a number of practices that vary widely in their significance and impact. However, they bear one thing in common: the death of a human being. Here is a brief analysis of practices that all fall into the category of euthanasia.

Voluntary Mercy Killing

This practice most closely conforms to the dictionary definition of euthanasia. It would permit the direct killing of a person upon that individual's request. One might feel that the term "assisted suicide" would be more appropriate; however, there is a subtle shade of difference. The phrase "voluntary mercy killing" carries with it the implication that some physical disorder resulting in the imminence of death and probably associated with the person's increasing deterioration or some degree of pain is the motivation for the request (Anon., 1962). The phrase assisted suicide carries with it no such implication, but merely denotes those instances when an individual for a variety of reasons (dishonor, disgrace, despair, etc.) may request assistance in the act of suicide.

An example of voluntary mercy killing may well be the case of George Zygmaniak. Mr. Zygmaniak was a patient in the intensive care unit of Jersey Shore Medical Center in Neptune, New Jersey. He had been paralyzed from the neck down in a motorcycle accident and had begged to be killed. His brother, Lester, smuggled a sawed-off shotgun into the intensive care unit and fatally wounded George.

Death Authorized by the Individual

Prior to the onset of the disease or disability and presuming that the individual is no longer capable of expressing personal wishes, the individual may execute a document authorizing this death (Mannes 1974). It would seem that the phrase "mercy killing with prior authorization" would be a more accurate description of this practice.

An example of legislation permitting such a practice was introduced into the Idaho State Legislature (H.B.143) in 1969.

Death Not Authorized by the Individual

Death may be induced with the consent of those empowered to act in someone's behalf. Such a practice is referred to as noninvoluntary euthanasia (Kole 1975: p. 143). The word noninvoluntary would appear to need some clarification. *Websters New World Dictionary* defines the word voluntary as "brought about by one's own free choice," and the word involuntary as "not by choice, not consciously controlled"; the prefix "non" meaning "not . . . and is used to give a negative force, especially to nouns, adjective and adverbs; non- is less emphatic than in- and un-, which often give a word the opposite meaning." The word noninvoluntary, although not found in any dictionary of the English language, has been manufactured to describe those situations in which a proxy authorization is obtained for mercy killing. According to *Webster's New World Dictionary*, the word proxy means "the agency or function of a deputy; the authority to act for another" and would seem a most appropriate descriptive word for this practice. The phrase "mercy killing with proxy authorization" would appear to be a more accurate description of this practice than euthanasia or even noninvoluntary euthanasia.

An example of "mercy killing with proxy authorization" could well be the administration of an overdose to a child in the final stages of Tay Sachs Disease upon the authorization of the child's parents (Fletcher 1973).

Death for Merciful Reasons

Euthanasia may refer to the practice of directly inducing death for merciful reasons without the consent of the individual or anyone empowered to act in his behalf (Fletcher 1973).

Some may feel the word "murder" would be more appropriately used to describe this action; however, there are significant differences. The word "murder" means by dictionary definition, "the unlawful and malicious or premeditated killing of one human being by another." The definition of mercy when used in this context would appear to conform to the fourth definition of mercy as presented in *Webster's New World Dictionary*: "kind or compassionate treatment; relief of suffering." It would seem that the qualifying adjective "mercy" would preclude the use of the word murder to describe this practice as the inclusion of the one (mercy) precludes the other (malice). Perhaps a more accurate description of this practice would be involuntary mercy killing.

An example of involuntary mercy killing would be as follows:

a mass of broken cranial and cerebral tissue emerged, the head was born to everyone's horror and the emaciated fetus began to cry—everyone was equally horrified. The mother would soon come out of the anesthetic and demand to see the baby. I undertook to bathe the baby myself. . . . I . . . immersed the baby head first.—Lord Segal of England, describing how he drowned a newborn baby who had been mutilated at birth ("Mercy Killing" 1973)

Withholding of Life Support Systems or Treatment

Euthanasia is often used to refer to the withholding of artificial life support mechanisms or treatments. There are several instances.

1. When such mechanisms or treatments offer little, if any hope of benefit to the individual, life support systems may be voluntarily withheld (*Interim Hearings on the Rights of the Terminally Ill 1974*). This practice would involve considerations regarding the benefits, or lack thereof, of treatment for a given patient. Once in possession of the known facts regarding his physical condition, the patient might freely opt for no treatment. Such a practice could be more accurately referred to as the patient's right to refuse treatment, even though such refusal might mean death or the hastening of the moment of death.

An example of this practice could well be the person with kidney failure who refuses to undergo dialysis or the individual with oat cell carcinoma of the lung who refuses chemotherapy.

2. Artificial life support mechanisms or treatments may be withheld with the prior voluntary authorization of the individual—i.e., before the onset of the disease or disability and presuming that the individual were then no longer capable of expressing her wishes, she executes a document authorizing the withholding of such artificial life supports or treatments under certain conditions. This is generally the practice referred to in the "Living Will."

3. Euthanasia may refer to a noninvoluntary withholding of artificial life support mechanisms or treatments when such mechanisms or treatments offer little, if any hope of recovery (Duff and Campbell 1973). Such a practice might be more accurately referred to as a proxy authorization to withhold treatment.

An example of proxy authorization to withhold treatment would be a decision not to treat a newborn with significant defects upon the authorization of the parents. One such example follows in the case of a hopelessly ill baby:

The hospital gave the baby no treatment other than pain killers—no antibiotics to fight infection and no oxygen therapy to aid his breathing. Just good nursing care and a diet of milk. As the baby lost strength, the nursing staff became so upset the hospital speeded up the hours of rotation. Peter couldn't hold down his food, so at his death, dehydration was severe. Meningitis had reoccurred. . . . Severe retardation, a mindless existence, would have been certain (Pell 1972).

4. Euthanasia may refer to the involuntary withholding of artificial life support mechanisms or treatments when such mechanisms or treatments offer little, if any hope of recovery or when such treatments might prove to be excessively inconvenient to the family (Hall and Cameron 1976). Such a practice would imply that there was no consent from the individual even though he would be capable of giving consent or from those empowered to act in his behalf. Such a practice might more accurately be referred to as the involuntary withholding of treatment.

An example of the involuntary withholding of treatment would be as follows:

The night before surgery, the woman's son-in-law called, reminded the doctor that he had performed approximately the same surgery on the woman several years earlier and asked him to cancel the surgery. If the physician operated the next day, the family savings would be wiped out and they would have to go without a color T.V. a second car and a larger home. [The physician] explained that the few extra years she would gain from this operation would hardly justify the privation to which this young family would be subjected (Hall and Cameron 1976).

5. Euthanasia may be used to refer to the practice of the voluntary withdrawal of treatment or artificial life support mechanisms when (a) they have not significantly benefited the individual, (b) they are no longer effective in the treatment of the individual, (c) they prove to be excessively painful to the individual or (d) they offer little if any hope of recovery to the individual. Such a practice could more accurately be referred to as the patient's right to withdraw from treatment (Fletcher 1973). An example could well be illustrated by the kidney dialysis patient who refuses to undergo further dialysis or breaks the prescribed diet.

6. Euthanasia may well refer to prior authorization to withdraw treatment or artificial life support mechanisms under the same conditions listed above, while presuming that the individual is unable to communicate her wishes. Certainly the phrase "prior authorization to withdraw treatment" would be far more accurate and specific than the general term euthanasia. An example might well be the removal of a respirator from an individual who had executed a Living Will and who is now comatose.

7. Euthanasia is commonly used to refer to the practice of nonin-

voluntary withdrawal of treatment or artificial life support mechanisms (Curtin 1976) when such mechanisms have not significantly benefited the individual, are no longer effective in the treatment, prove excessively painful, or offer little, if any, hope for recovery. Such a practice, however, would be more accurately described as proxy authorization to withdraw treatment than as euthanasia. An example would be the celebrated Karen Ann Quinlan case wherein the parents authorized the removal of a respirator from their apparently irreversibly comatose daughter in the full expectation that it would hasten the moment of her death.

8. Euthanasia may be used to refer to the involuntary withdrawal of treatment or artificial life support mechanisms (Colen 1974) under the same conditions listed directly above. Such a practice would be more accurately described as "involuntary withdrawal of treatment."

One example of involuntary withdrawal of treatment would be the following:

About four times in the past year, doctors at the Maryland Institute for Emergency Medicine turned off the respirator that was maintaining the life of a quadriplegic patient whose body was completely and irrevocably paralyzed—but whose brain was functioning. . . . The quadriplegics are never told their respirators are going to be turned off, and their families are told only obliquely, according to Dr. William Gill, clinical director of the institute. . . . Their spinal cords have been severed at the base of the skull, usually in an accident, and they cannot live without mechanical aids. . . . They can think, see and hear" (Colen 1974).

Aesthetic or Eugenic Killing

Euthanasia may be used to describe a practice wherein those who "would be certain to suffer any social handicap—for example any physical or mental defect that would prevent marriage or would make others tolerate [their] company only from a sense of mercy," (Will 1974) are put directly and painlessly to death. The principal concern in this practice is not the individual, but the aesthetic sensitivities of other persons in society. An aesthete may be defined as "a person highly sensitive to art and beauty; a person who exaggerates the value of artistic sensitivity or makes a cult of art or beauty." The "goodness" of this death, or the "mercy" exercised is therefore for the aesthetic values of society, a society that places the highest value upon youth and beauty. It would therefore seem more appropriate to refer to this practice as aesthetic killing. Some may feel that murder would be a more accurate term, but there is a subtle difference. Murder by definition implies a malicious intent while the intent here is not strictly malicious, but rather characterized by a sincere desire to spare society the "pain" of viewing or supporting "those whom some persons would have difficulty in recognizing as human" (Will 1974).

A second motive for aesthetic killing may be to promote the "improvement of the race," (Alexander 1971) in which case it might be more accurately referred to as eugenic killing.

Medical Triage

Euthanasia may be used to describe the practice wherein those who have little or no hope of recovery or who offer no potential benefit to society are *refused* treatment (Wertz, 1973:146). The individual's potential and probable contribution to society is stressed; his wishes or potential for human fulfillment are not factors in the decision-making. In such a practice the concern is clearly for the welfare of society rather than a concern for the individual or his family. Such "selective utilization of medical resources inadequate to care for all those in need," (Wertz 1973:154) would more accurately be described as "deliberate medical triage." An example of deliberate medical triage might well be Dr. Walter Sackett's 1974 proposal in Florida for "Death With Dignity."

Sackett wants to include retarded citizens, especially profoundly retarded ones (he calls them grotesques), in the category of "terminally ill" people. He thinks the second and especially the third provisions of his bill would permit Florida to extinguish the lives of 90% of the 1500 most retarded people in state hospitals. This, he says would save billions of dollars that could be used for "good social purposes" (Will 1974).

Therapeutic Euthanasia

Euthanasia has been defined as "institution of therapy that it is hoped would hasten death" (Williams 1973). The word therapy is a derivation of the word therapeutic which Websters defines as "serving to cure or heal; curative; concerned in discovering and applying remedies for diseases." The word death is defined as "the act or fact of dying; permanent cessation of life." It would seem antithetic to use the word therapy in conjunction with the hastening of death unless we are to redefine either death (e.g., as a cure for disease) or therapy (e.g., as serving to kill, killing; concerned with hastening death), or possibly both. For this reason, this contemporary definition is rejected as paradoxical and nonsensical.

Summary

In summary, then, the word euthanasia as used today may refer to any one or all of the following: voluntary mercy killing, mercy killing by prior voluntary authorization, mercy killing with proxy authorization, involuntary mercy killing, the patient's right to refuse treatment, prior authorization to withhold treatment, proxy authorization to withhold treatment, involuntary withholding of treatment, the patient's right to withdraw from treatment, prior authorization to withdraw from treatment, proxy authorization to withdraw treatment, involuntary withdrawal of treatment, aesthetic killing, eugenic killing, or deliberate medical triage.

However, euthanasia may actually come closest to conforming to its etymological origins when used to refer to the care and treatment of dying patients as epitomized by St. Christopher's Hospice in Sydenham England (Morrison 1973). Such a practice, for clarity's sake, would be best referred to as humane and reasonable care for the dying patient.

We have, therefore, discovered the ambiguity of the word euthanasia so far as to see that, as it is commonly used in the contemporary English language, the word connotes many diverse and widely divergent propositions related only insofar as they all imply the death of an individual human being. The means (if any) used to induce death, the reasons for the inducement of death, and the ramifications of the acceptance of these various practices are so widely divergent that the continued use of one term to apply to all of these (i.e., euthanasia) would appear to promulgate confusion rather than promote clarity. I conclude, therefore, that the word euthanasia should be eliminated and replaced with more appropriate terminology—a course of action that would allow for a more cogent exploration of the various ethical, legal, social, and medical factors of the various practices. It would also promote rational dialogue among those most seriously concerned and most directly involved with such practices.

REFERENCES

Alexander, L. 1971. "Medical Science Under Dictatorship." *Child and Family* 10(1):40.

Anon. 1962. *A Plan for Voluntary Euthanasia*, 2nd rev. ed. Euthanasia Society of England.

Callahan, D. 1976. Lecture presented at the International Institute of Health Care, Ethics and Human Values held at Mt. St. Joseph College, Mt. St. Joseph, Ohio, July.

Colen, B. H. 1974. "Doctors Decide Life Support End." Washington *Post*, March 10.

Curtin, L. 1976. *The Mask of Euthanasia*. N.C.F.L., Inc.

Duff, R. and A. G. M. Campbell. 1973. "Moral and Ethical Dilemmas in the Special Care Nursery." *New England Journal of Medicine* (October 25), p. 894.

Fletcher, J. 1973. "The Control of Death." *American Journal of Nursing* (April).

Hall, E. and P. Cameron. 1976. "Our Failing Reverence for Life." *Psychology Today* (April), p. 106.

Interim Hearing on the Rights of the Terminally Ill. 1974, p. 38. San Francisco, October 8.

Kole, M., ed. 1975. *Beneficient Euthanasia*. Buffalo, N.Y.: Prometheus Books.

Mannes, M. 1974. *Last Rights: A Case for the Good Death*. New York: Morrow.

"Mercy Killing: When Doctors Play God." 1973. Zalienpole, Pennsylvania *News*, November 3.

Morrison, R. S. 1973. "Dying." *Scientific American* (September).

Passmore, J. 1968. *A Hundred Years of Philosophy*. Baltimore: Penguin Books, p. 427.

Pell, R. 1972. "The Agonizing Decision of Joanne and Roger Pell." *Good Housekeeping* (January), p. 135.

Ryle, G. 1966. "Systematically Misleading Expressions." In M. Weitz, ed. *Twentieth Century Philosophy: The Analytic Tradition*, New York: The Free Press. p. 183.

Webster's New World Dictionary, Second Edition. 1966.

Wertz, R. ed. 1973. *Readings on Ethical and Social Issues in Biomedicine*. Englewood Cliffs, N.J., Prentice-Hall, p. 146.

Will, G. F. 1974. "Death With Dignity?" Cincinnati *Post*, May 20.

Williams, R. H. 1973. "The End of Life in the Elderly." *Postgraduate Medicine* (December).

PART TWO

THE KILLERS AND THE VICTIMS

7

MILITARY HOMICIDE
It Is Still Murder

Harold J. Bynum

◇

Murder in Normandy

In 1942, at the age of 27 (with only a tenth grade education), I went from my job as a machinist into the U.S. Infantry. In less than a year I rose through the ranks from a buck private to second lieutenant. Counting the time spent in hospital with wounds, in German Prisoner of War camps, and as an escaped P.W., I was in combat for almost a year. I received one promotion in combat and was an infantry Company Commander for a short time. During that period, my outfit fought from the breakout on the beaches of St. Lo to the front lines of Bastogne when most of us were wounded, killed, or captured at the very center of the Battle of the Bulge.

My first combat experience occurred in late June 1944, after the invasion. Before leading my own men in combat, I was attached to another front line infantry division as an extra officer to get experience. First, I was aware of the awful stink of death and gun powder; then, I saw Germans who had been left unburied and were swelling and bursting open in death. This was a quiet time; preparations were being made for the breakout from the beaches. As the attack began, the attached officers, like me, were sent back to their own units. We were lucky, for some of these men were killed by our own aircraft bombs which were supposed to clear the way for them when the yellow target smoke marking the front lines blew back over them. Try to imagine what it was like to be bombed, wounded, or killed by your own air force. Crazy murder!

I rejoined my own company and saw my first action at a small town which at least two of our divisions had been trying to take for a day or two. We went into action in the afternoon. I remember seeing a dying G.I. with a large bloody wound in his chest. A company medic cried while he tried to help him. As I watched, the G.I. died with a smile on his face. He seemed to be saying, "I feel sorry for you guys. It is all over for me now. But you have to go on."

We were in a skirmish line fighting our way down a slight hill, going from hedgerow to hedgerow with no covering artillery or mortar fire. Someone had failed to give us this cover, nor did we have the experience to form a protective covering of fire from our light weapons. It was pretty much an individual or buddy affair. As I moved down the hill, I heard a loud popping noise which sounded like two flat boards being slapped together. This noise seemed to come from behind my head, as if someone was shooting at me from behind. A lot of others were fooled by this too. Some of them actually turned and fired into the rear, no doubt hitting some of our own men. More crazy murder! We had not been trained to locate where the bullet would come from when someone was trying to kill you. But if you lived, you learned quickly that you heard the pop and then the thud of the recoiling gun being fired at you. And to locate the guy trying to kill you, you had to shoot at the thud or recoil sound or flash of his weapon and not at the pop of the bullet that seemed to come from behind as it passed by your head. There is no imagining the confusion and death this caused with green, untried troops with no covering fire, against experienced Germans with superior weapons.

Fear? I was afraid without knowing it. My mouth felt dry, as if full of cotton; my guts were tied up in knots; my sex organs were trying to pull back into my body. I had all those sensations, but it never entered my mind that they were caused by fear. Immediately, I drank all my water. I watched two friends from A Company go over a corner of a hedgerow about 100 yards in front of me. They were the lead company. I followed across the field and lacking experience jumped over the hedge at the same spot they had used. I landed in the pool of their blood collecting between them. They had been killed crossing the hedgerow. For a minute I froze. Then I heard my platoon sergeant, say, "Where is Lieutenant B?" I said, "Here I am. Let's go." We continued to fight our way on down toward the sunken road at the edge of town. This was our immediate objective. I don't know how we made it. You saw nothing to shoot at. You shot at sounds of guns recoiling, at gun flashes, at sounds of German voices and smells. Yes, if the wind was right, you could smell wine and the leather odor of German soldiers. It took all afternoon to go about 500 yards. During that time, I saw only one walking German. He had a Red Cross on him so no one shot him. Yet we killed and wounded several of the enemy.

All sorts of things happen while men are murdering each other, even things that make you laugh. When we reached the sunken road, we joined up with A Co. Lieutenant M. and I shared the same foxhole and were trying to protect ourselves from incoming German mortar fire. We had formed a line along the road and were expecting a counterattack which never came. While we were ducking the mortar fire, one of Lieutenant M.'s men crawled over and said, "Lieutenant M., I got to shit. Where should I shit?" We couldn't believe our ears but Lieutenant M. said, "Jimney Censor fires, man! Shit on the ground." We laughed at this poor soldier. Yet, he relieved himself right there and never got a scratch.

When the counterattack failed to materialize, my company was ordered to take the town. By the time we got started it was about 11 P.M. We were lucky. As we attacked, the Germans pulled out and we got through the town before they leveled it with 88s. Our friends in reserve were caught and lost many killed and wounded. I remember what a good feeling it was to expect the worst up front and get the best despite the fact that my friends were being killed.

My first action is described at some length to offer some idea of the experiences of green troops—the fear, confusion, crazy killing, lack of realistic training, and lack of any real feeling for anyone but yourself and the friends who are right next to you, whom you depend on as they depend on you. And while this is happening, the enemy isn't looked upon as something human. He is mainly a force of noise, smells, death, pain, and terror. He is trying to kill you, and you are trying to kill him. But there is more to it than that: we did not kill their Red Cross man.

Different Types of Killers and Murders

If you survive about three days in combat, this changes. First of all,
you learn that only about 12 out of 40 men are any good at killing.
The others are there just to get killed, wounded, or to break down. I
remember ordering these men to fire their weapons and having them
fire one or two rounds while I was present, then trying to hide after
I had moved on. What is the difference between men who kill and
those who will not? I do not know. Perhaps it is fear of being killed
themselves. They seem to think that if they didn't fire their weapons
no one would see them and they would be safe. But that was not true.
The good soldier, the best killer, lasted longer than the nonkiller or
poor soldier.

If you survived, you learned that the best combat men, the best
killers in the outfit, were the bravest, most dependable, best liked, and
most quiet-spoken men. No "loudmouths" made the grade. No drink-
ers did either. In our outfit, there were two psychopaths who, at times,
were good, but generally were undependable. You, or they, never
knew what they were going to do next. They acted mainly on impulse.
There was one loner, hunter type. He made a very good "sharp-
shooter." Then there was the death lover who took crazy chances, like
riding a bicycle in the front lines. He didn't last long. You soon learn
whom you can count on, and the outfit settles down into different
small "in groups." They respond to whatever comes up. They develop
pride in their own ability and in their outfit. Replacements have to
prove themselves before they are accepted.

It should be added that just as there are all types of men and killers
in combat, these men kill for different reasons and, at times, for no
apparent reason. They kill to win the war or to get it over with so they
can go home. They kill to protect themselves and their friends, to
prove themselves, to save face. They kill on impulse. There even
comes a time when they kill because they enjoy it. After all, men have
been satisfying their needs and solving their problems by hunting and
killing a lot longer than they have by using their reason.

Here are a few examples. We have fought our way against light
resistance to the top of a hill in a woods. At the time, the Germans
were fighting a delaying action in Normandy. We dig in for the night.
Three German soldiers came down a road toward us. The order is

passed along to let them come on in and be captured for information. Corporal C., a combat veteran, kills one of the Germans for no apparent reason. The other two ran back to their lines. Corporal C. gets up, runs around in a circle shouting, "I got the S.O.B." He has to be knocked down to keep from being killed because the Germans really open up on us now. We are pinned down. The first sergeant had to bring up the remainder of the company at a great cost of killed and wounded to form a firing line so we can move to a more protected position. All because of Corporal C's killing for no apparent reason.

Or there is the example of reflex killing. You go over a hedgerow and surprise two Germans who are trying to duck your artillery fire. You kill them on reflex or they kill or wound you. (By the way, much of the time you hope you get the "million dollar" wound which will not cripple you too much but will get you out of combat. I remember seeing a G.I. coming back holding a wounded arm with a big smile on his face and his friends congratulating him.)

Another example: after fighting for days and nights to the point of almost complete exhaustion, you discover many strange things happening to you. You are afraid before an attack, you feel sick, you ache with exhaustion. You hate the killing. You wonder what people are doing at home. You pray for it to end, yet there seems to be no end in sight. Then the attack and killing start, and from somewhere you get the energy to do your job. You lose ordinary human feeling and for a brief instant you feel all powerful, fearless. You get a terrific thrill or kick out of it. You have a strange peak experience, probably because you are so miserable death would be a relief. Or, perhaps at times, you have a feeling of what it is like to be a god, to have the power of life or death over other human beings. Maybe it is like the feeling the criminal has when he kills a holdup victim. You can get rid of a lot of frustration, anger, and hate. You can satisfy many self-centered desires by killing.

Very small things can get innocent people killed in a war. For example, we were going through Normandy without too much resistance when suddenly from a hill top I caught a glimpse of what appeared to be a part of a German machine gun squad walking in a small town a few hundred yards to my front. I asked for and got artillery fire which did a lot of damage to the town. We took it without firing a shot. There were no dead Germans, but there were dead civilians. One of my men looked at an old lady and then at me and asked, "Why?" My answer was wouldn't you rather see her there than your own mother? Who knows what would have happened if I hadn't caught that glimpse of the Germans?

Murder in the German Prisoner of War Camps

The final examples of war murders and reasons for killing will be taken from the Battle of the Bulge and my experiences in and out of four different German Prisoner of War camps in Bavaria. After recovering from wounds received as we approached Paris, I returned to my company which was in an outpost position a few miles in front of Bastogne. I was told it was a rest area. I got to my old Company C one day before the Germans attacked.

On the morning of the first day of the battle, the Company Commander turned the company over to me with the mission of helping B Company which was also in an outpost position a short way down a highway we were trying to hold. After about two miles, we ran into resistance from a group of Germans located in the edge of a woods with machine guns, apparently an advance recon outfit. We formed a firing line, called for artillery fire, advanced, and knocked them out.

There was a lot of snow on the ground and as I led the Company past the first destroyed German machine gun position, there was what appeared to be six dead Germans with their red blood running over the clean white snow. As I got by them, I suddenly heard a rifle shot from behind. One of the dying Germans was raising up to shoot me in the back when Corporal S., who was following me, saw him and blew his brains out. A brave man? Actually, he was a blond-haired teenager. I remember he had "God with us" stamped on his German belt buckle. It occurred to me the kid prayed to the same God I did. Why did God let him die instead of me? Cain and Abel?

We went on to relieve B Company and then were called to our own outpost which was preparing for an attack. By the next afternoon we were in position. While checking my men, I looked out from a hilltop and saw enemy tanks, armored carriers, and infantry as far as I could see across a valley. Our patrols had been reporting a German massing of forces for an attack, but no one in the high command believed them. That failure to believe led to thousands of casualties. As the fighting continued, we believed we were being used for "hamburger" because it would be easier to destroy the Germans outside of their own land. Besides, we could see P38s flying over us on the first day of the battle. They had to see what was going on, yet we could get no air support.

We had two tanks, two anti-tank weapons, four 105s, and what was left of C Company to fight the large German force. I sent Corporal S. to tell the Company Commander what was coming and got as many of my men as I could behind a stone wall where they could help protect the anti-tank weapons. These two weapons were the first to get it. I was then ordered to take what men I had left and defend the 105s. We did that until the enemy tanks ran right over them and their crews. We were in a small ditch, and the tanks ran over us. We escaped down into a woods firing whenever we saw something to shoot at. By then, we were surrounded by Germans. Late that night, Sergeant W., Sergeant K., and I tried to locate company headquarters. We found only Germans. In this action I received a wound in my hand and injured my leg going over a fence. We heard firing back in the woods and decided to go back hoping to find help. Instead, as we walked across a bridge, three Germans stepped out from the side of the bridge. I could have shot one of them, but I noticed a machine gun on the side of the bridge aimed at us. I became a P.O.W. for the first time.

Many horrible killings and heroic actions occurred on the way to and in the P.O.W. camps. After being worked over twice by front line German officers and complimented by a German Captain for giving nothing but my name, rank, and serial number, I was placed in a motorcycle sidecar, because of my wounds, and driven to a P.O.W. collecting point where I was loaded on a freight train with other captured officers from my division and men from other divisions. This train took us to Bad Orb, Bavaria, to our first P.O.W. camp. On the way there something happened which showed how killing can be stopped if we really want to stop trying to solve our problems by murder.

On Christmas Eve 1944, the P.O.W. freight train was parked on a siding in Dietz, Germany. At about 11:45 P.M., the British air force began to bomb the railroad yards where the train was standing. Lieutenant H. and I were watching the flashes made by the bombs and, in order to tell how close the bombs were falling, counting one thousand, two thousand, etc. until we heard the explosion. Suddenly, an explosion hit and rocked the train. This caused smoke and dust to fill the air and the 67 men packed in the car, many of whom were wounded, panicked. Many tried to break down the door and escape. This caused even more confusion because the German guards were in protected positions outside of the train, and they began to fire machine pistols at the train door. Unless something happened quickly to stop the confusion and attempted breakout, many of our men would be killed.

It happened! Chaplain K. of our battalion, a man who had proven many times in combat that he was a man who realized desireless love, choiceless awareness, in some way made his voice heard. He called out, "Men, let us pray!" We said The Lord's Prayer. Then he said, "Let's sing 'Silent Night, Holy Night.'" And while the bombs were still falling we sang that song, "Oh, Come All Ye Faithful," and "God Bless America." When we sang the last song, the men in the other cars began to sing it too. The confusion died down. There were no direct hits on the train. No one was killed that I know of. Once again, in the midst of hell, it was proven that unconditional or desireless love was stronger than death on Christmas.

After that experience my whole value system began to change. I began to wonder if it is possible for human beings to be expressions of unconditional or desireless love to satisfy their needs, to solve problems, and to find real, material, and loving security by realizing such a love instead of by killing. I still wonder if it is possible to fulfill these ideals. Later, I heard that Chaplain K. was killed while saving another P.O.W.'s life. That P.O.W. had often made fun of and laughed at Chaplain K.

After a brief stay at Bad Orb, we were shipped to a P.O.W. camp near Hammelburg where more men were to die from illness, become mentally ill from mistreatment and starvation, and be murdered for no apparent reason. Here is just one example. As I stood looking out of the window one afternoon, I noticed Lieutenant W. walk by on his way to the latrine. As he passed me, he was shot through the head and fell dead. The German guard who was standing on the other side of the fence had shot him for no reason. What made that guard choose Lieutenant W. and not me or someone else? The guard didn't know any of us. What motivated him to blow a defenseless human being's brains out? Was it heredity? Was it the lack of unconditional love in his childhood? Was it because of some deep anxiety, frustration, hostility? Was it the lack of faith and understanding that life itself has intrinsic value or worth? Was he a self-centered puppet of a scientific age, living at a dim level of awareness, ruled by the pleasure principle where all absolutes except blind chance and the scientific method are dead? Was he a product of a culture and civilization whose educational system had taught him to believe that he was a superman from a super race that could conquer and control all of life and nature? In other words, did he believe he was God or someone especially chosen by a God to carry out a paranoid mission? Or was he some kind of insane savage? What was the difference between him and Chaplain K.? Are all wars and murders acts of insanity? Or, are they necessary for life as we know it? Is life really a matter of survival of the fittest? If so, who are the fittest—people like Chaplain K., or people like the guard, or some other kind?

These and many other questions and guilt feelings began to fill my thoughts during my days as a P.O.W. and began to change me from a happy-go-lucky, carefree, successful machinist to what I am today. I am still looking for the answers. It seems to me that we must find the answers to these and other related questions if we are to understand and put an end to murder whether in war or in peace.

The experiences described above and, especially the following one, began to cause me to have anxiety attacks and deep depression. I began to feel that fate was really against me and to lose hope. Before losing his sanity, hope was the last thing a P.O.W. lost. While we were at Hammelburg, General Patton sent a decoy task force of about two tank companies several miles behind the German lines to liberate the P.O.W. camp there. The rumor was that he had a relative there whom he wanted to free. The task force succeeded in breaking into part of the camp and we thought we were all free. Then we were told that we were on our own to make it back to our lines many miles away. The task force took some volunteers to help them fight their way back. A few of us tried to make it on our own. Lieutenant P. and I started out alone, and, if I remember correctly, we were free for about four days and nights before we ran into an ambush and were recaptured.

Being recaptured after coming so close to freedom brought on my first attack of deep depression and caused me to have a strange "out of body" experience. The Germans collected 12 of us and, without giving us any food or water, marched us back to Hammelburg. I don't remember too much about that march except the strange mental experience and that if you fell out of the march you were never seen again. I also remember seeing the remains of the task force which had come to free us. They had all been wounded, killed, or captured on the way out, including my closest friend, Lieutenant H. He had volunteered to man the 50 caliber machine gun on the lead tank. He had asked me to go with him, but since I never volunteered for anything, I had refused. In addition to being recaptured, I lost my best friend, and this added to my depression. How could a good general like Patton send a boy to do a man's job and get them all killed, wounded, or captured? This is just one more example of how crazy, useless murders occurred in World War II.

We were put on a train at Hammelburg and sent to Nuremberg, Then to a P.O.W. camp outside of Munich, where we were finally liberated by Patton. I believe it was April 21, 1945.

After liberation I almost died of dysentery. I was sick for days and lost more weight. I was never placed in a hospital. They didn't have room for all of us. I remember waiting in line four hours in Camp Lucky Strike in France for a piece of boiled chicken. I also remember "liberating" food from that camp's officer's mess. In time, we were shipped back to the States and fattened up for the invasion of Japan. That never happened because of the atomic bombs. So I was honorably discharged after about four years in the Army.

What Life Is Like Now

What is life like now for this 63-year-old, ex-clinical psychologist? I am still a prisoner of guilt, anxiety, depression, failure, and some unknown hidden force. I feel guilty over my share of the crazy killings. I remember the civilians, especially the old woman. She was probably someone's mother. I think of the young kid whose brains were blown out when he tried to kill me. What would life have been like for him if he had lived instead of me? Would he have been a failure? I am depressed not only over losing my friends but also thinking about all the others who suffered or died. What good did it do?

I am a prisoner of this emotional and physical illness which has made me fail in my career as a clinical psychologist and other jobs, fail in my marriage, and fail in my health to the point where I am not able to do a simple job, like my last one in 1976 as caretaker of an apartment building. Yes, from an economic point of view I am a prisoner. I'm now dependent on my V.A. Compensation which is $155.00 a month—30 percent for nervous disorder, 10 percent for wound in left hand—and my Social Security of $152.90 a month. This allows me just to get by in a one-room apartment on the edge of the ghetto in the city that has been called the "murder capital" of the world. Even more important, I am a prisoner of a *self* based on conditional love and self-centered desire, and all that goes with that kind of self, making it impossible for me to express unconditional or desireless love, which is the only kind of love there really is as far as I can understand.

A Typical Day

As this 63-year-old self wakes up on a typical day, usually around 3 A.M., my first thought is what is this strange force which makes me a prisoner? My first feeling is one of anxiety brought on by dreams of driving a car, or sometimes a train, without brakes or steering; or by dreams of being lost in a large city looking for home but unable to find it. This feeling is followed by one of frustration and then hostility. I wonder, would it be possible to blow up the whole universe? That would do away with awareness and solve all of man's problems. Then I narrow this destructive feeling down to people who have given me a bad time. I plan ways to kill them. Then the word ambivalence comes to mind. I say, "This is insanity." Then the attack of depression comes, and I want to kill myself. I try to figure out the best way to do this. There is the feeling that I would like to push my brains out with my fists, but that seems impossible. Then I plan to use poison. I have some hidden away, but I'm afraid it would fail to work. I settle on using a shotgun, putting it in my mouth and blowing my brains out. But that would make a terrible mess.

You are chicken, something says. That is the real reason you don't kill yourself. Then ambivalence again. Something says life has intrinsic value. As a man you have no right to play God and destroy life. This is followed by a feeling of respect for my mother, and religious thoughts and feelings taught by her and the church when I was a child. Then I say the Lord's Prayer and go through a series of relaxing exercises. Then I try to figure out something to do that will be helpful for the few older people who still live in the apartment. Just another ego trip like all the rest of my life but maybe one which will help me get rid of some of my guilt and depression.

Then the thought, you are prisoner of your war experiences and of some unknown force, some preverbal, subcortical, pre-ego conditioning which has caused your life to be "one big ego trip" based on self-centered desire and a conditional love *self*. This makes you see yourself as something apart from the universe or life instead of seeing your real self as life expressing itself through you in the form of unconditional love or desireless love. This unknown force has caused your failures and your illness.

I ask myself, what is this unknown force? How do I get off this merrygoround ego trip? Is there some way to be reborn so that the real self of unconditional or desireless love may be realized, actualized? In other words, how do I escape from my self-centered prison and become a free, loving, spontaneous expression of the wisdom of life? How do I escape so I can view and live life from a wholistic point of view—as it really is—instead of looking at life from my self-centered point of view and trying to see and make it what I want it to be? How do I stop trying to be God?

No schizophrenic rebirth or regression to a pre-ego state will free me. Sitting with my hands folded in prayer or meditation waiting for some great cosmic force to solve my problem will not work. Doing my best in every way I can, for everyone I can, in every place I can, has failed. It is obvious that nothing I have learned from psychology has freed me. The knowledge gained from psychology has helped me to change and exist in my prison of ego defenses or symptoms at a certain level of illness. But I am still a prisoner of my self-centered problems.

But I must not lose hope. So I force myself to get up around 8 A.M. with the hope that I will be able to free myself with the help I get from the V.A. Hospital. I should mention here that it takes about 90 percent of my energy to fight off the daily anxiety attacks, depression, and physical illness. Only with the help I get from the V.A. am I able to do this. There is barely enough energy left in me to do the ordinary things that must be done in order to just exist.

My Problems and the V.A.

I first applied for V.A. Compensation in 1975. I was too proud, sick, or ignorant before that. But in that year I became so ill with foot trouble, a heart problem, high blood pressure, hiatial hernia, diverticulosis, Menière's Disease and emotional problems that I had to be hospitalized in a V.A. hospital. While I was a patient there, I applied for service-connected compensation for the above ailments. After a long delay I was granted 60 percent service connected disability, 50 percent for psychoneurosis with anxiety and depression, and 10 percent for the wounded left hand. The other claims were denied because I could not prove that they resulted from my P.O.W. experiences.

After being discharged from the hospital, I returned to my job as caretaker of a 31-unit apartment building and continued to work there until I fell down the stairs while having an attack of vertigo caused by Menière's Disease. Because of that and because that same disease has reduced my hearing to around 50 percent and because of my nervous condition I had to quit, move to a small apartment, and live off my Social Security and compensation.

Then the big blow hit me. Early in the spring of 1978, after 31 years of marriage, my wife divorced me because of my illnesses and my inability to give her any real material security. She took all of our savings except for $2500 I got from the divorce. After the divorce, the V.A. cut my compensation to 40 percent or $155.00 a month. This really brought on an attack of depression. I went to the D.A.V. for help and they told me to go to the Mental Hygiene Clinic for outpatient therapy.

I now go there once a week for supportive psychotherapy. It is very helpful. I also go to the High Blood Pressure and Heart Clinic, the G.I. Clinic, and the Ear, Nose, Throat Clinic for treatment and medicine on a regular basis. The latter is now fitting me with a hearing aid that I have been trying to get since 1975. Finally, I have seen two outside psychiatrists, and they agree that I have a psychoneurosis with anxiety and depression, caused by my war experiences, and that my compensation should have been increased to 100 percent instead of being cut to 40 percent. These reports were given to the V.A. The V.A. had one of their psychiatrists interview me. At present I'm still a prisoner, waiting and wondering what is going to happen to me.

What Was Life Like Before the Above Experiences?

What was life like before the war experiences? I was born in Mayfield, Kentucky. My first memory is a hazy memory of something being held by something at around the age of three. I later learned *that* something was me being held by my mother, and we were on the way to my father's funeral. They were separated at the time of his death. One of my next memories was seeing what I later learned was my dead father on his deathbed with bright coins over his eyes to keep them shut. So my first introduction to life was love—being held in my mother's arms—and death—seeing my dead father.

I was told I was bowel-trained in two weeks. I never found out how long it took to wean me. Come to think of it, I still haven't been weaned. I'm still dependent on the V.A., my therapist, my ego defenses, my conditioning.

Life was rough without a father. How does a boy learn to be a man without a father or someone to substitute for a father? My mother had to spend all her time as a dressmaker making a living for three small children—my older brother, my older sister, and me. There wasn't much time to spend loving her children. What attention and love you got you bought with work and good behavior. I don't know how she was able to do all the work she had to do to keep us together. There were times when we had nothing to eat but navy beans. She seemed to derive her strength from religion. When I was very young, we went to church three times a week. Mother read the Bible to us every night before we went to bed. I received a very strong religious training and joined the Baptist Church at the age of twelve.

Apparently I was blessed with a high IQ. I was taught to read around the age of four. I won my first prize for being the best boy reader in the first grade. I actually read the Bible at the age of six but didn't understand it. I still don't. However, I did read something at that early age which has influenced my whole life. It had to do with how man had to be born again before he could enter the kingdom of heaven. The question of how this is to be done has been a main interest throughout my life.

All of us in the family went to work at a young age. We had to earn money for the food we ate. I started somewhere between the ages of nine and twelve washing dishes in a hometown cafe on weekends, with time off for church. Then I became a waiter and a "soda jerk." Along the way I was a "houseman" in a local pool hall where I learned to bet on horses, shoot dice, and fight. I received my first sex education there and made my first visit to a whorehouse at the age of fourteen. At that time I lived alone in a furnished room over a cafe where I worked over the lunch hour and from five to twelve at night. I went to high school about half time but made good enough grades to play football and earn my sweater and letter as fullback on the high school team.

When I was a junior in high school, I became homesick for my family, quit my job and school, hopped a freight, and went from my hometown to live with them in Chicago where they had moved. Times were rough; it was during the depression. They had no room for me there. So I went on the bum, riding freight trains all over the western states, working wherever I could. Finally, I wound up back in Chicago, where my sister got me a job in a machine shop. I served my apprenticeship and became a successful and well-paid machinist.

I was happy. I made a home for my mother and had enough money to go to the horse races, have the average number of girl friends, and enjoy watching the Chicago Bears football games.

I worked at the same machine shop for seven years and advanced steadily. Then World War II came. I didn't have to go because I was a machinist, but being patriotic, looking for adventure, and perhaps because of some unconscious death wish, I joined the U.S. Infantry right after Pearl Harbor.

I was honorably discharged in 1946 and returned to my family and job in Chicago. I began to have attacks of depression. The girls, horse races, football, work—nothing seemed to be fun or important anymore. My whole value system had been changed by the war. The horror of it can't be described. It has to be experienced to be believed. Shortly after my discharge, I went to see a V.A. psychiatrist and told him I was so depressed I wanted to kill myself. He turned me over to a psychologist who talked to me for about a half hour and told me to come back in two weeks.

As I left I thought, "Hell, I'm either going to get help now or kill myself." So I went to my minister with my problem. He suggested that I go to school, become a social worker or psychologist, and get rid of my guilt feelings and depression by helping others.

In the meantime I had married a former Red Cross woman. I had met her first while recovering from wounds in an Army hospital in England. She went along with the idea of my going to school and went back to her teaching job to help out. I didn't want her to do this, as I believed we could make it with me working part time and the G.I. Bill. But she insisted. We moved from Chicago to Detroit, where she got her old job back and, with her help, I went to college, made almost straight A's, and became a clinical psychologist who was successful at first (in a state mental hospital) and then a failure because of my nerves. I tried being program director of a boy's club, private practice, cattle farming on my wife's family farm, running a small store and being caretaker of an apartment building, among other jobs, but failed at every one of these because of my emotional problems.

One final word—You cannot have any idea how difficult it has been for me to write this paper unless you have been a psychologist on the sick side of the desk. I have been able to do it because I am willing to try *anything* that might help us solve the problems of our emotional and mental illnesses that make us prisoners of our memories and our conditioning and cause us to murder each other.

One final question: Who was the real prisoner, Chaplain K. or the German guard who shot Lieutenant W. for no apparent reason?

8

TERRORISTIC FADS AND FASHIONS:
The Year of the Assassin

H. H. A. Cooper

◇

> To achieve notoriety it is enough,
> after all, to kill one's concierge
> Albert Camus[1]

A former Guatemalan foreign minister; an Italian prosecutor; an American oil executive in Iran; the Military Governor of Madrid; a close personal aide to Yasir Arafat; a Turkish newspaper editor; a Spanish Supreme Court Justice; a communist trade unionist in Genoa; and a number of ordinary Spanish policemen. What do these people have in common? The somewhat cheerless answer is that they were victims of terrorist assassins during the opening months of 1979. Not a very spectacular total, perhaps, when contrasted with the ordinary criminal homicide statistics of a major city in the United States. It is, nevertheless, of more than passing interest to those whose business it is to keep a watch on terrorist tactics and techniques. While projections and trends in the fluid, volatile area of terrorism are always difficult to establish on other than a speculative basis, these indicators, at least impressionistically, must be a source of special concern to anyone charged with the provision of protective services.[2] It is therefore worthwhile looking at some of the problems of assassination within the context of that difficult subject area called terrorism.

Terrorism is a hard concept to pin down; it means different things to different people.[3] Accordingly, definition is an exercise in futility;

it is simply impossible to satisfy all of the people all of the time. While strict definition may be hopelessly elusive, certain ingredients are impressively stable.[4] Three of these are material for the present purposes. The notion of terrorism, in anybody's definition, must involve the generation of a high level of fear; its direction or application for coercive purposes; and a human audience. Terrorism is something done, calculatedly, by human beings to impress other human beings. Terrorism has its expressive as well as its instrumental side. But it is its symbolic side that looms especially large and gives it a characteristically potent quality. Terrorism moves progressively from the grossest of exaggerations to the subtlest of understatements.[5] Successful terrorism is an object lesson in nonverbal communication; the message is self-evident. The meaningful transition from death and mutilation to the casually raised eyebrow which might immediately accomplish the same end is no easy one. It is largely a matter of establishing an effective track record. Overall, terrorist strategy is much concerned with matters of this sort. To be effective at all, terrorism has to be cost effective; otherwise it is simply a grand but empty gesture. How much actual terroristic activity is consciously (and conscientiously) planned with such neat analyses in mind is debatable; the management consultants have not yet invaded that area in force. But there is an almost instinctive feeling about these things that serves to guide the practicing terrorist. Hence, he quickly learns to choose among a limited array of options for the one that suits his purposes best. How these choices are made is very much influenced by prevailing sentiments. What seems to work is quickly imitated, hence the cyclical nature of terrorist modalities. So we seem to have arrived, almost after the fashion of the Chinese calendar, at the Year of the Assassin.

Assassination is a rather special kind of homicide.[6] As a term of art, it certainly presents fewer definitional problems than terrorism. It is characterized by intentionality and a certain perception of the target figure. People are assassinated because of who they are or for what they are believed to represent. At the heart of every assassination there is a definite power play. The death of the chosen victim is seen as a way of influencing events and, through them, the power relationships with which that person is vitally connected. It will be immediately apparent that assassinations are not necessarily terroristic when measured by the criteria set out above. The secretive nature of assassination is sometimes emphasized and, where elimination as a purely instrumental purpose is predominant, fear may simply be crowded out by mystery. Where assassination is consciously used as an instrument of terror, the message must perforce come over loud and clear. A terroristic assassination is one which is designed to impress.[7] It must, therefore, strike at what was felt to be inviolate or invulnerable, or it must do so in a particularly horrible way. Assassination is one of the finer weapons of the terrorist armory calling for precision in its use if the desired results are to be achieved. Assassination cannot be undertaken indiscriminately or the effect is lost and the message goes astray. Carefully employed, as the Old Man of the Mountain[8] well knew, assassination can have a decisive effect upon the course of events. The secret lies in knowing whom to remove from where, when to do it—and how. The assassin who has no conscious terroristic purpose or commitment can well ignore the niceties imposed by such considerations. He may be no less of a craftsman for all that, but his ends are different. The terrorist is playing to the gallery, and he must have a fine sense of the temper of his audience if his performance is to bring him, metaphorically, applause, rather than catcalls or stony silence. The terrorist as assassin is seeking much more than notoriety.

It is trite, but nevertheless worthy of observation here, that there is a right and a wrong way of engaging in every activity, best expressed perhaps in the apothegm that there is a time and place for everything. A circumspect examination of the possibilities discloses a surprisingly limited range of options available to the terrorist according to time, place, and purpose. Obviously, these may be classified in a wide variety of ways, but it is useful to see them, in the present context, in terms of communication: is the terrorist setting up the framework of a dialogue or merely giving forth with an unanswerable (for the moment) monologue? The most common of the dialogue type of terroristic actions are kidnapping, hostage taking, and extortion bombing. In each case, implicitly or explicitly, a bargaining situation is created. Something of value is put at risk by the terrorist who creates a substantial fear of its destruction in order to obtain what he wants. The message is thrown out, and a response is expected. If all goes the terrorist's way, the tragedy can, it is inferred, be averted. There is a pause, an interval for reflection, or whatever other reaction might be considered appropriate by those to whom the opportunity for dialogue is thus extended. A number of assumptions are necessarily made (albeit un-consciously in most cases) by the terrorist, but only one need concern us here. What is jeopardized must have some value for the party at whom this undisguised power play is directed, or no dialogue is likely to result at all.[9] Otherwise, ignoring considerations of humanitari-anism or civic duty, it is rather as if, having secreted a bomb in the headquarters of General Motors, one were to direct the concomitant demands to the Ford Motor Company.

But a more insidious calculation going to the root of the matter is a further obfuscation that the terrorist anxious for dialogue must face: what is put at risk may have some value, but how much? This is the true dynamic of every bargaining situation and that which, individ-ually, gives them their interest. There is no need, here, to pursue this line of thinking down the labyrinthine corridors into which it is capable of intrusion. Suffice it to say that in every bargaining situation there comes a point at which values are weighed; some are discarded, while others are deliberately, if reluctantly, sacrificed to preserve those con-sidered more important.[10] In short, if the game goes on long enough the terrorist may get something less than he bargained for—or no bargain at all.

Over the last few years, there has been a steady, if not always con-sistent, hardening of attitudes governing official dealings with terror-ists. Some countries have traditionally adopted an inflexibly hard line which, if it does not inhibit dialogue altogether certainly has a chilling effect.[11] The message to the terrorist, even where it is not precisely articulated, is unmistakably clear: do your worst, you will get nothing from us. Rarely, however, have the lines of responsibility been so exactly drawn as to permit of such a decisive confrontation. More usually, other considerations have entered the picture—the need to safeguard international relations, the pressures of domestic politics, and the like. There is generally some motive to talk, if not to bargain, and this has been encouraging to the politically inspired terrorist even at times when the current has run most strongly against any sort of dialogue at all.[12] Yet there are inbuilt biases against dialogue with terrorists that are extremely difficult to overcome, save by a massive exertion of force that most terrorists find hard to generate and apply. The terrorist is constantly faced with the problems of escalation; viol-ence must become more and more novel and spectacular to capture the imagination of the audience to which the terrorist must appeal for results. And all the while, the forces of counterterrorism are gathering strength and growing more painfully effective. It becomes more and more difficult to establish and manage a dialogue with the hunters breathing down one's neck. Such a situation had built up, internationally, in 1977 and 1978. While it was still very difficult in the wider, international forum to reach agreement on what to do about terrorism and terrorists, a consensus of sentiment was clearly growing among those nations most closely affected. The killing of Hanns-Martin Schleyer and Aldo Moro signaled that; in the absence of some entirely new and unforeseen dimension, the end of the dialogue had been reached.

While this must not be understood as foreclosing, once and for all, the possibilities of a successful politically inspired kidnapping, hostage taking, or extortion bombing, these events have certainly caused terrorists generally to reassess their options. Schleyer and Moro were, at least in theory, regarded as extremely valuable bargaining counters. Yet when their lives were placed on the line, they were simply not heavy enough to tip the scales in the terrorists' favor.[13] More valuable targets are hard to find, harder to take, and harder still to hold securely while the delicate dialogue is proceeding. Then, again, the crucial question looms: what is *more* valuable? The power to go much beyond a Schleyer or a Moro is simply not there in most cases and, in any event, who is so unique, so irreplaceable in these times, that a more malleable attitude might be reasonably expected? What these events have produced is a kind of terrorist disillusionment with the politics of this style of activity. The terrorist has come to realize that he must count less and less upon the cooperation of his victims to make his operations work. Slowly but surely, his own success in the past and the reaction this has induced have forced the terrorist back to a unilateral demonstration of his power: do first, talk later. To stage a comparatively faint-hearted retreat into a campaign of bombing is designed more to do economic damage rather than to take lives.

The more intransigent turn to assassination. The terrorist can ill afford to tread water; he stands too much chance of drowning in the oceans of apathy. He must maintain the momentum of his undertaking if he is to be in business at all. With each reduction in his options, operationally, his political base comes increasingly under pressure.

For those terrorists who still entertain the hope of appealing to an enlarged political constituency, a policy of mass destruction of lives and property is virtually unthinkable.[14] Assassination is, for them, an acceptable alternative designed to maintain or even step up the pace of their operations. This is, substantially, the point at which the more dedicated of the Italian terrorists arrived. Frustrated in their attempts at "dialogue-type" terrorism as an instrumental device, and tiring of the largely expressive tactic incorrectly referred to in this case as "knee-capping," they are turning more and more to assassination in the hope of turning the tide of events once more in their favor. The political alienation that this must eventually produce has evidently not been discounted in advance, but as its impact comes to be felt, who is to say that these terrorists, their options reduced below an acceptable operational minimum will not, finally, turn their thoughts to the un-thinkable? Meanwhile, we pass somewhat apprehensively through the Year of the Assassin.

A brief word or two may be usefully interpolated here on the at-tractiveness of assassination for the terrorist. By comparison with, say, kidnapping, assassination is a very economical undertaking. Fewer personnel and support resources are needed and the act, once com-mitted, is over in the instant as far as the terrorist is concerned. There is no need for a hideout, elaborate communications and security sys-tems, the agonizing negotiation of the matter to a satisfactory conclu-sion. As a demonstration of raw power, it can be exemplary. And, if the victim is carefully chosen and the task executed to perfection, it can be most influential upon the course of events. None of this is the product of original thinking on the part of modern-day terrorists. These are merely the beneficiaries of a body of learning going back to the earliest times, for assassination has always been a well-honed tool of government and, even today, there exist among the grand family of nations, those who would not scruple to employ assassination as a form of international power politics if it were expected that the ap-propriate results might flow from its use. The risk of assassination is one of the unhappy burdens of high office which must be prudently balanced against the perquisites of correspondingly great power. The terrorist simply rises to the challenge when he believes it to be in his interests to do so. Moreover, perfect protection against the risks of assassination is a utopian dream; the resourceful assassin can always penetrate any protective screen.[15] The ratio of completed assassinations to attempts must be, in itself, a source for concern to potential victims.[16] Lastly, it may be observed, that assassination is not simply a burden of high office; given the right set of circumstances, it might well make a lot of sense to the terrorist assassin to start his work at a much lower point on the scale. The degree of protection that can be accorded this enlarged class of victims is much diluted and the element of fear engendered thereby greatly enhanced.

Who are these modern terrorist assassins? A definitive answer is very difficult to give with any degree of academic honesty. Few indeed are those serious students of the subject who have even seen a working terrorist let alone subjected that exotic creature to anything like an appropriate regimen of scientific study. Our knowledge of the subject, such as it is, has to be gleaned from a variety of circumstantial sources, including the recollection of those who have engaged in such terroristic enterprises in the past. This latter is mainly like trying to get a feeling for the life of lepidoptera from a study of dessicated butterflies.[17] Nevertheless, some of these materials, properly interpreted are of at least impressionistic value in putting together a picture of what it takes to engage in such nefarious activity. Of course, it is axiomatic that these former terrorists do not think of what they have done in such terms, so that, in the main, their accounts are laudatory and justificatory of the assassinations they have undertaken. Few would regard themselves as terrorists although their activities were manifestly designed to terrorize.

For the serious student, there is one little-known memoir of considerable interest in the light of the terrorist situation in Italy. It is that of Giovanni Pesce,[18] a communist partisan, who was no stranger to death in combat, having served with the International Brigades during the Spanish Civil War. He recounts vividly, and with patent sincerity, the personal difficulties he experienced in undertaking his first assassination assignment. The account is most useful not only in evaluating what personal qualities are needed to undertake such missions, but also as a reminder of how little matters have changed in the 30 odd years that separate Pesce's partisans from Front Line and the Red Brigades. The type of terrorist assassin employed by political extremist movements may be a criminal or a psychopath (or both), but he is rarely psychotic. He is often a True Believer (and he may well have something in which truly to believe).[19] It has been said of such persons that they are ordinarily misfits in the society they reject.[20] It is this rejectionist quality that is a distinctive feature of terrorist assassins, and it is no semantic accident that the term, in a variety of languages, has come to be applied in our times to the most uncompromising and hard-line of terrorist groups. Those likely to trouble the peace of the world further are most likely to be associated with such groups. As the opportunities for dialogue become fewer, their shrill monologue is likely to become more strident and increasingly heard in high places.

And what of the victims? Kings, princes, and presidents are usually well paid for their trouble and correspondingly well-protected. But, given a choice, it is in the nature of things for the terrorist to seek out the "soft" target. Such targets abound, and more and more we can expect them to receive attention from the terrorist assassin. It may be feasible for the head of state to travel in a bulletproof limousine, with advance guards and outriders, phalanxes of protectors and food-tasters, but what of the bank manager whose only "crime" is that he represents a symbolically detested element in a hostile environment?[21] Such protection as can be afforded potential victims at this lower level involves, substantially, a change of lifestyle. In the long term, the quality of life is quite gravely impaired, as witness the modern tragedies of Belfast and Beirut. This is in the nature of assassination by degrees and serves well to accomplish the terrorists' overall task. It is no longer, then, necessary to shoot, say, a chief of police to convey a message of fear; it will suffice to kill the policeman on point duty, if you do it frequently enough and with evident malice. In Italy, it has reached the stage where it requires extraordinary courage or a degree of near disqualifying stupidity to be a juror in a terrorist trial. In Spain, the ordinary police officer who dons his uniform in the morning may well pause to wonder whether he will be alive to take it off by the time his tour of duty ends. This is a most fruitful field of study for the victimologist, but for those who might fall to the terrorist's bullet, the Year of the Assassin is a grim season indeed.

Assuming these unpleasant speculations to be well-founded, how long are we likely to have to endure under the cold chill of the terrorist assassin's shadow? It is cold comfort to consider that we are but at the beginning of the cycle and that many more lives are likely to be claimed before this trend gives ground before another terroristic fad or fashion. Assassination has been with us for a long time and, as a terrorist modality, it will doubtless be with us to eternity. What is presently disturbing, if one may be so indelicate as to suggest it, is the way in which, like so many other things in our life and times, it has become debased and cheapened. There is a certain gallows humor about this that recalls the touching story of the concentration camp victim who, to comfort his wife, urged her to hurry so as to be in the early vans while they were still taking a decent class of person. It would doubtless have appealed to Marie Antoinette's sense of the fitness of things to know that she at least was a victim of the Great Terror while it had in prospect persons of *her* station. The terrorist assassin is now reaching down for victims among those that Marie Antoinette would have had eat cake. This is an ugly portent for the future, for it means that the Year of Mass Destruction that may well follow the Year of the Assassin is not too many months behind.

NOTES

1. *The Fall* (New York: Vintage Books, 1956), p. 26.

2. This is an increasingly important area of activity for "terrorist watchers," but the quality and completeness of the data collected and published is, in most cases, questionable. Perhaps the best service in the area of international terrorism is that provided by Risks International, Inc. of Washington, D.C.

3. On this, generally, see H. H. A. Cooper "Terrorism: The Problem of the Problem of Definition," *Chitty's Law Journal* (March 1978) 26(3):105–8.

4. A real understanding of the definitional problems requires a thorough analysis of the many definitions that have been offered. When this is undertaken, it becomes apparent that there is almost universal agreement on certain elements, while others remain the subject of intractable debate. The categorization of these various elements is not subject to much fluctuation.

5. Much the same has been observed about the more violent aspects of organized crime. The strategy of the political terrorist has long been developed along roughly parallel lines by the mobster, and in countries such as Italy there has probably been some cross-pollination of ideas.

6. See, Richard W. Kobetz and H. H. A. Cooper, *Target Terrorism: Provoking Protective Services* (Gaithersburg, Md.: International Association of Chiefs of Police, 1978), p. 25.

7. The curious, extraordinarily technical assassinations and attempted assassinations of Bulgarian exiles during 1978 illustrate the point. So, too, does

the assassination of Orlando Letelier, former Chilean ambassador to the United States and other Chileans associated with the Allende regime. For an interesting sidelight on the Bulgarian case see William Schwabe, "The Sentry and the Dog Revisited," *Soldier of Fortune*, May 1979, pp. 32–35.

8. The legendary Sheikh Hassan i Sabbah of the Ismaili sect, spiritual founder and guiding spirit of the twelfth-century assassins, an aberrant order of fanatical Muslims who provide the name if not the earliest point of reference for terroristic activity of this kind. On the *hashishin* generally see, Bernard Lewis, *The Assassins* (New York: Basic Books, 1968).

9. See, on this generally, H. H. A. Cooper, *Hostage Negotiations: Options and Alternatives* (Gaithersburg, Md.: International Association of Chiefs of Police, CTT Series, 1978).

10. This is what stands behind the declared United States policy of not paying ransom and not freeing prisoners. See, generally, "Hard-line vs. Conciliatory Policies: The International Experience," in *Disorders and Terrorism* (Washington, D.C.: U.S. Government Printing Office, 1976), pp. 430–35.

11. Foremost among these is Israel, which has, nevertheless, been brought on more than one occasion to the brink of negotiation with terrorists, notably at Entebbe. Given the right combination of factors, even Israel may yet be forced into the dialogue that has been successfully resisted up to now.

12. This was clearly the position in the Schleyer case where, following the skyjacking of flight 181 all kinds of international pressures built up. See, on this, H. H. A. Cooper, "Hostage Rescue Operations: Denouement at Algeria and Mogadishu Compared," *Chitty's Law Journal*, (March 1978) 26(3):91–104.

13. In the case of Schleyer, the terrorists threw yet another element of the greatest weight upon the scale by the skyjacking of Lufthansa flight 181. This element, putting another 92 lives in jeopardy, might have been decisive in the terrorists' favor had the near-wondrous assault by the West German GS-9 not succeeded in freeing all save the pilot at Mogadishu.

14. This, which remains the classical view, seems to be borne out by most of the recent terrorist campaigns. Terrorists do not turn against a friendly or neutral populace unless they perceive themselves to be in dire straits. The situation in Northern Ireland is a case in point.

15. The assassination in Mexico of Leon Trotsky is a case in point. The German priest Brocardus, advising Philip VI of France said: "I therefore know only one single remedy for the safeguarding and protection of the king, that in all the royal household, for whatever service, however small or brief or mean, none should be admitted, save those whose country, place, lineage, condition and person are certainly, clearly and fully known." Lewis, The Assassins, pp. 1–2.

16. See, on this, James F. Kirkham, Sheldon G. Levy, William J. Crotty, *Assassination and Political Violence: A Staff Report to the National Commission on the Causes and Prevention of Violence*, (New York: Bantam Books, 1970), p. 117.

17. This picturesque notion is taken from an allusion by Robert Allerton, a confessed professional criminal, who was referring to the methodological problems involved in the study of such personalities. See, Tony Parker (with Robert Allerton), *The Courage of His Convictions* (New York: W. W. North, 1962).

18. Giovanni Pesce (Visone), *And No Quarter*, trans. Frederick M. Shaine, (Athens: Ohio University Press, 1972).

19. See Eric Hoffer, *The True Believer* (New York: New American Library, 1951).

20. C. Eric Lincoln, *The Black Muslims in America* (Boston: Beacon Press, 1951), p. 100.

21. On May 11, 1978, the Italian manager of the Milan branch of New York's Chemical Bank was shot in the legs. Two political terrorist groups claimed credit for shooting and it is noteworthy that many of the published statements of Italian political extremist organizations have labeled United States multinational corporations as prime enemies.

9

BLACK HOMICIDE

Alton R. Kirk

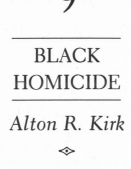

Vital statistics in America show that the mortality rates for blacks are generally higher than those for their white counterparts. The difference in mortality rates between blacks and whites in the United States has been evident since vital statistics have been kept. In 1978, according to the U.S. Public Health Service, the resulting life expectancy at birth showed that the average nonwhite male and female lived about six fewer years than the average white male and female. White women can expect to live 77.7 years, nonwhite women 73.7; white men, 70.2, nonwhite men 65.3. The difference between the rates for the highest and lowest groups is a span of approximately 14 years. (Dennis 1977).

Violence and violent deaths are increasing in both races and sexes in this country, and homicide is one of the major forms of violent destructive behavior. According to Hirsch et al. (1973), "homicide represents the ultimate deterioration of personal interactions, its frequency in a given population furnishes an objective index of violent reactions to the cumulative stresses in a group. Moreover, problems generated by these tragic losses of life are larger than a simple summation of individual misery." This is especially true for the black population where homicide is a major cause of death among younger blacks, especially men.

I shall examine homicide as a leading cause of death among blacks and review some trends in black homicide in order to see how they compare with nonblack homicide trends. I shall also make some consideration of the theoretical aspects of homicide. Additionally, I shall examine some of the psychosocial factors that may be contributing to this high rate of homicide. Finally, I shall suggest some changes that may aid in the reduction of these high rates.

The data in this analysis for blacks will be represented by nonwhite statistics, since census data reveal that blacks constituted from 90 to 94 percent of the total nonwhite population between 1950 and 1970. We realize that the various groups that make up the nonwhite population are quite divergent. However, there are no data specifically for blacks. The data for nonwhites other than blacks tend to minimize the extreme; therefore, while it may affect the degree, it does not affect the direction.

Marked patterns in the occurrence of homicide appear during the period 1940–1976. According to *Health—United States* (1978), the homicide rate has risen in every age group since 1940. It should be noted, however, that in 1930, during the country's most serious economic depression, the homicide rate was about as high as it was in 1970 for virtually all age groups. The increase in homicide that began in the early 1960s reached a high in 1974 but decreased in 1975, and 1976. These figures show that males are more likely to be victims than females. The usual murder victim is a male 25 to 34 years of age. After age 35, the older a person becomes the less likely he or she is to be murdered. People other than white are six times more likely to be murder victims than are white people. Nonwhite males are 20 times more likely to be murdered than are white females.

Homicide rates were at their lowest in the 1950s and 1960s. For example, the homicide rate in 1960 for people 15 to 24 years of age was half of what it became in 1976 and one-third less than for people 25 to 34 years of age. Living conditions for young adults appear to have changed drastically during the 1970s—for the worse, as indexed by homicide rates.

Dennis (1977:315–28) reports that "homicide enters as the fifth leading cause of death for all non-white males. However, it is the leading cause of death for young non-white males in practically every urban area where their numbers in the population are substantial. In 1972, homicide death rates emerged as the leading cause of death for non-white males ages 20–24, 25–29, and 30–34. However, in 1973 accidents had taken the lead in all age groups except 30–34" (see tables 9.1 and 9.2).

Most of these murder victims are killed not by white racists, but by other blacks. According to an article in *Ebony* (1979), more blacks were killed by other blacks in 1977 than were killed in the entire nine-year Vietnam War. During that year, 5,734 blacks were victims of other blacks. The Vietnam War claimed 5,711 black lives. Black self-destruction and especially black homicide have become an increasing problem among the nation's black communities.

Many diverse factors account for this high black homicide rate. Some social investigators have studied the predictability of high homicide rates by identifying sociocultural correlates. Thus, several demographic, sociological, and psychological variables have been, and are being, investigated with respect to homicide incidence. Investigators have reported relationships between violence and business trends, race, age, geographical location, socioeconomic status, day of week, and time of day.

Henry and Short (1965) showed a negative correlation between homicide and the business cycle for high status whites, but a positive correlation for subordinate blacks. These investigators also found that the overwhelming majority of murders were intraracial. Vital statistics show that blacks are victims and perpetrators of violence at a rate that is disproportionate to other groups. In all groups, males are more likely to die violent deaths than are females, and young males are more likely to die violent deaths than are older males.

Geographically, the southern part of the United States has been reported to show a higher level of violent deaths. This trend still holds for whites. However, recent statistics show that homicide rates are higher in the north-central region for blacks (*U.S. Vital Statistics*, 1975; Federal Bureau of Investigation, *Uniform Crime Reports*, 1952). The highest rates of violence or violent deaths are being reported in states experiencing the fastest growth in population (Reckless 1967). Homicide rates are higher in central cities than in suburbs or rural areas. Klebba (1975) reported that 58 percent of the black population lived in central cities, compared to 28 percent of the white population. The homicide rates in the central cities were 84.5 and 8.8 for black and white males, respectively. According to Graham and Gurr (1969) and Pyle (1974), the disorganized sectors of cities where violence is

Table 9.1
Leading Causes of Death for Nonwhites at All Ages, 1974

Males	*Rate (per 100,000)*
Diseases of the heart	291.0
Malignant neoplasms	173.5
Cerebrovascular diseases	89.4
Accidents	85.3
Homicide	67.2
Certain causes of mortality in early infancy	33.9
Influenza and pneumonia	32.9
Cirrhosis of liver	26.7
Diabetes mellitus	16.3
Suicide	10.2
Females	*Rate*
Diseases of the heart	227.9
Malignant neoplasms	117.2
Cerebrosvascular diseases	92.3
Accidents	29.3
Diabetes mellitus	27.1
Certain causes of mortality in early infancy	24.6
Influenza and pneumonia	19.2
Cirrhosis of liver	14.7
Homicide	14.5
Arteriosclerosis	8.7

SOURCE: U.S. Vital Statistics

committed are characterized by high unemployment, mobility, anonymity, low income, poor housing, and so forth to a greater degree than in other sections of the city or in rural areas.

Wolfgang (1958) reported that in 64 percent of all homicides, alcohol was present in the victim, the offender, or both. He reported further that 65 percent of homicides in his study were committed during weekend periods.

In addition to these easily identifiable correlates of homicide and violence, there are other situational or background variables that may influence violence and, relatedly, the high rate of homicide among blacks. The increased availability of hand guns, for instance, is reported to be a factor in the increased homicide rate. Zimring (1972:303–5) noted that "homicide by fire arms increased by 169 per-

Table 9.2

Leading Causes of Death for Nonwhites by Selected Age Groups by Sex, 1973

Ages 15–19, Males	*Ages 20–24, Males*	*Ages 25–29, Males*	*Ages 30–34, Males*
1. Accident	1. Accident	1. Accident	1. Homicide
2. Homicide	2. Homicide	2. Homicide	2. Accident
3. Malignant neoplasms	3. Suicide	3. Suicide	3. Heart
4. Suicide	4. Malignant neoplasms	4. Heart	4. Cirrhosis of liver
5. Heart	5. Heart	5. Cirrhosis of liver	5. Suicide
6. Influenza, pneumonia	6. Influenza, pneumonia	6. Malignant neoplasms	6. Malignant neoplasms
7. Cerebrosvascular diseases	7. Cerebrovascular diseases	7. Influenza, pneumonia	7. Cerebrovascular diseases
8. Nephritis, Nephrosis	8. Cirrhosis of liver	8. Cerebrovascular diseases	8. Influenza, pneumonia
9. Anemias	9. Anemias	9. Diabetes mellitus	9. Diabetes mellitus
10. Bronchitis, Emphysema, Asthma	10. Bronchitis, emphysema, Asthma	10. Nephritis, nephrosis	10. Nephritis, Nephrosis

Ages 15–19, Females

1. Accident
2. Homicide
3. Malignant neoplasms
4. Heart
5. Influenza, pneumonia
6. Complication of
   pregnancy
7. Suicide
8. Cerebrovascular
   diseases
9. Anemias
10. Diabetes mellitus
11. Bronchitis,
    Emphysema, Asthma
12. Nephritis, Nephrosis

Ages 20–24, Females

1. Accident
2. Homicide
3. Heart
4. Malignant neoplasms
5. Suicide
6. Influenza, pneumonia
7. Cerebrovascular
   diseases
8. Complication of
   pregnancy
9. Cirrhosis of liver
10. Anemias

Ages 25–29, Females

1. Accident
2. Homicide
3. Heart
4. Malignant neoplasms
5. Cirrhosis of liver
6. Cerebrovascular
   diseases
7. Influenza, pneumonia
8. Complication of
   pregnancy
9. Anemias
10. Diabetes mellitus

Ages 30–34, Females

1. Homicide
2. Accidents
3. Malignant neoplasms
4. Heart
5. Cerebrovascular
   diseases
6. Influenza, pneumonia
7. Complication of
   pregnancy
8. Suicide
9. Nephritis, Nephrosis
10. Hypertension
11. Diabetes mellitus

cent in Chicago between 1965 and 1970, three times as fast as homicide by all other means." Preliminary data from a study by Dennis, et al. (1979) show high correlations between homicide and sociopathological variables such as family background factors, school problems, trouble with the law, or unemployment.

Under the direction of the Office of the Surgeon General of the United States, a group of researchers (Leifer and Roberts 1972; Murray, et al. 1972; Greenberg and Gordon 1972; McLeod, Atkin, and Chaffee 1972) extensively investigated the behavioral and attitudinal influences of media presentations of violence. It is generally agreed that many blacks, especially those of low socioeconomic status, spend a significant amount of their recreational time watching television. Crime and violence on television are in abundant and continuous supply. The viewing of this violence may have a desensitizing effect on many blacks who may participate in real life violence. It may also contribute to children becoming more physically aggressive. Similarly, movies can have the same type of influence. This was evidenced in the black communities by the so called "blaxploitation" films of the early 1970's. Such films as *The Legend of Nigger Charley*, *The Mack*, and *Superfly* portrayed blacks as rough and tough. They had the women, the clothing, and the big fancy cars. Following these films, many blacks began to imitate the dress, speech, and behavior of the characters.

Relatedly, social learning theorists have stressed the role that imitative learning may play in the behavior of young people. Thus, in the study of aggression, many investigators have examined the influence of aggressive behavior in films (Bandura and Houston 1961; Lovaas 1961; Mussen and Rutherford 1961; Bandura, et al., 1963a). At least in laboratory test situations, results of these studies have indicated an increase in the probability that subjects will behave aggressively immediately following exposure to aggressive roles.

The way in which a number of experimental conditions and social factors affect the behavioral consequences of witnessing models' aggression also has been assessed (Bandura et al. 1963b; Hicks 1968; Walters and Willows 1968; Hanratty, et al. 1969; Nelson, et al. 1969; Dubanoski and Parton 1971; Meyer 1972; Noble 1973; Lockert 1974). Frustration, competition, justification of aggression, and emotional deviance are among the several factors that have been manipulated as independent variables in one or more of these studies.

Bandura and Walters maintain that "societies that provide approved aggressive modes are likely to produce aggressive children" (1963:369). They note the prevalence of aggressive peer models as delinquent youth in such subcultures and assert that, in such groups, the crucial process in the development of aggressive behavior patterns may be "identification with an aggressive prototype rather than a hostile reaction to emotional deprivation" (*ibid.*, 370). Further, Bandura and Walters emphasize that differences in aggressive expression "appear to be at least in part, a function of the extent to which members of a particular group tolerate and show approval of aggressive actions" *ibid.*, 381). According to Bandura and Huston (1961), when a parent hits or whips a child, even in response to the child's aggressive acts toward peers, a degree of incidental learning of aggressive responsiveness from the parental physical behavior may be expected to occur in the punished child through imitation. The theoretical explanation for increases in aggressive responses among observers of modeled aggression (Bandura and Walters 1963b) is that the display of aggression in models not only signals permissiveness for such behavior, but also (1) facilitates the acquisition of new aggressive responses and (2) weakens the strength of competing inhibitory responses in subjects. This increases the probability that previously learned patterns of aggression will occur in response to aggressive modeling.

According to *Ebony* (1979), "there is a square mile of Urban badland [in New York City] that law enforcement officials have dubbed 'Dodge City.' And rightly so. In the last five years, 430 men, women and children have been shot, stabbed, beaten, bludgeoned or otherwise battered to death there. Last year, 69 people were killed in this community of 110,000, and so far this year, 38 people have been murdered at a startling rate of one every four days." The area described is, of course, Harlem. Harlem is simply a magnification of other black communities within the United States. Violence and, more specifically, homicide is out of proportion to such occurrences in similar nonblack communities.

In order to examine some of the psychosocial factors that may contribute to the high rate of homicide among blacks, we must review the niche of blacks in this society from a historical perspective. The history of American blacks abounds with racism and oppression that directly or indirectly touch all aspects of black persons' lives. From the basic acquisition of food, shelter, and health care, racism and oppression affect blacks socially, economically, educationally, legally, politically, and, perhaps most of all, psychologically. In all these aspects, blacks suffer disproportionately to any other group in this country.

As a result of the history of this ubiquitous oppression, blacks are angry. They are angry because for many years they were told where they could live, where they could work, how much money they could earn, where to go to school, what professions to pursue, how they should talk, how they should act, whom they could marry, and how many children they should have. At the present time, almost everyone can point to at least one black who has "made it" in the various positions of employment, politics, education, and so forth. However, no black has been able to escape all the restrictions placed on him or her by this society.

Blacks are angry because they live in a system which views them as being "abnormal beings," a system that regards them as being "culturally deprived" and "socially disadvantaged." They are angry because the majority culture has acknowledged, by virtue of the Civil Rights Laws, that they have legitimate grievances and has "promised" that something would be done to improve their situation. Consequently, black aspirations and expectations have risen, only to be blocked by the same oppressive forces that existed before the Civil Rights Movement. The constant pressures of institutional racism and oppression leave blacks with a sense of frustration, hopelessness, and powerlessness beyond compare.

This anger is internalized and long simmering. Too often it manifests itself in aggression against those who are physically close, against family members or friends, who, for the most part, are other blacks. According to Poussaint (1972), "It is as if, in a mood of sheer desperation, blacks seek to become a part of the white mainstream and obtain so-called manhood by turning to physical brutality and petty crimes against one another. Violence can be a potent drug for the oppressed person. Reacting to the futility of his life, the individual derives an ultimate sense of power when he holds the fate of another human being in his hands."

Many people fail to see that black homicidal behavior is symptomatic of more general societal problems and that the anger, hatred, and frustrations that very often lead to blacks killing blacks are not inherent in the "black personality" but result from generations of oppression. One may then ask the questions, "Why is black on black homicide so high? Do not other ethnic minorities suffer from discrimination and oppression?" The answer, of course, is, "Yes." The difference is that American blacks are the only ethnic group in this country introduced to it as slaves. Additionally, blacks have not been granted the opportunity to rise above their low status as have other minorities.

According to Guthrie (1976), whites "believed that 'original' man was white, [and that] attempts to explain the presence of blacks in foreign lands often came from interpretations of religious writings. One view held that the African's dark skin and his consequent enslavement by other men had been a proclamation from God."

There have been minorities of lighter color skin pigmentation who have been discriminated against in the history of this nation. All of them have been able to overcome the prejudices against them to a greater or lesser degree. Although each has had to struggle for acceptance, none has had to overcome the assumption of "subnormality" and theological rationalization of a "deserved lesser state of being." If original man was white, then to be other than white is to be not just different, but wrong. One can prove his capability and worth, thus overcoming assumptions of "inferiority," through deeds of accomplishment. If his skin is black, he is unacceptable and accomplishments will not make him otherwise. Moreover, the black person cannot choose to give up his blackness at times of convenience as a means of escape or a vacation from oppression. The pressure is ever there, impossible to escape from.

Unkept promises, impenetrable walls, anger, violence—a violence now contained within a subgroup of our society; black homicide is not a black problem but a human problem. It is a problem which we must work vigorously to solve. Currently, blacks are venting their anger and frustrations at other blacks within their own communities. We know from history that the oppressed ultimately direct their aggressive actions toward the oppressors. All members of this society need to work together in all areas to remove the causes of this anger and frustration if we are to prevent the human tragedy of black homicide from becoming an expanding and uncontrollable societal problem.

REFERENCES

Bandura, A. and A. Huston. 1961. "Identification as a Process of Incidental Learning." *Journal of Abnormal and Social Psychology* 63:311–18.

Bandura, A., D. Ross, and S. Ross. 1963a. "Imitation of Film-Mediated Aggressive Models." *Journal of Abnormal and Social Psychology* 66:3–11.
—— 1963b. "Vicarious Reinforcement and Imitative Learning." *Ibid.* 67:601–7.
Bandura, A. and R. Walters. 1963. "Aggression in Child Psychology." *Yearbook of the National Society for the Study of Education* 1963 62 (part 1):364–415.
Dennis, R. E. 1977. "Social Stress and Mortality Among Nonwhite Males." *Phylon* 38:315–28.
Dennis, R. E., E. Lockert, and A, Kirk. 1979. "Profile: Black Male at Risk to Low Life Expectancy" (Research in progress). Department of Psychiatry, Meharry Medical College, Nashville, Tennessee.
Dubanoski, R. A. and D. A. Parton. 1971. "Imitative Aggression in Children as a Function of Observing a Human Model." *Developmental Psychology* 4(3):489.
Ebony, 1979. "Black on Black Crime" (August).
Federal Bureau of Investigation. 1952. Uniform Crime Reports for the United States and Its Possessions 22:31.
Graham, H. G., and T. R. Gurr. 1969. *Violence in America. Historical and Comparative Perspectives: A Report to the National Commission on the Causes and Prevention of Violence.* New York: Signet.
Greenberg, B. S. and T. F. Gordon. 1972. "Children's Perceptions of Television Violence: A Replication." In HEW publication no. HSM 72-9060, eds. J. P. Murray et al. (vol. 5). Washington, D.C.: U.S. Government Printing Office.
Guthrie, R. V. 1976. *Even the Rat Was White: A Historical View of Psychology.*
Hanratty, M., R. Liebert, L. Morris, and L. Fernandez. 1969. "Imitation of Film-Mediated Aggression Against Live and Inanimate Victims." *Proceedings of the 77th Annual Convention of the American Psychological Association* 4:457–58.
Health—United States. 1978. U.S. Department of Health, Education and Welfare, Public Health Service, Office of the Assistant Secretary for Health. Washington, D.C.: U.S. Government Printing Office.
Hendin, H. 1963. *Black Suicide.* New York: Basic Books.
Henry, A. F. and J. F. Short. 1965. *Suicide and Homicide.* New York: Free Press.
Hicks, D. J. 1968. "Effect of Co-Observer's Sanctions and Adult Presence on Imitative Aggression." *Child Development* 39:303–10.
Hirsch, C. S., N. B. Rushforth, A. B. Ford, and L. Adelson. 1973. "Homicide and Suicide in a Metropolitan Country." *Journal of the American Medical Association* 223(8).
Klebba, A. J. 1975. "Homicide Trends in the United States, 1900–1974." *Public Health Reports* 90(3):195–204.
Leifer, A. D. and D. F. Roberts. 1972. "Children's Responses to Television Violence." In HEW publication no. HSM 72-9057, J. P. Murray, E. A. Rubenstein, and G. A. Comstock, eds. *Television and Social Behavior*, vol. 2. Washington, D.C.: U.S. Government Printing Office.

Lockert, E. 1974. "A Study of the Relationship Between Social Class and Imitation of Peer Modeled Filmed Aggression." Doctoral Dissertation, Nashville: George Peabody College, Vanderbilt University.

Lovaas, O. I. 1961. "Effect of Exposure to Symbolic Aggression on Aggressive Behavior." *Child Development* 32:37–44.

Meyer, T. P. 1972. "Effects of Viewing Justified and Unjustified Real Film Violence on Aggressive Behavior." *Journal of Personal and Social Psychology* 23(1):21–29.

Murray, J. P., E. A. Rubenstein, and G. A. Comstock eds. 1972. *Television and Social Behavior: A Technical Report to the Surgeon General's Scientific Advisory Committee on Television and Social Behavior.* HEW Publication no. HSM 72-9057. Washington, D.C.: U.S. Government Printing Office.

Mussen, P. H., and E. Rutherford. 1961. "Effect of Aggressive Cartoons on Children's Aggressive Play." *Journal of Abnormal and Social Psychology* 62:461–64.

Nelson, J. D., D. M. Gelfand, and D. P. Hartman. 1969. "Children's Aggression Following Competition and Exposure to an Aggressive Model." *Child Development* 40:1085–97.

Noble, G. 1973. "Effects of Different Forms of Filmed Aggression on Children's Constructive and Destructive Play." *Journal of Personal and Social Psychology* 26(1):34–9.

Poussaint, A. F. 1972. *Why Blacks Kill Blacks.* New York: Emerson Hall.

Pyle, G. 1974. "The Spatial Dynamics of Crime." University of Chicago, Department of Geography, Research Paper No. 159, p. 123.

Reckless, W. C. 1967. *The Crime Problem.* New York: Appleton-Century-Crofts.

U.S. Life Tables. 1959–1961 and 1969–1971.

U.S. Vital Statistics. 1975.

Walters, R. and D. Willows. 1969. "Imitative Behavior of Disturbed and Non-Disturbed Children Following Exposure to Aggressive and Nonaggressive Models." *Child Development* 39:79–89.

Wolfgang, M. E. 1958. *Patterns in Criminal Homicide.* Philadelphia: University of Pennsylvania Press.

Zimring, F. E. 1972. "Some Facts About Homicide." *The Nation.* March 6.

10

WOMEN AND HOMICIDE

Elissa P. Benedek

◇

The murderess is a topic of particular fascination for Americans. A murderess steps out of her traditionally perceived role as a passive, dependent, and quiet creature. Her image is transformed. The murderess may be thought of as insane, mentally ill or, at the very least, emotionally disturbed. The contemporary mass media have emphasized women's greater involvement in spectacular violent crime (Rosenblatt and Greenland 1974).

In this paper I explore women and homicide, particularly women and uxoricide (spouse murder). I review the meager existing literature about women as murderers from the perspective of their biology, sociology, and psychology, and then turn to contemporary thinking about women who murdered their husbands. Finally, I discuss existing strategies for their legal defense. However, it is clear that our knowledge about the murderess is incomplete; existing information is mostly theoretical, only occasionally grounded in research, and more often representing an extrapolation from data garnered about males who commit homicide.

Our knowledge of the character and causes of female criminality is at the same stage of development that characterized our knowledge of male criminality some 30 or more years ago.

The most current data about the incidence of female homicide are available from the Uniform Crime Reports of Crime in the United

States (U.S. Department of Justice 1977). In the Uniform Crime Reporting Program murder is defined as the "willful killing of another." Classification of this offense, as in all other crime index offenses, is based solely on police investigation as opposed to any determination by a court, medical examiner, coroner, or other agency. Therefore, the actual number of murders by females in the United States are probably not even accurately reported in this document. It has repeatedly been emphasized that homicide offenders, like other offenders, are lost (statistically) as they pass through the legal process (Widom 1978). Not all murder is detected nor are all murderers identified or investigated. Even when investigated, a number of offenders are diverted from the process of prosecution. Others are diverted from the Criminal Justice System, and still others are acquitted. Deaths caused by negligence, suicide, accident, or justifiable homicide are not included in this classification; attempted murder might well be counted as aggravated assault. However, arrest statistics provide some measure of involvement in criminal acts by sex, age, and race and allow us to compare changes in rates over the years (Widom 1978).

In 1976, there were an estimated 18,780 murders committed in the United States. This number is approximately 2 percent of the total of violent crimes. Of these 18,780 murders, victim and offender were identified in 10,847 cases where there was a single victim and a single offender. The offender could not be identified in 3,596 of the murders, and, in the remainder of the murders, there was a multiple situation involving more than one victim or offender. Of the 10,847 identified cases, 8,190 cases were male victims, murdered by 6,432 males and 1,758 females. Unfortunately, from the FBI Uniform Crime Statistics, it is not possible to tell the relationship of the male victim to the female offender, nor is the age of the victim addressed. Thus, a proportion of the male victims may have been young children and another fraction may have been strangers, neighbors, or criminals. However, we can extrapolate from other information and hypothesize about the relationship of the female murderer to many of her victims (Rasko 1976; Totman 1971; Wolfgang 1958; Ward et al. 1969).

Rasko, in a comprehensive study of homicides and attempted homicides committed by female killers in Hungary, provides one set of observations of the relationship of the victim to the female killer. She notes that in a study of 125 female murderers, most of their 140 victims were their husbands, common law husbands, or lovers (40 percent), and 20 percent were their children. In her study she excluded infanticide victims as they would constitute the largest class of victim. Thus, two-thirds of victims are persons with a close relationship to the offender. She cites Totman's data collected in the United States (Totman 1971). These data revealed that 40 percent of victims of female murderers were husband, common law husband, or lover, 21 percent were children (excluding infanticide), and 29 percent were other relatives. It is her belief that the distribution of victims of female killers in Hungary by type of victim–offender relationship is comparable to that of the United States. The 1976 Uniform Crime Reports reveal that 27 percent of all murder victims in the United States were related to the offender and 54 percent were "otherwise acquainted." Thus, it appears that 81 percent of all murders, whether murderer–female victim or murderess–male victim might be classified as "interacting" as compared to "stranger" murders. Newspaper and television coverage of female homicide might lead one to believe that Jean Harris, Emily Harris, Ma Barker, and Bonnie Parker are the typical American violent female criminal, and the more recent study of women in violent crime by Ward et al. (1969) supports the hypothesis that the role of women in murders and their choice of victim are closely tied to the female sex role. According to Wolfgang's data (1958), 51.9 percent of female victims had a family relationship to the offender whereas the rate for male offenders was 16.4 percent. Ward's data, drawn from populations of women incarcerated in state prisons for crimes of violence, support these findings. Women involved in murders in the Ward study were the sole perpetrator in 77 percent of the cases and in over half of the cases, a family member or lover was the victim.

A careful study by Ward et al. (1969) suggests some conclusions about Uniform Crime statistics on women and homicide. These authors have carefully evaluated the national crime statistics collected by the FBI:

It is not possible to draw accurate conclusions about crime trends from this [sic] data because changes in population are not taken into account when increases in crime are cited. The fact that more arrests are reported may also reflect in the increase of the number of police officers available, the increased efficiency of law enforcement efforts, greater uniformity of police record keeping operations, and that more law enforcement agencies are contributing to uniform crime reports. These qualifications should be kept in mind as we look at arrest and commitment data to try to determine trends in the rates of crimes of violence by women.

These authors, although disclaiming the accuracy of their data, nevertheless state:

The percent that women represent among persons arrested in the United States for violent crimes has been declining for homicide and assault from 15.3 percent to 12.9 percent for assault respectively. The percentage of women arrested for violent crimes out of the total number of women arrested has remained fairly stable over the last eight years.

Simon (1976) reviewing 1972 Uniform Crime data notes that there is an increase in part I crimes for both males and females. The increase comes, according to her interpretation of the data, in an increase in property crime not an increase in homicide (Klein and Kress 1976).

Biological Theories of Female Criminality:

At the turn of the century, Lombroso offered one of the earliest biological explanations for female criminality. In *The Female Offender*, originally published in 1903, Lombroso described female criminality as an inherited tendency which could be regarded as a biological atavism. Such cranial and facial features and their accompanying behavior could be eliminated if atavistic people were prohibited from breeding. At this time, criminality was regarded as a physical impairment similar to epilepsy. Lombroso theorized that individuals developed differently within sexual and racial limitations. They ranged from the most developed (the white male) to the most primitive (the nonwhite female). Lombroso compared in great detail the crania, moles, heights, and weights of convicted criminals and prostitutes with those of "normal women." Any trait that he found to be more common in a criminal group, he pronounced as an atavistic trait—a mole, dark hair, and so forth. A woman with a number of telltale traits could be regarded as a potential criminal. This was clearly an unscientific and irrational basis for prediction. He specifically rejected the idea that certain traits, such as obesity, could be the result of differences in lifestyle due to poverty rather than representing a prediction of criminality. He said, "Women have many traits in common with children, that their moral sense is deficient, that they are revengeful, jealous. In ordinary cases, these defects are neutralized by piety, maternity, want of passion, sexual coldness, weakness and an underdeveloped intelligence." He characterized the female offender as being more masculine as compared to the more normal woman who lacked intelligence and was weak. Thus, he noted that the anomalies of skull, physiognomy, and brain capacity of female criminals approximated more closely that of males, normal or criminal, than those of the normal woman.

Another theoretician who saw women as somewhat biologically deficient was Sigmund Freud (1933). He described women as being passive, masochistic, and narcissistic. He felt these defective qualities existed because women lacked a penis. This "physical deficiency" made them unable to resolve the Oedipal conflict. Thus, they became inferior in a moral sense and were less able to control their impulses. Although Freud does not directly relate superego weakness to female criminality, he implies women are inclined toward amorality because of their anatomical "deficiency." His general view of deviant behavior, a variety of sorts manifested by women, results from the "masculinity complex" or penis envy.

Most biologists and neurophysiologists who have looked at violence have found no neurological, neurochemical, or physiological basis for violent behavior and homicide. It has not been possible to differentiate between men and women. Those who have studied hormonal imbalances have commented, "Before psychology, sociology and criminology can be convincingly written as merely special aspects of endocrinology, many more facts than are now available will have to be collected and integrated (Hoskins 1941). Studies of testosterone levels (for the most part in males) correlate neither with fighting nor with psychological tests nor with histories of violent behavior. Studies of urinary and plasma testosterone concentration in prisoners have yielded contradictory results (Nassi and Abramowitz 1976). Unfortunately, though women have not been subjects and there has been an extrapolation of data from men to women, there has also been extrapolation of data from animal research to man. Thus, most of the research models for both sexes are animal models.

Sociology of Criminal Behavior

Research on the sociology of female homicide is clearly much more impressive and informative. Martin (1976), Hilberman and Munson

(1977–78), and others describe the classic picture of the battered wife who eventually murders her husband. Such a woman often comes from a home where she has observed and experienced parental violence and sees violence as a norm in social interaction and as a solution for conflict. Marriage is frequently seen as an escape route, but her choice of husband is not intelligently determined. Thus, the potential offender often chooses a mate with a high penchant for violence. She has been beaten repeatedly and brutally for a period of years by a spouse or lover who may be drunk, sober, tired, depressed, elated, mentally ill, or just angry. Lacking educational and financial resources, she describes a feeling of being "trapped." This feeling increases proportionately with the number of young children she has. Community resources are disinterested, ineffective, or unavailable. Information about homicides reveals that the battered wife has turned to social agencies, police, prosecutors, friends, ministers, and family, but they have not offered meaningful support or advice. Interviews with abused women who have murdered their spouses reveal that they feel that homicide was the only alternative left to them.

In reality, obviously, this is not the case. Their exploration of the real world and its resources has not been complete or skillful; however, their restricted and distorted conception of reality is perhaps more important than the reality itself. Sociologically, they are impoverished and undereducated. Psychologically, they are depressed, helpless, and hopeless. More important, as a group, they are filled with an impotent rage which has no legitimate channel of expression.

Thus, what is actually premeditated homicide often appears unpremeditated. It may or may not be connected with voluntary alcohol or drug ingestion which can serve as a facilitating or disinhibiting factor. It may follow an actual incidence of abuse. However, it may follow the reawakening memory of a past abuse, that is, the offender may kill the victim months after an earlier abuse when present actions arouse recall of the previous episode. On the basis of her limited predictive skills, she anticipates that she will be abused again.

CASE 1

Mrs. R., a 40-year-old mother of four, was accused of the first degree murder of her 45-year-old husband. During a clinical interview, she recounted a 22-year history of violent abuse and beatings at the hands of her jealous husband. These beatings occurred regularly and resulted in life-threatening injury on at least two occasions. Mrs. R. finally separated from and divorced her husband, although she claimed she still loved him. Six months after the separation, and last beating, her husband returned unexpectedly to claim his property. Mrs. R. was very frightened. When her former husband approached her in anger, she remembered the last episode of violence and picked up a gun to frighten him. As he advanced toward her, she felt threatened (although according to witnesses he had not overtly threatened her) and shot him. She claimed she was in terror because of past abuse.

The most carefully assembled and succinctly presented analysis of crimes of violence committed by women is a study conducted by Ward et al. (1969). This study is based on demographic characteristics of personal histories and institutional experiences of a large sample of women incarcerated in the California Institute for Women. This cited population included all the inmates housed in that institution between 1962 and 1964 and a comparable sample collected in 1968. After an analysis of the data, the authors commented on what they found to be the characteristics of women sent to prison for homicide, assault, or robbery. When considering the characteristics of women committed for homicide, the authors observed that these women were more likely to be white, tended to come from homes which were relatively stable, had infrequent reports of previous criminality, and little history of parental divorce. They were noted to have drinking problems but not to have been involved in narcotic abuse. Few had an extensive criminal record; a large percentage was diagnosed as having some type of psychological disability. Women committed for assault and battery, on the other hand, were more likely to come from minority groups and from families in which there was criminal behavior and separation or divorce of parents. Like the women imprisoned for homicide, women committed for assault and battery also had serious drinking problems but were more likely to be involved in use of narcotics. They also had a history of prior criminal offenses but to a lesser extent than the homicide group and were diagnosed as having psychological difficulties also.

Physical strength was not used in committing a crime in 51 percent of the cases. Over one-third of the weapons were knives or other household implements. Another one-third of the weapons were guns. Women tended to use household objects, a reflection, perhaps, that the homicide was committed in their own homes, against their own children, lovers, and husbands. Also interesting is the degree to which the victims were unable to defend themselves. Of the victims in this sample, 42 percent were ill, drunk, off guard, asleep, or infirm. Another 19 percent were children (this differentiation is confirmed by Wolfgang).

Totman (1971) also studied the psychological and sociological characteristics of women committed for homicide of a spouse or infant. She interviewed 120 murderesses during their prison sentences. Her data supported the notion that murderesses were largely unsuccessful and dissatisfied with their previous educational and vocational achievements. She found their lives barren, focused superficially on traditional wifely or maternal activities. The women prisoners could not believe that additional satisfaction, intellectual outlets, and pleasures or achievements were possible through employment or education. In fact, the opposite was seen, as they were poorly educated and had no form of vocational training. They did not share personal concerns with, nor were they able to get support or help from, significant others or community resources. Ultimately, when caught in a crisis, these women defined and reinterpreted their negative situation so that it called for an action they previously had not considered—murder. These women exhausted all possible courses of action for solving their personal dilemma, and having no recourse (at least from their perspective) chose murder as a solution. If they could have used fantasy, they would not so readily have killed. Frequently, they are fantasy deprived.

Totman described in great detail women who murdered a spouse rather than killing a child. These women consciously perceived their relationship to a mate (either boyfriend or spouse) as a negative one. They often hoped the relationship would change, but if change was recognized as impossible, they still felt committed to their relationship. Even though these women recognized that their relationship with a mate was traumatic, they were unable to communicate openly their feelings about their mates and rarely communicated such feelings about problems with others outside their families. Such others would include police, lawyers, and family members. When women were asked why they had chosen murder as a way of handling a difficult personal situation, every woman in the study denied having conscious thoughts of murder, except in the last few moments before the victim's death. Even those who had taken a weapon and gone to another location to find their victim were clearly in the minority and tended to explain their behavior in two alternative ways, either to frighten someone with a weapon or having "flipped out."

Twenty-eight out of thirty murderesses studied reported that they had been subject to undeserved and unreasonable amounts of physical and/or verbal humiliation by their victim. They saw marriage as a way out of a difficult family situation, a situation where no other exit was offered. They had no way to support themselves because they had no educational or vocational training. They could not imagine themselves as doing anything but being married and having children. Once married, their experiences outside of the home were limited. The only group affiliation mentioned more than once by these murderesses was membership in Alcoholics Anonymous. They had no hobbies, no outside interests, and no involvement with other men or women.

In Totman's group, as compared to the Ward et al. group, all of the patient subjects had been subjected to or had witnessed violence with their parents, in the general neighborhood environment, (the ghetto), their work setting (prostitute or barmaid), or in their relationships with their mates. Some reported a combination of these experiences. These women typically had had more past arrests for assaultive behavior.

Totman questioned her subjects as to why, after assessing their situation, they felt they had no other alternatives. Why had they chosen murdey? All of her respondents reiterated their ambivalence about their situation. It was, indeed, destructive, but it was also attractive in that their mates were exciting or needed fulfilling. The ambivalence, in combination either with a hope for favorable change of a spontaneous nature or feeling trapped, created inaction or inertia. Occasionally, a woman would temporarily leave an abusive mate. However, women who fled reported themselves as returning to or being chased by the spouse victim. Suicide was an alternative considered by some of this group. Rarely, a woman would attempt suicide and, in some situations, she dared her victim to kill her.

In this selected group of 28 female spouse killers, none used the defense of insanity. Some indicated confusion, distress, anxiety, and fear. Psychiatric diagnoses on their chart reflected personality disorders in 16 subjects and psychotic or borderline disorders in seven subjects.

CASE 2

Mrs. X., a 45-year-old woman, described the murder of her abusive husband as if she had watched a third party take a shotgun and kill him. Mrs. X. had a past history of psychiatric disability—but even more importantly, she described other stressful occasions when she had felt herself "float out of my body and watch." One of those crises was a childhood rape.

CASE 3

Mrs. Z., a chronic schizophrenic, abused alcohol during periods when her illness exacerbated. During one such period this guilt-withdrawn woman began to believe her abusing husband had another girlfriend. She drank wine to fortify herself as she waited for her husband to return home from his job. As he entered their apartment she killed him.

Totman (1971) also interviewed five women guilty of first degree murder—a charge that requires premeditation. These women were clearly above average in intelligence, had no previous arrests, and were middle or upper middle class. Their motivation, as seen by the district attorney, was a combination of wanting insurance money and having a boyfriend. These subjects, in contrast to those who committed manslaughter, denied serious relationship problems with their mates and complained they had been unjustly dealt with by the criminal justice system that sent them to prison. They were more like the stranger murderer than the family murderer.

A more recent study by Hilberman (1977–1978) supports the descriptions of women assailants by Ward et al. Her group were gathered from a rural medical clinic where inquiry was made about family violence. Their social situations were very much like the pictures of women who eventually murdered their spouses, but for the most part they were more passive and suffered more psychiatric symptomatology. Hilberman states, "The few women who resorted to counterviolence did so as an act of desperation associated with the failure of other options. They fought back with kitchen knives, broom handles, frying pans, hot grease and lye, hammers, screwdrivers and rarely, with guns. In contrast to the husband's violent behavior, the violence by women was related *to a direct threat to life* and usually came as a surprise since they themselves were unaware of the extent of their rage."

Hilberman notes that psychiatric history suggested prior psychological dysfunction for more than one-half of the women. The single most frequent diagnostic category was manic depressive psychosis. Schizophrenia, alcoholism, and personality disorders were found less frequently. (This was in contrast to Totman's sample, where personality disorder was the most common diagnosis.) Hilberman noted that, among her sample, fear of loss of control was a significant concern. She wrote, "These fears were often expressed in vague abstract terms but were unmistakably linked to aggression."

She noted that some of her patients fantasized detailed plans for murdering their husbands as a way of coping with anger. One woman who had been explosive in the past began throwing the shotgun at her husband instead of firing it. Others locked up guns and knives to prevent easy access to weapons without knowing why they did so. Some displayed outward aggression by verbal retaliation while others fought back physically. However, these cases were the exception. Passivity and inhibition of action were found in the majority. Thus, Hilberman has described a group of potential murderesses, a group more likely to have psychiatric disturbance in the form of depression and more likely to be concerned about control of aggressive impulses.

An additional study by Widom (1978) reports the observation that murderesses have, like their male counterparts, various problems in the handling of aggression. Widom studied 73 women awaiting trial at Massachusetts Correctional Institution for violent offenses using a variety of psychological tests derived from the MMPI. She was able to develop four personality profiles or four distinct types into which 76 percent of the sample fell. Type I: Women differed in terms of their higher levels of hostility, impulsivity, and aggression and low levels of anxiety. Type I women were labeled as primary psychopaths, similar to males described by Cleckley (1964) or, as described by Megargee (1966), undercontrolled. Type II: Women were secondary or neurotic psychopaths, seeming to experience guilt and showing a high level of anxiety and depression. Type III: Women saw themselves as being basically free from psychological disturbance. Their pattern was that of a high lie score, low levels of anxiety and hostility, although they seemed to resemble the Overcontrolled Personality type suggested by Megargee (1966). Type IV: Women were identified as psychologically normal criminals with few personality problems. Interestingly enough, those women who had previous convictions for homicide were either in the Type I group (Cleckley psychopath or Megargee's undercontrolled), or the Type IV group, similar to Totman's group of 10 murders. However, as compared to the general population, the level of hostility in all four groups of women awaiting trial was higher.

In summary, it seems as if women who murder husbands belong as a group to that distinct population type that Megargee has identified as people who overcontrol violent and aggressive impulses. These women typically cannot directly express aggressive or hostile feelings. Their actual violent act occurs only after a long accumulation of aggressive and violently provocative acts directed against them. Megargee calls them the "worm turns" type.

Defense Strategies

Independent of psychological data, two female attorneys, Schneider and Jordan (1978) have developed a new strategy for defending women who murder in response to physical or sexual assault. They suggest a strategy of self-defense. In the past, the defense of impaired mental state was traditionally used for women charged with homicide. Such defenses tended to imply that women who responded to life-threatening situations by murder were either mentally deranged or insane. These lawyers suggest that an impaired mental state defense should be considered only as a last resort, with full awareness that should such a defense be used the social implications are that the woman is both a criminal and insane. Additionally, they feel it is undesirable, because the insanity defense often leads to commitment to a mental hospital for indefinite treatment. The impaired mental state defense may lead to a diminution of sentence, but a period of time will be served in jail. Although current beliefs about incarceration tend to focus on its use as an agent of punishment rather than its deterrent and for rehabilitative functions, it is clear that for most women a period of incarceration will serve only to alienate them further from their family and to reinforce their lack of self-esteem.

Because of the small numbers of women incarcerated and because sexist bias still prevails, there are relatively few women's prisons with any form of sophisticated rehabilitation available to them. Thus, a defense focusing on self-defense ought to be considered when it is appropriate. The outcome, if successful, would be acquittal. These attorneys stress that the person claiming self-defense must have a reasonable apprehension of danger and a reasonable perception of the imminence of that danger. Though divisible into two parts, the legal standard is often expressed as reasonable grounds to apprehend imminent death or grievous bodily harm. The authors stress that although the standard to evaluate reasonableness differs from state to state, it is generally defined as the perception of both apprehension and imminent danger from the individual's own perspective. They remind attorneys that a woman's perspective is different from that of a man—that is, a woman who is regularly abused perceives the fist or body of a large male as a deadly weapon and may feel ill-equipped to defend herself with her own fists. Her only resort may be use of a weapon. These attorneys have stressed the importance of presenting evidence of a homicide victim's general reputation for violence or his prior commission of specific threats or acts of violence. They felt this was as clearly relevant and crucial to the reasonableness of a woman's conduct in perceiving the imminence of bodily harm. This propensity for violence can be used to support the reasonableness of a woman's conduct in defending herself.

One should not assume from this discussion, which comes from a psychiatric perspective, that all women who murder abusing spouses are either mentally ill, suffer from an impaired mental state, or are involved in self-defense. The motivation of murderesses, as we have seen, is complex. Such women cannot be easily described. They have diverse personality patterns and are also diversely categorized biologically, psychologically, and sociologically. Unfortunately, our state of knowledge about the female criminal and the female murderer is similar to our knowledge about children in the early 1800s; we then considered children as mini-adults. Today, we tend to consider women murderers as mini-males. In this article, I have attempted to show that at least one class of women murderers—those who have been abused by their spouses—differ in significant ways from other murderers. Their personality, social history, socioeconomic status, and lack of opportunity form a complex web of factors contributing to the criminal action. Homicide by them is an act of desperation. It is the result of the conversion of these complex psychological, physiological, biological, and social forces.

REFERENCES

Cleckley, H. 1964. *The Mask of Sanity*. St. Louis: Mosby.

Freud, S. 1933. *New Introductory Lectures on Psychoanalysis*. New York: Norton.

Hilberman, E. and M. Munson. 1978. "Sixty Battered Women." *Victimology: An International Journal* 2:460–71.

Hoskins, R. 1941. *Endocrinology*. New York: Norton.

Klein, D. and J. Kress. 1976. "Any Woman's Blues—A Critical Overview of Women, Crime, and the Criminal Justice System." *Crime and Social Justice*, no. 5, Spring–Summer.

Lombroso, C. 1903. *The Female Offender*. New York: Appleton.

Martin, D. 1976. *Battered Wives*. San Francisco: Glide.

Megargee, E. 1966. "Undercontrolled and Overcontrolled Personality Types in Extreme Antisocial Aggression." *Psychological Monographs*, 80.

Nassi, A. and S. Abramowitz. 1976. "From Phrenology to Psychosurgery and Back Again: Biological Studies of Criminality." *American Journal of Orthopsychiatry* 46:591–607.

Rasko, G. 1976. "The Victim of the Female Killer." *Victimology: An International Journal* 1:396–402.

Rosenblatt, E. and C. Greenland. 1974. "Female Crimes of Violence." *Canadian Journal of Criminology and Corrections* 16:173–80.

Schneider, E. M. and S. B. Jordan. 1978. "Representation of Women who Defend Themselves in Response to Physical or Sexual Assault." New York: Center for Constitutional Rights.

Simon, R. 1976. "American Women and Crime." *The Annals of the American Academy of Political and Social Science* 423:21–46, January.

Totman, J. 1971. "The Murderess." *Police*, July–August.

Totman, J. 1971. "The Murderess: A Psychosocial Study of the Process." Ann Arbor: University Microfilms.

U.S. Department of Justice. 1977. Uniform Crime Reports, Federal Bureau of Investigation. Washington, D.C.: U.S. Government Printing Office.

Ward, D., Jackson, M., and R. Ward. 1969. "Crimes of Violence by Women." In D. Mulvihill, et al., eds. *Crimes of Violence*. Washington, D.C.: U.S. Government Printing Office.

Widom, C. 1978. "An Empirical Classification of Female Offenders." *Criminal Justice and Behavior* 5:35–52.

Widom, C. 1978. "Toward an Understanding of Female Criminality." *Progress in Experimental Personality Research* 8:245–50.

Wolfgang, M. 1958. *Patterns in Criminal Homicide*. Philadelphia: University of Pennsylvania Press.

11

CHILDREN
WHO KILL

Robert L. Sadoff

◇

Two youngsters hire a third and pay him $60 to kill their father. Two boys, age 16, strangle one boy's mother and his six-year-old sister. Mother and son plot to kill stepfather. Eight-year-old smashes the skull of his one-year-old brother. Four-year-old girl drowns baby sister. These news events reflect children who kill.

My own experiences with children who kill include several cases of parricide, young parents who kill their newborn offspring, youngsters who kill younger siblings, a 14-year-old boy who killed his teacher, a 12-year-old boy who killed his older brother, and a 15-year-old boy who killed a stranger in the course of a robbery. The diversity of killing by children is apparent, yet there are some common trends that occur. Mostly, homicide by children occurs within families or among acquaintances or friends. Except when committed during a felony, the killing is rarely done to a stranger. Parricide must be separated from fratricide, as indicated in at least one study showing that killing by children of other relatives is different from the killing of parents.

Killing by youngsters under 10 appears to be different from the killing by adolescents, which seems to have its own pattern related to acts of impulsive violence. Younger children seem to kill their own siblings or their parents for reasons of jealousy, demonstrating childish anger, where the behavior is expressed through loss of control.

Homicide by children and adolescents has been known for centuries but has been studied intensively only rather recently. Much of the early work has been ascribed to Lauretta Bender, who since 1935 had followed 33 boys and girls (initially under 16) who had been associated with the death of another person (Bender, 1959). She indicates, as do most studies in this area, that the overwhelming majority of youngsters who kill are boys. In her series 31 of the 33 children studied were boys between the ages of five and fifteen. A classification of the mode of death was as follows:

Mode of Killing	Number of Children
Fires	6
Drowning	5
Stabbing with sharp object	7
Repeated blows with heavy object	6
Shooting	6
Other	3

She found evidence of depression, schizophrenia, chronic brain disease, and epilepsy. (EEG's available on 15 boys reported five normal and ten pathological, indicative of epilepsy.) She found that three were finally diagnosed as intellectual defectives, twelve schizophrenics, three epileptics, seven chronic brain syndromes, and ten psychoneurotic depressions. Almost half had psychiatric evaluations preceding the incident which led to the death of another person. She concluded that there are

certain dangerous symptoms of a psychiatric nature which should be considered as significant, especially when they occur in combinations as follows:
1. Organic brain damage with an impulse disorder and abnormal EEG and epilepsy;
2. Childhood schizophrenia with preoccupations of death and killing in the psychoneurotic phase or with antisocial paranoid preoccupations in the pseudopsychopathic phase;
3. Compulsive fire-setting;
4. Defeating school or retardation (reading disability);
5. Extremely unfavorable home conditions and life experiences;
6. A personal experience with violent death. (Bender 1959)

Following Bender are a number of authors who present a series of youngsters who killed and have emerged with suggestions for psychodynamics or etiological factors involved in the homicidal behavior. In one early study, Bridgman (1929) described four young murderers and concluded, "In the cases of two of these children, it seems fair to say that environment has seemed a determining factor; in the other two, certain native traits seem greatly to be involved." The study is primarily empirical and based on her observations of the four youngsters ranging in age from 12 to 16.

Most early writers lacked a sense of specificity. Stearns indicates, that "In murder by adolescents with obscure motivation," four cases have certain elements in common, enough I believe to establish a clinical syndrome" (1957). He suggests that the male adolescents who killed had good reputations, the victims had all been females and the crimes were wanton and ferocious. No motive had ever been established and he presumes that there has been "gross mental disease to account for such crime." He believes these people should be confined for life since "there is indication of some morbid quality which would make it dangerous to ever release them."

Specificity began to emerge in the early 1960s when Sherwin Woods wrote on "Adolescent Violence and Homicide," indicating that ego disruption and the six and fourteen dysrhythmia found on the EEG may in some way be related to adolescent aggression and homicide. He noted, "It is my hypothesis that the dysrhythmia does not itself induce violence, but rather that it serves as a biologically determined stress on an already impoverished ego. In the resultant regressed ego state there is the emergence of primitive non-neutralized aggression, with the violent acting out of conflict previously held in check by the defensive system of the ego" (1961).

Similarly, Michaels (1961) presents a paper on "Enuresis in Murderous Aggressive Children and Adolescents" in which he states, "In a series of studies over many years I have shown that a history of persistent enuresis occurs more often in juvenile delinquents than in any other type of psychiatric disorder." He also showed that in a series of eight boys who killed, three had the presence of epileptiform or epileptic seizures and six had the presence of late bed-wetting. MacDonald (1969) has been credited with the development of the "triad" in juveniles to evaluate dangerousness: enuresis, firesetting, and cruelty to animals. Others have later added a fourth factor— fighting among peers in school.

Most reports on murder in juveniles relate to adolescents. McCarthy

(1978) discusses "narcissism and the psychodynamics in the self in homicidal adolescents," where he concludes: "In my view, their expression of the homicidal rage can be understood as an attempt at reparation of the self. Its expression affirmed a sense of reality and restored infantile omnipotence." He believed the youths who killed had an underlying narcissistic rage and an impaired capacity for self-esteem regulation. He believed the homicidal assaults appeared to be "multi-determined by early deprivation and disturbances in object relations that paralleled a lack of solidity of the self. Homicidal assaults were also related to the presence of dehumanization, loss of control and sadistic fantasies."

Marten (1965) discusses the overcontrolled, quiet, deceptive youth who becomes involved in homicide, and Smith (1965) describes "the adolescent murderer" from a psychological standpoint; he indicates that he has studied a group of eight murderers from ages 14 to 20, of which he has presented three in detail. He states: "Characteristically, these patients suffer early experiences of deprivation which result in an under-developed ego and a vulnerability to outbursts of violent aggression." He believes the act of murder for these patients is characteristic "of a type of ego failure which is, on the one hand, superficially incongruous with the rest of the patient's life and, on the other hand, a defense against a threatened disintegration not apparent in the surface symptoms."

Walsh-Brennan (1974) of England ascribes much of the etiology to juvenile homicide to environment and parental rearing rather than psychodynamics. He found, for example, in a study of 11 youngsters who killed that eight had "overdominant mothers." He believes the answer to prevention of further adolescent homicide lies in the mother–child relationship and factors within the parent as well as the adolescent.

By far the greatest number of children who kill take parents, siblings, or relatives as victims. They kill strangers infrequently, except in gang situations or in the perpetration of other violent crimes. Tanay (1973) has written extensively on reactive parricide, and I (Sadoff 1971) have written on clinical aspects of parricide, indicating the ambivalence of the juvenile to the victim and the sense of relief experienced after he has killed his mother or father.

Duncan and Duncan (1971) present five cases in which the adolescent had an abrupt loss of control associated with a change in his interpersonal relationship with the victim. They postulate that a history of parental brutality is significant in the consideration of adolescent homicide.

Perhaps the clearest article is by Easson and Steinhilber (1961), who document clearly, with a series of cases, that murderous behavior by children and adolescents is related to the wishes of the parent who fosters such behavior. In at least one of the cases they demonstrate this conclusion by showing that the mother recalled several times indicating to her child that she wished the victim (his father) were dead, and on another occasion the mother had said to her son that he would not be able to live with her until his father were dead.

Sargent (1962) underscores that conclusion when he presents a series of cases all of which were related to parental wishes. He concludes with the two following hypotheses: "(a) The first corollary suggests that the stimulating adult accomplishes his goal by inflaming in the child latent hostile feelings toward the victim. (b) The second corollary suggests that the child's susceptibility to the unconscious stimulation of the parent or adult rested upon both the immaturity of the child's ego and the presence of a special bond between stimulating adult and child."

Others have suggested that other family psychodynamics are involved in youngsters who kill. Paluszny and McNabb (1975) treated a six-year-old who committed fratricide, an event also related to intrafamily dynamics. Foodman and Estrada (1977) discuss family reaction to members who commit accidental homicide within the family.

Tooley (1975) discusses murderous six-year-old children who set fires, who demonstrate murderous rage related to the ambivalent relationship with mother.

Podolsky (1965) indicated that about 700 children commit murder each year. He asked why they kill and proposed a number of dynamics. For one, he said, "The death wish is strong in children who are likely to kill."

Many authors have been struck with the apparent calmness of the killer and the total concession that is made without remorse when confronted by the authorities. Adelson (1972) presents "the battering child" in which he reveals five infants less than one year of age who were killed by children eight years of age or younger. He points out how easy it is to kill infants by battering since their brain is so vulnerable and the skull barely able to protect the vital organ.

Perhaps one of the most remarkable studies is that by Sendi and Blomgren (1975) who studied three groups of adolescents—10 who had committed homicide, 10 who had threatened or attempted homicide, and 10 hospitalized controls. They found that the adolescents who did commit homicide were psychotic-regressive and those who threatened or attempted homicide were organic-impulsive. They believe their study suggests the importance of environmental factors in reinforcing homicidal behavior.

Following this brief discussion of the psychodynamics or etiological factors involved in adolescents or children who kill, what productive factors have emerged to aid us in the detection of individuals who may become killers? Duncan and Duncan (1971) indicate the following assessment for prediction:

1. The intensity of the patient's hostile destructive impulses as expressed verbally, behaviorally, or in psychometric test data.
2. The patient's control over his impulses as determined by history and current behavior, particularly in response to stress.
3. The patient's knowledge of and ability to pursue realistic alternatives to a violent resolution of an untenable life situation.
4. The provocativeness of the intended victim and the patient's ability to cope with provocation in the past and currently.
5. The degree of helplessness of the intended victim.
6. The availability of weapons.
7. Homicidal hints or threats.

Malmquist (1971) discusses (1) behavioral changes that occur in the prodromal period prior to homicidal behavior, (2) a call for help that perhaps was not properly heard, (3) use of drugs to stimulate violent behavior or decrease inhibitions, (4) the presence of object losses, primarily close complex relationships such as lover or mother or threats to manhood, by provocation or incitement by teenage girls. He also discusses somatization, hypochondriasis, or recurrent medical problems before the homicidal behavior. He notes there can be an emotional crescendo, or a buildup of agitation just before it, and also a threat of homosexual behavior or homosexual threats to the potential killer. He concludes that the homicidal behavior which may be very close to suicidal behavior could be interpreted as "a last desperate effort to survive," and asks "whether one can hypothesize juvenile homicide as a miscarried triumph based on a continuing desire to live rather than to die?"

Miller and Looney (1974) reveal the following factors related to an actual homicidal episode: "All the patients studied had a history which included: (1) parental violence, (2) severe early emotional deprivation, and (3) erratic control over aggressive impulses. Psychological examination indicated that the patients had: (1) ego images of themselves as physically inferior, weak and inadequate, (2) a violent and primitive fantasy life, (3) blunted and shallow emotional reaction, (4) severe sexual inhibitions." They conclude, "The likelihood of murder is thought to be extremely high in the presence of either total dehumanization or partial dehumanization when part objects are aggressively eroticized." Finally, Miller (1974) lists the following nonspecific indicators in youngsters who show a propensity for injuring others:

1. History of having been beaten as a child
2. History of head injury
3. Stubbornness
4. Temper tantrums
5. Emotional deprivation
6. Alcoholic parents
7. Preference for knives over guns

Having discussed dynamics and etiological factors of childhood and adolescent homicide and predictive factors, what now can we conclude regarding treatment for adolescent murderers? Shall we be as pessimistic as Stearns, who concludes that adolescent murderers are internally depraved as well as deprived and must be confined for life, or may we be more sanguine and outline a program of treatment for such young killers? It seems to me that the review of the literature and my own experience with youngsters who kill indicates a need, first, to conduct a thorough physical examination, a neurological examination, with electroencephalogram, skull X-rays, and brain scan, if warranted; a comprehensive psychological test battery; and a complete family and individual psychiatric assessment. Once the factors involved in the perpetration of the violence are known, then adequate treatment may be instituted. This may consist of medication, confinement, hospitalization, psychotherapy, family therapy, educational and occupational rehabilitation or separation of the individual from the tension-producing family environment. The point is the treatment must be geared to the etiology and the illness. All adolescent killers are not of a uniform group and may not all be treated similarly. As we have noted, some suffer from brain damage, others from schizophrenia, others from psychoneurotic tension, and still others appear to have either a normal personality or a character and personality disorder that had become aggravated under the stress of familial and environmental pressure. For some adolescents, especially those who kill parents, the treatment would focus on the preexisting morbid situation which led to the homicide. Further treatment would be for depression or other reaction to the violent behavior.

Corder et al. (1976) found, in their study of adolescent parricide, significant differences as compared with other adolescents who have murdered relatives or strangers. They conclude that the adolescents charged with murdering strangers were significantly more likely than the parricidal group to have a history of poor impulse control, aggressive behavior, and previous arrests and sentences to training schools. The parricide group showed more indication of chronic physical abuse by parents, more indications of overattachment to their mothers, more evidence of atypical sexual stimulation by parents, and more incidences of amnesia for the act of murder.

Thus, it seems clear that adolescents or children who murder usually do so within the family or toward parents but may also act violently toward strangers. There appears to be a difference in the psychodynamics and family dynamics of the different groups. Children who kill often are acting out the fantasies, wishes, or unconscious urges of their parents, and very often have disturbed family relationships. In addition to treatment, we must consider the predictive elements outlined by Miller and others, and begin to work in a preventive capacity by recognizing disturbed families before violence occurs and beginning intervention to avoid adolescent murder whenever possible. In the parricide cases that I have studied, it has been noted by family members or neighbors on very many occasions that they were able to predict that the youngster would one day kill his father or mother because of the manner in which he was treated. It is this type of prediction by neighbors and relatives which has to be brought to official attention for adequate professional intervention and prevention of homicide.

The subject of children who kill, thus, is vast and there is no apparent uniformity. We must be aware of the multiple factors that occur in any behavior and especially that leading to such extreme behavior as murder. The study of children who kill is as complex and important as that for adults who kill. There may be greater ability to prevent homicide by children than homicide by adults, where the behavior is even more varied and the possibility of control less adequate. The important lesson in studying children who kill is that a number of the homicides could have been prevented by adequate intervention, proper medical care, or appropriate separation of perpetrator from victim.

Another important aspect is the treatment of families in which a child has killed, and where the pathology is directly related to the deprivation and the concern about the violent behavior of one of the family members. The family of a child who kills is usually totally disrupted by the behavior and requires reintegration, therapy, and skillful management and followup.

REFERENCES

Adelson, L. 1972. "The Battering Child" *Journal of the American Medical Association* (October 9) 222(2):159–61.

Bender, L. 1959. "Children and Adolescents Who Have Killed." *American Journal of Psychiatry* 116:510–13.

Bridgman, O. 1929. "Four Young Murderers." *Journal of Juvenile Research* (February) 13(2):92–96.

Corder, B. F., et al. 1976. "Adolescent Parricide: A Comparison With Other Adolescent Murder." *American Journal of Psychiatry* (August) 133(8):957–61.

Duncan, J. W. and G. M. Duncan. 1971. "Murder in the Family: A Study of Some Homicidal Adolescents." *American Journal of Psychiatry* (May) 127(11):1498–1502.

Easson, W. M. and R. Steinhilber. 1961. "Murderous Aggression by Children and Adolescents." *Archives of General Psychiatry* (January) 4:1–9.

Foodman, A. and C. Estrada. 1977. "Adolescents Who Commit Accidental Homicide." *Journal of the American Academy of Child Psychiatry* (Spring) 14(2):306–18.

McCarthy, J. B. 1978. "Narcissism and the Self in Homicidal Adolescents." *American Journal of Psychoanalysis* (Spring) 38:19–29.

MacDonald, J. 1969. *Psychiatry and the Criminal*, 2nd ed. Springfield, Illinois: Charles C. Thomas.

Malmquist, C. P. 1971. "Premonitory Signs of Homicidal Aggression in Juveniles." *American Journal of Psychiatry* (October) 128(4):461–65.

Marten, G. W. 1965. "Adolescent Murderers." *Southern Medical Journal* (October) 58:1217–20.

Michaels, J. J. 1961. "Enuresis in Murderous Aggressive Children and Adolescents." *Archives of General Psychiatry* (November) 5:490–93.

Miller, D. 1974. "Identifying and Treating the Potential Murderer." *Roche Report: Frontiers of Psychiatry* (March 15) 4(6).

Miller, D. and J. Looney. 1974. "The Prediction of Adolescent Homicide: Episodic Dyscontrol and Dehumanization." *American Journal of Psychoanalysis* (Fall) 34:187–98.

Paluszny, M. and M. McNabb. 1975. "Therapy of a Six Year Old Who Committed Fratricide." *Journal of the American Academy of Child Psychiatry* (Spring) 14:319–36.

Podolsky, E. 1965. "Children Who Kill." *General Practitioner* (May) 31(5):98–102.

Sadoff, R. L. 1971. "Clinical Observations on Parricide." *Psychiatric Quarterly* 45(1):65–69.

Sargent, D. 1962. "Children Who Kill—A Family Conspiracy?" *Social Work* (January) 7(1):35–42.

Sendi, I. B. and P. G. Blomgren. 1975. "A Comparative Study of Predictive Criteria in the Predisposition of Homicidal Adolescents." *American Journal of Psychiatry* (April) 132(4):423–27.

Smith, S. 1965. "The Adolescent Murderer." *Archives of General Psychiatry* (October) 13:310–19.

Stearns, A. and A. Warren. 1957. "Murder by Adolescents with Obscure Motivation." *American Journal of Psychiatry* 114:303–5.

Tanay, E. 1973. "Adolescents Who Kill Parents—Reactive Parricide." *Australian and New Zealand Journal of Psychiatry*, 7:263.

Tooley, K. 1975. "The Small Assassins." *Journal of the American Academy of Child Psychiatry* (Spring) 14(2):306–18.

Walsh-Brennan, K. S. 1974. "Psychopathology of Homicidal Children." *RSH* 6.

Woods, S. M. 1961. "Adolescent Violence and Homicide." *Archives of General Psychiatry* (December) 5:528–34.

12

ACUTE PSYCHIATRIC HOSPITAL TREATMENT OF ASSAULTIVE AND HOMICIDAL CHILDREN

Cynthia R. Pfeffer

<>

A universal developmental task is the mastery of aggressive drives. Psychiatric hospital treatment is commonly the first phase of a lengthy process of therapy for pathologically aggressive children. Therefore, it may present a unique opportunity to understand the treatment issues of children in whom normal development of aggressive impulses has not occurred. In a study (at Bronx Municipal Hospital Center) of 58 psychiatrically hospitalized latency age children, Pfeffer et al. (1979) noted that approximately 80 percent showed severe aggressive tendencies. Tooley (1975) described the hospital care of two six-year-old children who had murdered their younger siblings.

A comprehensive review of the literature reveals a relative paucity of reports about the psychiatric treatment of children whose actions are potentially so dangerous that loss of life may occur. My article is based upon relevant reports from the literature and primarily upon several years of experience with such children, ages 6 to 12 years. My purpose is to discuss both the role of the hospital milieu and individual treatment.

Pathologically aggressive behavior includes aggression toward objects, aggression toward others, and aggression against self. Pfeffer et al. (1978) defined a spectrum of suicidal behavior that included suicidal ideas, threats, and attempts. Similarly, a spectrum of homicidal behavior may be outlined as follows:

1. *Homicidal ideation:* thoughts of wanting to kill or harm someone.
2. *Homicidal threats:* ideas or a precursor assaultive act. For example, a child picks up a knife with the thought of harming or killing someone.
3. *Homicidal attempts:* Aggressive actions which may have seriously injured or killed someone.
4. *Homicide:* An action which caused the death of the victim.

I shall specifically focus on aggression directed toward others and objects. However, many of the assaultive youngsters also exhibited self-directed aggression.

Treatment of homicidal and dangerously assaultive children often involves an initial phase of intensive hospitalization and subsequent long-term treatment. Carek and Watson (1964), describing the inpatient treatment of a 10-year-old boy, elected an initial phase of hospitalization for three stated reasons: (1) to promote a therapeutic grip on the child's family; (2) to uncover and work through the conflicts leading to the homicide in a setting that can manage repetitive acting-out behavior; (3) to provide an opportunity to study the family and the child more closely. King emphasized that the hospital phase of treatment offers "reconditioning of perceptions with constant attention being paid to the legitimate operations of feeling, in contrast to total reliance upon feelings from outer world assessment" (1975: 143). He found that a most disabling deficit in the development of assaultive youth was educational deprivation, specifically with marked deficiencies in language, use of abstraction, and facility with symbolic communication. He believed that a fundamental benefit of hospitalization was to provide academic remediation. Tucker and Cornwall (1977), detailing the hospital treatment of a 10-year-old boy, noted that the most therapeutic aspect of hospitalization was separation from the mother.

Essential to effect the most successful therapeutic outcome is a holistic treatment approach that encompasses extensive diagnosis of such complex factors as constitutional vulnerability, environmental stress, intrapsychic conflict, and the child's state of ego functioning. Children with neurological deficits, environmental stresses, and psychopathology—including such diagnoses as sociopathic reactions, borderline personality organization, and psychosis—are all vulnerable to homicidal behavior. Specific types of interventions can be suggested when such a variety of variables are evaluated.

Most reports to determine risk factors for potentially homicidal behavior have focused primarily on adolescent behavior. Such risk variables help define areas upon which to focus treatment. All reports emphasize family disorganization, exposure to violence, family patterns of violence, and marked family psychopathology (Bender and Curran 1940; Corder et al. 1976; Duncan and Duncan 1971; Easson and Steinhilber 1961; Foodman and Estrada 1977; Patterson 1943; Scherl and Mack 1966; Sendl and Blomgren 1975; and Smith 1965).

A. Freud stated that "unsatisfactory libidinal reactions to unstable or otherwise unsuitable love objects during anal sadism will disturb the balanced fusion between libido and aggression and give rise to uncontrollable aggressivity, destructiveness, etc." (1963: 249). Tooley observed that her two homicidal children intuitively realized that their mothers found their large families a burden. The homicidal children "enjoyed a special relationship with her because of their willingness in several ways to share her burden, to 'mother' her, and to act out for her" (1975: 307). In accord with Scherl's observations of unusually conflict-laden mother–child relationships in three cases of homicidal adolescents, Easson and Steinhilber pointed out the striking finding in all eight cases of children and adolescents who assaulted or murdered that "one or both parents fostered and had condoned murderous assaults" (1961: 35). Therefore, a family intervention approach is one aspect of the treatment of the severely assaultive child. Bender and Curran (1940) studying 33 children under 16, and Sendl and Blomgren (1975), studying 30 adolescents, believed that organically derived deficits in impulse control and psychotic states of regression were factors contributing to a child's potential homicidal behavior. Sendl and Blomgren (1975), in a controlled study of 10 adolescents who committed homicide, 10 adolescents who had threatened or attempted homicide, and 10 hospitalized nonhomicidal adolescents, observed that adolescents who threatened or attempted homicide were impulsive and organic but those who committed homicide were in a regressed psychotic state. As a result one must be concerned with strengthening ego functioning and improving object relations as an essential aspect of the treatment.

Beres (1952) outlined three categories of aggressive reactions as manifestations of ego development, expressions of sadomasochistic relations, and reactions to frustration. He used these concepts to develop treatment interventions. For example, in cases of primarily disturbed ego development, the interventions are to promote opportunities for development of relationships with adults with whom identifications may rectify problematic relationships during an earlier period of life. The interventions of predominantly sadomasochistic relationship involves effecting an integration of aggressive and libidinal impulses and the resolution of ambivalent relations primarily through intensive psychotherapy. The treatment of aggression that is predominantly a response to frustration includes education and parental guidance so that realistic restraints and limits can be enforced on the child while also promoting the child's need for independence and ego development. Therefore, the aim of treatment is not to abolish aggressive impulses but to promote sublimation of such impulses and to diminish the destructive element of aggression.

Characteristics of Treatment

The techniques of treatment for assaultive and homicidal children are not radically different from the hospital treatment of other symptoms and behaviors. However, the degree of anxiety is often considerably greater for the therapist and hospital staff when coping with the behavior of a dangerously aggressive child. For example, a main reaction of the hospital staff to one 10-year-old severely aggressive boy during the first month of his hospitalization was fear and a conviction that he was weird and could all too easily become violent. Several staff members talked about how the intensity of his eyes suggested his involvement in another world. He could not develop any real attachments to staff, although there were a few nurses who began to like him more. The anxiety tends to be more personal—that is, fear about the therapist's own safety is an issue in marked contrast to the anxiety in treating a suicidal patient where the anxiety relates to concern that the patient may kill himself. Often hospital staff adapt an ultra-cautious "hands off" policy and do not want to interact with an aggressive patient. This is true even for a hospital staff working with a child who physically is relatively smaller and weaker than the adult staff.

Potentially homicidal behavior is an acute psychiatric emergency in which immediate treatment is required to protect the child and others and to decrease the severity of distress so that more intensive evaluation can occur. Hospitalization may be the best first phase of intervention. Special techniques focus on dealing with the homicidal impulses. Containing and redirecting such impulses in a socially useful way by means of discussion and play become a goal of treatment. Methods of empathic, firm physical holding or isolation from ward activity often are beneficial to diffuse the impending or actual eruption of uncontrolled aggressive impulses. Medication may be an adjunct to maintenance of stable ego control over impulses. A vivid example of these techniques is exemplified in an 11-year-old boy who was hospitalized after pushing a girl down the stairs at school. The intensity of his behavior on the unit reflected the urgency of his needs to be understood by someone. He talked about his desire to kill his peers, and he was convinced that no one ever believed that his intentions were serious. The therapist's decision to put him on constant observation was the first symbolic means that he could experience of being taken seriously. It was also decided to medicate him for the degree of dangerous and agitated behavior. He reacted to medication with fear, anger, relief, and eventually a beginning recognition of his need to be taken care of. Medication gave him the chance to achieve greater self-control and distance from the intensity of his feelings. Therapeutic intervention that acknowledged both his anger and love led him to confess his struggle between his "good side" and his "evil side." The therapist's ability to withstand his anger seemed to free him to exhibit more active and creative play.

Prediction of outcome and prognosis is derived from assessment of whether aggressive behavior is ego syntonic, repetitive, and without remorse or guilt or whether it is the result of a sudden breakthrough of conflictually determined aggressive impulses. Prognosis is somewhat better for the latter type of behavior, since the conflict of the patient can be utilized to strive for relief and change in responses. Ego syntonic behavior must first become ego dystonic with evidence of concern about the consequences of such behavior. This is often a long, arduous, less hopeful therapeutic task.

The treatment of assaultive children includes those whose homicidal behavior has not resulted in death or serious injury to others as well as those who have actually murdered. Bender and Curran (1940) pointed out that young children, not having developed a mature concept of the finality of death, often do not appreciate the serious outcome of their actions. By means of magical fantasies or insufficiently developed concepts of causality, their actions are not associated with a sense of the future. The treatment of assaultive and homicidal children involves strengthening ego deficits of reality testing, judgment, object relations, and impulse control. However, for those children who committed homicide another treatment dimension results which relates to the intrapsychic and family responses to the actual loss of the victim. The finality of the loss must be discussed, although defenses against this fact are often maintained.

The Therapeutic Milieu of the Hospital

Acute hospital treatment includes a variety of available multiple modalities of interventions such as individual, group and family therapy, school remediation, and psychopharmacology. The hospital provides a distinctly unique experience for the child: it focuses on socialization and daily self-care skills; it functions to strengthen and support reality testing, impulse control, object relations, and the expression of emotion. Specifically, the hospital provides opportunities for the assaultive child to sublimate aggressive drives, increase tolerance for frustration, and perceive reality appropriately.

In the treatment of the severely aggressive child, the milieu offers specific types of structure, supports, constancy, protection, and opportunities for transference reactions. The structural organization of the unit with dependably occurring daily routines, group living, and clearly defined rules offers opportunities to work through anxieties and frustrations related to inconsistent and confusing family experiences. An atmosphere prohibiting harm to self or others strengthens the realization that the ward is a protective atmosphere.

The explicit message is that no child will be hurt. The constantly available unit staff provide ego support when a child is feeling desperate, frustrated, and hostile so that containment of dangerously aggressive impulses and redirection of them into more appropriate channels of discharge can occur. The staff provide an opportunity for the development of more appropriate object relations through a source of identifications and role models who are empathic and not destructive. The staff present themselves as individuals who will not be harmed, murdered, or chased away by the wishes and actions of the assaultive child. Specific intense transference phenomena may be readily observed. Recognition that the behavior of the assaultive child who is demanding, provocative, and hostile is a reenactment of his vulnerability, helplessness, and distress derived from conflicts with significant family members is the main feature of hospital therapy.

Individual Treatment

Genetic factors, transferential components, and specific moment-to-moment meanings of behavior are the focus of individual therapy. The therapist must be prepared to cope with intense uncontrolled aggressive impulses focused at him and at objects in the treatment office. By the promotion of an empathic, inquisitive, and objectively neutral attitude toward the child, an atmosphere of trust and a therapeutic alliance may develop. Channeling aggressive impulses into play elaboration and verbal communication offers immediate goals of intervention. Once these conditions are reasonably established, further elaboration and detailing of conflictual and transference manifestations become apparent and can be worked through. Smith in his discussions of assaultive children clearly stated that "the crux of the therapeutic process is being able to enter into a regressive transference that momentarily reinstates the patient's symbiosis with the mother" (1965: 318).

Sam, a nine-year-old, is an example of such treatment issues. The relationship of Sam to his therapist fluctuated between a desire for fusion stemming from love and his wish to kill his therapist. He admitted he was scared his mother would never come back from a trip to Puerto Rico. In play he related that he only felt happy when his mother was happy, inferring a regressed symbiotic pull in this relationship. Sam became increasingly possessive of his therapist. His rage at his therapist was expressed by destruction of a doll that he labeled with the therapist's name. His fear of being abandoned by his mother paralleled his violent rage at his therapist, who told Sam that therapists are not omnipotent, and needed intelligible cues from him as to how he felt. This led to Sam's more explicitly discussing his feelings. He wanted the therapist to control him from his violent feelings. He felt lonely and misunderstood, and believed that no one cared about him.

Cases Illustrating Treatment Issues

Several cases will clarify relevant types of conflicts noted in assaultive children. The treatment goal is to clarify and work through such conflictual issues.

1. ATTEMPTS TO MASTER TRAUMA

Leroy, a 10-year-old boy, displayed escalating, uncontrolled attacks on his grandfather, who was progressively becoming blind. Leroy was subject to rapid mood swings. He threw chairs and had temper tantrums. Following his grandfather's blindness and retirement, Leroy's behavior became increasingly worse. He needed and demanded constant attention and did not follow rules.

Leroy's sole attachments, however, were with his grandparents. His parents had separated shortly after his birth and at four months of age he was given to his grandparents. Leroy's father, a musician, had died from a drug overdose. Leroy had been told that his father's death was an accident. His grandfather, who was very concerned about Leroy, described himself as a strictly moral man who tolerated no lying, cheating, stealing, or disobedience. For discipline, the grandfather reported being very forceful when giving commands to Leroy and occasionally whipping him. However, he tried to be fair with the child. Leroy depended upon his grandfather to take him everywhere. His grandfather stated, "We changed our whole life for this little boy. We are all he has. We never let him down. We are his mother and father. All our love is concentrated on him."

In therapy sessions, Leroy, an intelligent boy, repeatedly played with dolls. He would inspect the genital areas of both the Mommy and Daddy dolls. He rotated and twisted the arms and legs of the Daddy dolls roughly. He asked about his natural mother and father. He did not know how his father had died but imagined his father had been shot. Clearly Leroy wanted to know the truth but felt helpless and desperate about getting information. When asked about his grandfather, Leroy became agitated. Once with clay he aggressively made a face with sharp teeth and enlarged eye sockets. He was preoccupied with eyes. When asked why he had not gone on trips recently, he professed not to know. When questioned, he said perhaps it was because his grandfather could not see to drive him there. During sessions, Leroy said his eyes hurt. When asked whether he liked his grandfather to be home or at work during the day, he responded ambivalently, "Oh, I like it with him at home. No, at work. No, I like him better at home."

Traumas, resulting from loss or physical damage, stimulate for the child active attempts to diminish the distressing feelings resulting from the trauma. Such emotions are intense, and when their sublimated or verbal expression is problematic, a motoric mode of expression of such feelings often occurs. Aggressive behavior may become repetitious in an active attempt at mastery. In this case, Leroy was responding intensely to the deteriorating condition of his grandfather with extreme anxiety, depression, and loss of impulses. Fear of loss of his grandfather stimulated fantasies about his unknown parents. The lack of clarity about how his father had died increased his worries about his grandfather's condition. The strict discipline of the grandfather stimulated aggressive impulses of retaliation. Frightened by his own death wishes, he attempted to deny what he believed about his parents and about his grandfather's condition. The manifest aggression toward his grandfather served not only to ventilate his ambivalence and frustration but more importantly as a positive means of maintaining attention from his grandfather. The attacks upon his grandfather were a means of recapturing his previously close active relationship with a strong disciplinarian. By hitting his grandfather and provoking punishment and discipline, Leroy attempted to deny the fear and trauma of his grandfather's impending death. Treatment focused on providing a substitute empathic adult who could help Leroy understand his problems with control of impulses, sadness, loneliness, and fear of abandonment.

2. REPETITION OF PARENTAL VIOLENCE

Daniel, seven, was hospitalized because of disruptive and assaultive behavior and his mother's statements that she "would kill him" if she did not have relief. Daniel, using a knife and scissors, cut furniture, curtains, towels, his mother's clothes, and his sister's hair. His mother beat him and once cut his chin with a knife when she "was at the end of her rope." To protect his mother from charges of abuse, Daniel told the assigned social worker that he had cut himself when he fell. He told his therapist that "I didn't want my mother to be in the newspaper with headlines that she cut her child. I was afraid that she would go to jail or that she might beat me."

Daniel's mother, adopted when she was three, believed her mother had given her away because she was bad. Daniel's father separated from his mother because of numerous arguments about his drinking.

Daniel, alert, cooperative and polite, was precocious. He worried about his mother, believed he was bad, and wanted help to be good so that his mother would like him. He did not understand the reasons for his behavior. He repeatedly played with "wild animal dolls" and arranged fights with the lion, "King of the Jungle." At other times, he played that he was the baby "because I didn't get whipped." He talked about his mother's favoritism toward his younger sister. He admitted saying he was responsible for things that happened even when he was innocent.

Identification with the aggressive behavior of others is a form of coping with anxiety derived from states of extreme vulnerability and helplessness. Such anxieties are often mastered, overcome, and defended against by active repetition of the threatening situation which is initially encountered in a passive way. This example illustrates how the ambivalent relationship with the mother is the focus for behavioral symptoms. By identifying with his mother's low self-esteem and feelings of badness, Daniel believed that his mother did not love him. He believed that he deserved punishment, and his behavior provided a reason for him to be punished. His wishes to be close to his mother are forbidden except by provoking her intense wrath and severe punishment. Her style of discipline was reflected in his form of destructive behavior. In treatment, his ability to relate to his empathic therapist freed him sufficiently to reveal his intense longing for a warm relationship and his anxiety about punishment and retaliation for his secret desires. His ability to verbalize and divert his feelings and fantasies into play promoted a means of sublimation of his aggressive impulses and eventual diminution of his assaultive behavior.

3. PAUCITY OF INTERNALIZED POSITIVE IDENTIFICATIONS

Larry, eight, fiercely attacked children at school. After his grandparents, who were instrumental in raising him, moved away, his behavior worsened. His mother refused to allow him to live with grandparents. Larry asked for them, denied that they had moved away, or insisted they were his real parents. He had little trust in people, especially his mother, and had difficulty forming a significant attachment to anyone.

Larry, intelligent and verbal, was often angry and spoke about dreams of monsters. Access to violent fantasies overwhelmed him, leaving him unable to maintain control. Play themes were replete with homicidal ideas in which everyone was killed. He felt he lived in a world where no one could be trusted because everyone was capable of violence. Several concerns were of infidelity. His play lacked any good objects. Mothers were depicted as aggressive. He illustrated this by describing playing with a mother doll, who gave her "son" a bath and then cooked and ate him. The sadism was revealed in his portrayal of a wife who tied her husband to a train track and laughed when a train ran over him. All characters fought with each other, had forceful sex, and killed each other off. Parents were portrayed as children who needed to be taken care of and difficult.

This case illustrates that intense ambivalence, lack of internalized good objects, and minimal control of aggressive and libidinal impulses can be a developmental product of an extremely chaotic and inconsistent family situation. In this example, the relationship with the therapist strikingly mirrored the ambivalence and lack of trust. As the therapist was felt to be a potentially good object and a source of safety from uncontrolled emotions, the child produced play elaboration. The play occurred as long as the child received support from his therapist as an aid to defend against feelings becoming overwhelming and out of control. Violent fantasies were vividly projected into play where it became evident that the world was considered a very dangerous place to live.

4. THE EFFECT OF SEVERE EGO DEFICITS: RETARDATION AND PSYCHOSIS

Wayne, 11, moderately retarded, was unmanageable after the birth of his brother. Although his school had attempted to prepare him for the birth and show him how to be careful around the baby, Wayne was intensely jealous. He demanded his mother's attention whenever she was with the baby. If she did not respond to him, he retaliated by breaking windows. He once grabbed his mother by the neck and attempted to knife her. He pushed his nine-year-old sister down the stairs. He did not understand that he could cause irreparable harm, did not realize the force of his strength, and had no comprehension of danger.

Wayne's aggression was heightened by the major shift in the family organization. The combination of ego deficits, of low intelligence, poor control of impulses, poor reality testing and judgment increased his vulnerability when supports and attention were diminished. The need for firm limits, the sense of deprivation of his mother's love, and rivalry with the infant were experienced with great intensity. Frustrated, anxious, and enraged, Wayne provoked attention by the manifestation of his uncontrolled impulses. Treatment included concrete separation from the stimulation generated by the infant and maintenance in a well-structured environment. Continued contact with his mother was encouraged.

Another case illustrates the issues of psychotic reaction. Sam, seven, was hospitalized after he attempted to stab his three-year-old sister with a butcher knife. His chronic behavior problems were a reflection of the chaotic home situation. His parents were unable to control their children and were afraid of their own hostile feelings. In fact, Sam's father's loss of control resulted in frequent beatings with a belt.

At school, Sam walked around the class pointing scissors at children's faces, and screamed at them. He talked about responding to frightening voices telling him to "hurt other children."

In therapy sessions, fantasies of ripping up and eating mother and father were elicited. His desire for protection and empathy was impressive. His emotional state easily fluctuated from moments of aloofness to states of exuberance which gave way to intense hostility. Delusional and paranoid ideas were expressed as statements of "don't look at me. Leave me alone." He constantly worried about "scarey ideas in my head." His thoughts were illogical. For example, he spoke about "a turtle under my bed, a turtle named Gina who I will stick with nails."

The relationship with the therapist offered a constant trusting person to whom the child could reveal his thoughts without fear of retaliation. Expression of frightening delusional fantasies was encouraged, while demands for reality oriented functioning were made. Sublimation of aggressive impulses into play is a goal. Psychopharmacological approaches were essential to diminish delusional and bizarre ideation.

5. SUCCESSFUL HOMICIDE

Paluszny and McNabb (1975) discussed the two year treatment of a six-year-old girl in outpatient and day hospital treatment. The child had killed her four-month-old brother. Her parents had separated when she was three because of her father's alcoholism and abusive behavior. The child's mother, a high school dropout, was a housewife who took care of her three children while being supported by welfare.

The murder occurred when the child was left to babysit for her two younger siblings. When the mother returned, she found the infant dead. The patient stated she had taken the infant out of his crib. He fell off the sofa. To stop him from crying the patient repeatedly hit his head against the floor.

The process of treatment will be briefly described. In the initial session, the patient depicted with dolls a boy and a girl playing and fighting. One doll fell and was dead. The patient stated that her brother was "buried and that some day" she would tell her therapist more about it "but not today." The initial treatment issues were massive repression of the events of the incident and resulting anxiety. Treatment at the day hospital allowed the child to be able to regress while in a therapeutic environment. The therapist frequently referred directly to the death. The patient defended against such open discussion fearing eruption of her out-of-control anger. Gradually repression diminished. The patient hit dolls and hit children in school. She expected and welcomed external controls. She even established test situations to see if the adult would stop her aggressive behavior. Guilt became apparent, and feelings of remorse and her own badness were gradually evident. This was followed by provocative behavior with the wish to be punished. Sadness and wishes for nurturance were expressed. Symptoms of stealing were interpreted as her belief that she was bad and needed punishment. Her longstanding wish for more attention from her mother was exposed and discussed in relation to the death of her brother.

In the cases of completed homicide by children and adolescents described by Carek and Watson (1964), Paluszny and McNabb (1975), and Scherl and Mack (1966), the treatment processes all were described as long and intensive. Initial reactions included intense anxiety, defenses against depression, denial, and other attempts to ward off recollection of the action. During treatment, when trust in the therapist was increased and empathic attitudes internalized, the children developed mechanisms to delay dangerous discharge of impulses and to begin to consider the details of the events and consequences of their actions.

Conclusion

The treatment of assaultive and homicidal children must occur simultaneously with the extensive evaluation of the complex issues contributing to such behavior. Hospital treatment is often an essential beginning phase of the process of treatment and, in most instances, long-term therapeutic intervention must be expected.

Return to the family may be problematic because of the intensity of stress and inability to make adequate changes which will provide a safe atmosphere. At Bronx Municipal Hospital Center approximately 40 percent of assaultive hospitalized children are able to return home and the remainder are referred to long-term hospital facilities for other therapeutic residential care.

Educating the staff to methods of management of the assaultive child will decrease anxiety, increase motivation, and decrease feelings of helplessness. The communication among the staff of their objective observations is essential to understanding the transference reactions of the child and in formulating appropriate curative interpretations.

Theoretical considerations about the outcome of such assaultive children may include questions about the specificity of types of interventions for various manifestations of homicidal behavior. Whether a family-oriented approach, a hospital setting, outpatient care, or psychopharmacology are most effective is not well documented. However, often a multimodality approach is recommended. Furthermore, early recognition of potentially homicidal youth and the effects of early intervention should be studied. Detailed case descriptions of such youngsters will help to enhance the skill of therapists as well as to illustrate significant psychodynamic factors of such behavior.

REFERENCES

Bender, L. and F. J. Curran. 1940. "Children and Adolescents Who Kill." *Criminal Psychopathology* 1:297–322.

Beres, D. 1952. "Clinical Notes on Aggression in Childhood." *Psychoanalytic Study of the Child* 7:241–63.

Carek, D. J. and A. S. Watson. 1964. "Treatment of a Family Involved in Fratricide." *Archives of General Psychiatry* 11:533–42.

Corder, B. F., B. C. Ball, T. M. Haizlip, R. Rollings, and R. Beaumont. 1976. "Adolescent Parricide: A Comparison with Other Adolescent Murder." *American Journal of Psychiatry* 133:957–61.

Duncan, J. W. and G. M. Duncan. 1971. "Murder in the Family: A Study of Some Homicidal Adolescents." *American Journal of Psychiatry* 127:74–78.

Easson, W. M. and R. M. Steinhilber. 1961. "Murderous Aggression by Children and Adolescents." *Archives of General Psychiatry* 4:27–35.

Foodman, A. and C. Estrada. 1977. "Adolescents Who Commit Accidental Homicide." *Journal American Academy of Child Psychiatry* 16:314–26.

Freud, A. 1963. "The Concept of Developmental Lines." *Psychoanalytic Study of the Child* 18:245–65.

King, C. H. 1975. "The Ego and the Integration of Violence in Homicidal Youth." *American Journal of Orthopsychiatry* 45:134–45.

Paluszny, M. and M. McNabb. 1975. "Treatment of a 6-Year-Old Who Committed Fratricide." *Journal American Academy of Child Psychiatry*, 14:319–36.

Patterson, R. M. 1943. "Psychiatric Study of Juveniles Involved in Homicide." *American Journal of Orthopsychiatry*, 13:125–30.

Pfeffer, C. R., H. R. Conte, R. Plutchik, and I. Jerrett. 1979. "Suicidal Behavior in Latency Age Children: An Empirical Study." *Journal American Academy of Child Psychiatry*, 18:679–92.

Scherl, D. J. and J. E. Mack. 1966. "A Study of Adolescent Matricide." *Journal American Academy of Child Psychiatry* 5:569–93.

Sendl, I. B. and P. G. Blomgren. 1975. "A Comparative Study of Predictive Criteria in the Predispositon of Homicidal Adolescents." *American Journal of Psychiatry* 132:423–27.

Smith, S. 1965. "The Adolescent Murderer." *Archives of General Psychiatry* 13:310–19.

Tooley, K. 1975. "The Small Assassins: Clinical Notes on a Subgroup of Murderous Children." *Journal American Academy of Child Psychiatry*, 14:306–18.

Tucker, L. S. and T. P. Cornwall. 1977. "Mother–Son Folie à Deux: A Case of Attempted Patricide." *American Journal of Psychiatry*, 134:1146–47.

13

HOMICIDAL AND ASSAULTIVE
BEHAVIOR IN THE ELDERLY

Joseph Richman

◇

For a variety of reasons, little attention has been paid to the dynamic and situational factors in the relatively infrequent occurrence of homicide and other violent behaviors among the elderly. First, there is a general tendency to dehumanize the elderly, in the sense that their behavior is seen as less dynamically meaningful or socially motivated than in the young. Second, there is a lower incidence of violence among the elderly, who are more often the victims of homicide and the other crimes of violence. Third, a too ready answer may be found in the biological decline that accompanies aging. The acknowledged fact of the association of homicide with cerebral organic mental conditions sometimes seems to preclude further investigation.

An organic mental syndrome is quite frequent but does not explain why a few individuals are violent while so many are not. What other factors may have been operative, and why has the person become violent just at that time? Roth (1968), who emphasized the organic component, also noted that the effects of brain damage depend upon the personality of the individual. Social and environmental pressures are also extremely pertinent. Nevertheless, both the psychological and the social aspects have been neglected in the general disregard of the problem in the published literature. As Epstein, et al. (1970) state, "The elderly offender has only rarely been a subject of study, and relatively little has been written about him other than what is given in annual arrest and prison reports."

Perhaps most of us are guilty of the attitude that events which are less frequent are therefore less important. Why talk about homicide in the elderly when the greater dangers are suicide and homicide against the elderly? Just look at the statistics.

But suicide and homicide may not be that separate. In a study of children who had attempted suicide (Richman and Pfeffer 1977), we found that most of them also had a history of aggressive behavior. Their psychological test data indicated that their aggressive and destructive impulses could go in either direction—against others or against the self. In another (unpublished) study (by Theodore Jacobs, Edward Charles and myself) of adult patients who had been seen at a psychiatric emergency room because of assaultive behavior or homicidal attempts, we found that over 75 percent also had a history of suicidal behavior or ideation. As we shall see presently, the same pattern holds with the aged, perhaps to an even greater degree; and the outward expression of their aggression may take place more often than we think.

While the overall incidence of crime in the elderly is low, the relative incidence of homicide and aggravated assault is high, and the percentage of elderly arrested for such crimes has risen steadily. Unfortunately, as Shichor and Kobrin (1976) report, little is known about the circumstances of such acts, the psychological dynamics, the settings, or the social and interpersonal relationships between the criminal and his victim. The two known facts are that such crimes are unrelated to robbery or any other direct personal gain, and that the victim is almost always someone known to the elderly murderer.

What has been well documented is the association of psychiatric and especially organic disorders with crimes of violence by the aged. Roth's comprehensive study of such crimes in England and Wales applies as well to the United States. Violent acts are almost always committed by men, and three major conditions or patterns are consistently found.

First, the violent acts "often arise in a setting of mental disorder with suicidal tendencies."

Second, a small number of aggressive acts are perpetrated by paranoid subjects, often pathologically jealous, their controls weakened by senility or chronic alcoholism. One example given by Roth was of a 67-year-old man with arteriosclerosis who killed his wife because he believed she was about to desert him to marry his former boss. "The act was perpetrated in a nightmare condition ('A bad dream'); there was nocturnal clouding of consciousness, without comprehension of the act itself."

Third, murderous attacks may occur without suicidal or paranoid tendencies, provoked sometimes by seemingly very trivial reasons. Examples of the latter included "a depressed 77-year-old man who killed his wife when she swore at him for sitting on her false teeth in the middle of the night"; and "a 75-year-old man who strangled his daughter-in-law after a quarrel. He was an irascible, difficult man who had engaged in many quarrels with his deceased wife and his children. Blunting and diminished control of affect had become more pronounced in the two to three years preceding the offense, but he was intellectually well preserved."

Crowell and Mark (1973) reported an unusual case of a man who developed normal pressure hydrocephalus following a car accident, after which he became agitated, paranoid, and aggressive. He attacked his daughter-in-law; he tried to hit her on the head with a lamp and chased her about the house with a razor, threatening to cut her throat.

These case histories were intriguing, but ultimately unsatisfactory: little or no attention was paid to a comprehensive assessment of homicidal potential. The more useful discussions tend to be found in the articles about younger aggressive persons, such as in the survey by Kozel (1972) on the diagnosis of dangerousness. The following outline on the major areas to investigate in the assessment of homicidal potential is based upon such studies. It was found helpful in understanding the cases from our own files, as well as those reported in the literature. The most important features included the following:

1. *Evidence of problems in impulse control.* Examples include a history of the use of force or violence; a tendency to react with violence to frustration; and, in general, an inadequate capacity to delay discharge.

2. *Evidence of a regression from a higher level of development.* Examples include the presence of impaired judgment and reality testing, as well as control. Such data would often be associated with the presence of an organic mental syndrome and other conditions leading to a decline in ego resources.

3. *An investigation of the purpose or meaning of the act.* "What

problem in his life was being solved by the offenses, and does that problem still exist?" This question is an important reminder for us to consider the situational crises that are relevant to the act, the personal and symbolic meaning to the individual and others involved, and the social function it may perform for the family and social network.

4. *The person's self concept and values.* For example, is violence considered an acceptable form of problem solving, and is it part of his image of masculinity?

5. *The nature of his social and interpersonal relationships.* Is conflict prominent? Does he feel loved, supported, encouraged? Or else, does he feel threatened, disdained, or rejected?

The foregoing material was most meaningful in connection with our clinical experiences with the elderly in a New York City hospital center. While no cases of completed homicide were examined at the geriatric unit of the Bronx Municipal Hospital Center, several came close; and they bore some interesting similarities to the cases reported in the published literature. One of my first cases was a 73-year-old man who was brought in by the police. He had threatened to kill his wife, then entered their neighbor's apartment and proceeded to break up the furniture. There was no clear precipitant. His wife stated that periodically "Satan got into him." There was a past history of alcoholism. Further neurological and psychological testing disclosed a seizure disorder and clouding of consciousness at the time of these episodes. A somewhat similar situation was that of a 78-year-old man who picked up a knife one evening and tried to enter the next door apartment in order to attack a neighbor. The diagnostic impression was that of a transient psychotic episode associated with an organic mental syndrome and states of confusion. He also had a history of alcoholism. He responded very well to phenothiazenes, and was in treatment only briefly.

Perhaps there should be some consideration of the question of homicidal ideation. It is present fairly frequently in our clinic population, and may be prodromal to the act itself in some cases. An example is one 84-year-old paranoid lady, who appears cognitively intact. She is a widow who lives alone in a housing project. Basically, she is a lonely, isolated woman with a lifelong pattern of few friends and conflicted relationships. During her sessions with her therapist at the clinic, she spent most of the time detailing the injustices to her committed by her neighbors, followed by fantasies of killing them. (More attention should be paid to the meaning of neighbors among the elderly.)

A more complex case was that of a couple, both 80 years old. The husband was severely impaired organically, and was becoming more so. However, it was the wife who was assaultive and subject to rages of homicidal intensity. She herself suffered from a cardiac condition, severe arthritis, and other ailments, and walked with a cane. When sessions were held with her and her husband and she lifted her cane and shook it in the air, everyone ducked. Meanwhile, he had become increasingly feeble, incontinent, aphasic, and otherwise impaired. His wife said she was enraged because she had "discovered" that he spent "hundreds of thousands" of dollars on whores all the years they were married. She would have liked to place him in a home, but was unwilling to use their funds. The wife's violence seemed to express her feelings of being trapped in an intolerable situation. She was a miser; and although their marriage had not been a good one, she was faced with the loss of money, of companionship, and of a familiar relationship through institutionalization or death.

The situation was a very different one with another couple where the husband was the violent individual, but both cases illustrated the central role of marital and family disturbances which can lead to violence. He had been referred from the courts, where his wife had taken him after he choked her and beat her up. He was 70, she was 53. He was very ill physically, feeble and failing, while she was healthy and worked full-time. He walked with difficulty and could not always reach the bathroom in time. She had taken him to court 25 years before, also for beating her up. Nevertheless, the marriage had been relatively stable until two years ago. At that time they bought a house with his money but in her name, since the banks would not give him a mortgage at his age and condition. Violent arguments then escalated. She stated that she had tolerated his bad temper until then, but could no longer stand him. He accused her of wanting to get rid of him now that she had the house.

The initial mental status examination revealed a man with a picture of wounded narcissism and self-esteem. He had always been a good provider and responsible family man. However, the content of his speech emphasized what a good street fighter he had been in his youth and what an outstanding soldier he had been during World War II. He exhibited a role immaturity in which being a man was seen as being tough with other men and insulting with women. While there was no clear evidence of organicity, he was tangential and preoccupied with the past. The quality was that of an overall decline in physical and mental health and resources. Placed on phenothiazines, and seen in weekly couple and family meetings, he quickly improved in functioning and mood. However, when his assaultive behavior did subside, his wife became more provoking, angry, and acting out. She refused to attend family meetings, and did not notify him of changes of appointments. According to his therapist, he decompensated again, and refused to attend any further sessions, saying that if he left the house they would not let him back in.

Both the literature and clinical experiences suggest a range of destructive and homicidal behavior, from direct murder and direct assaults that are associated with males to more indirect and less violent means that may be more associated with females. These include such acts as having someone else do the job, concealed homicide (e.g., with the use of poison); and a still more subtle destruction of the other, where the "homicide" is consequently even more sinister.

It is noteworthy that only one woman is mentioned as the perpetrator of violence in all these cases. One wonders, however, whether such homicidal or assaultive acts may occur in women, but with less violent methods. In a trial reported in the news media, a woman in her 80s was accused of hiring someone to murder her husband. Her lawyer implied that both she and her husband were peculiar and suffering from an organic decline. The second example concerns the grandparents of one of my youthful patients. They divorced many years before when he charged, among other complaints, that she had put ground glass in his hamburgers. Seen 30 years later, in a family meeting with her divorced husband, daughter, son-in-law, and grandchildren, her first words to me were, "I've been dying to meet you."

The third example was a 75-year-old man who had been treated, successfully, for cancer the year before, but who was now ending his days by refusing to return to the hospital for further treatment. He refused to leave his bed, refused to eat, and refused to move. Seen at a home, he was a wasted man, dying of depression and malnutrition, who voiced many angry accusations against the hospital and doctors for using him and wanting his money, although he was on Medicare. The physician and nurse who visited the home were sympathetic to his complaints, as well as those of his wife, and a very positive relationship was quickly established. When the visiting physician urged him to return for a further examination, the patient wavered and looked at his wife. She replied, "I would not do it, if I was you." He then resumed his paranoid complaints, and refused any further medical contacts.

Technically, this was not murder. However, if the definition is that of one person causing the death of another, then the question does arise.

Discussion

There is an increase of crimes against the elderly, and a decrease of crimes by the elderly. They are more often the victims of homicide (and suicide) than the perpetrators. The question of why there is not more crime, especially impulsive crime of violence, in the aged, is still an open one. With increasing decline there is a decreased tolerance for frustration and a decreased capacity to delay the discharge of impulses. Anything that weakens the ego decreases control. With many elderly persons there is such a weakening of the ego, with an attendant greater expectation of loss of control. Theoretically, one might predict an increased likelihood of homicide and other acts of violence. The unanswered question, therefore, is still: Why not more homicides? One possibility is that there *is* more than meets the eye.

What emerges from the literature and experiences with elderly violent persons, is that the infrequent phenomenon of homicide is the end result of biological, psychological, and social conditions that are present in a less extreme form in a much larger population. A related point is that when one takes into account homicidal ideation, homicidal attempts (in the form of assaults), and the more indirect and subtle forms of destruction of an other, the occurrence of such other-destructive behavior is actually higher than the statistics would indicate.

The absence of adequate information about those old persons who commit murder points to the need for more comprehensive studies. The cases of violence we have seen, while incomplete, are intriguing. Most of them could best be understood within a comprehensive systems framework. The homicidal or violent act is due both to an exacerbation of a lifelong pattern, *and* to a change in behavior and the entire situation as a result of age, illness, and decline.

The biological, organic components have been studied the most. In the published case histories all but one were clear-cut cases of organic mental pathology. That one exhibited blunting of affect and other signs of psychopathology, but his cognition was reported as clear (Roth 1968). The cases we have seen in the clinic of the elderly assaultive patients whose aggressive behavior stopped short of completed murder seemed similar in many respects to those published reports of elderly people who committed murder. Organic mental syndromes, for example, were common. One might hypothesize that there are similarities in the individual dynamics and situational factors of both homicidal attempts and completed homicide. An examination of all the cases, published and clinical, pointed to six major components of violence in the elderly.

1. A certain premorbid personality is present, in particular, one in which violence is ego and culturally syntonic and associated with social approval. Several of the assaultive husbands had a "tough kid" history, with much fighting, school failure, and an association of being a "real" man with being violent. Several had a history of alcoholism.

2. The individual is mentally and physically impaired, which has resulted in a drastic difference in his self-concept, his self-esteem, and the way he is regarded by significant others. The difference is due to a decline in the personal resources or coping abilities of the individual, usually on the basis of an organic mental syndrome or a general physiological decline, which weakens the ego, impairs impulse control, and sometimes judgment.

3. There is some provocation from the family and social network. In the majority of the assaultive patients in the clinic, their marriage had been unstable or unhappy, with marital problems that dated back many years. In a manner analogous to messages sent to suicidal persons to harm themselves (Rosenbaum and Richman 1970), homicidal or assaultive persons may receive messages from the family or significant others to harm others. The family and social network may have a stake in being provocative.

The importance of neighbors needs to be stressed, particularly among the elderly for whom the neighbors may have become the major part of their social network. Many old and fixed family patterns and conflicts with those who have died may be transferred with little basic change to these neighbors.

4. The act serves a social as well as psychological function. It may,

for example, occur as part of a process of extrusion of the older individual from the social network.

5. There is a crisis, which helps precipitate the homicidal behavior.

6. Society is brought in. As a result, what has begun as an individual
and family process becomes part of a social problem.

In summary, the act of homicide in the elderly can best be understood in the light of the personality of the murderer, the nature of the
relationship to the victim, and the circumstances surrounding the act.
When pursued with full lethal intent, homicide is the extreme example
of the effects of frustration and aggression unleashing the destructiveness inherent in human nature. However, conflict and hostility in
human affairs are inevitable. The problem, therefore, is not to eliminate aggression in the elderly (or at any age), since that is not possible,
but to learn how to be aggressive better. For this, the availability of
acceptable social outlets, of social resources, and the skills of the
psychotherapist can be most helpful.

REFERENCES

Crowell, R. M. and V. H. Mark. 1973. "Aggressive Dementia Associated with
    Normal Pressure Hydrocephalus." *Neurology*, 23:461–64.
Epstein, L. J., C. Mills, and A. Simon. 1970. "Antisocial Behavior of the
    Elderly." *Comprehensive Psychiatry*, 11:36–42.
Kozel, H. 1972. "The Diagnosis of Dangerousness." *Roche Report: Frontiers
    of Psychiatry* (Feb. 15), 2(4):5–8.
Richman, J. and C. Pfeffer. 1979. "Figure Drawings in the Evaluation of
    Suicidal Latency Age Children." Presented at the 9th Annual Meeting of
    the International Association of Suicide Prevention and Crisis Intervention,
    Helsinki, Finland (June 26).
Rodstein, M. 1972. "Crime and the Aged." *Journal of the American Health
    Association* 2:65–67.
Rosenbaum, M. and J. Richman. 1970. "Suicide: The Role of Hostility and
    Death Wishes from the Family and Significant Others." *American Journal
    of Psychiatry*, 126(11):1652–55.
Roth, M. 1968. "Cerebral and Mental Disorders of Old Age as Causes of
    Antisocial Behavior." *International Psychiatry Clinics* 5(3):35–58.
Shichor, D. and S. Kobrin. 1976. "Criminal Behavior among the Elderly: A
    Survey of the Arrest Statistics." Paper presented at the 28th Annual Meeting
    of the American Society of Criminology, Tucson, Arizona (November 4–7).

14

HOMICIDE AND THE FAMILY

Herbert Goldenberg
and
Irene Goldenberg

◇

The perspective on homicide and the family we wish to offer emerges from our experiences as family therapists. For us, this means first understanding all behavior in any individual as an interpersonal event. Homicide is no exception. In our view, it requires adopting an interpersonal frame of reference, rather than focusing on that individual's intrapsychic conflicts and inner dynamics. Secondly, we believe a person's behavior or problems or symptoms occur within a context and cannot be understood without examining that context. All behavior within a family expresses how that family system is functioning. Dysfunction indicates that stress has overloaded the system's usual adaptive and coping mechanisms. From such a systems viewpoint, as Minuchin et al. (1978) point out, the locus of pathology is not the individual but rather the individual in context. This brings us to a third issue—how to bring about change. We believe that changing the family environment—the context—will provide a new setting for the individual to have new experiences. On the basis of changes in experiences, his or her subsequent behavior patterns will begin to change. The focus of family therapy, then, is to help members of a dysfunctional family change their system—i.e., their characteristic patterns of interaction, their style and manner of communication, and the structure or organization of their relationships—so that each member is free to become independent, unique, and whole.

Having laid out a brief sketch of our approach, we shall delay its elaboration regarding homicide in the family until we consider alternative explanations of this phenomenon. That the problem is a very real and urgent one is seen immediately from FBI data (Anthony and Rizzo 1973) indicating that the murder of one family member by another constitutes about a third of all homicides. Primarily, this involves one spouse killing another (53 percent), although the killing of children by parents (17 percent) and parents by children (6 percent) are also significant. Twenty-three percent of all family homicides involve killings of other relatives, presumably including siblings.

How have such extraordinary statistics been explained? Grinker (1971) has suggested that the cause of human violence cannot be stated, since clearly aggression or violence is not a simple, unitary phenomenon. Even in specific cases, and sometimes contrary to appearances, an act of violence rarely stems from a single cause. He argues for the broad-based consideration of all of the following factors: *biological* (here he includes genetic explanations such as the reported link of an XYY sex chromosome condition in men and criminal behavior, as well as the possibility of brain damage as in psychomotor epilepsy or the effects of drug, including alcohol, abuse); *psychological* (in which he deals with such causes as maturational, developmental, or personality deformation); and thirdly, *social* (rapid changes in living, the absence of the traditional nuclear family, working mothers, increased social mobility, etc.).

Sadoff (1976), concerned with issues involved in the fields of law and psychiatry, supports Grinker's position, arguing for a view concerning violence within a family that includes medical, legal, and psychosocial considerations. He notes that wife-beating, child battering, sexual abuse of children, and corporal punishment are all prevalent in today's society and, although short of homicide, may be considered forms of emotional violence or physically destructive behavior within a family. Psychoanalytic formulations regarding family homicide have emphasized the unconscious motives for aggression in unresolved Oedipal rivalries, death wishes, or loss of ego control in the perpetrator. Anthropological explanations have been based upon studies of cultural and subcultural differences, and sociologists have investigated changing family structures (e.g., single-parent families, blended families, the loss of nuclear and extended family life, and the failure of community institutions to fulfill some of the nurturing and caregiving functions previously supplied by generations of intact families).

To these, we would add the systems view of the family. In a case of a 15-year-old girl who killed her father, Anthony and Rizzo (1973) describe both the family's "aggressive climate" and its "sexual climate." The father was the central figure in the household and his aggressive and erotic behavior, especially when drinking, became the main determinant of family transactions. A violent man, he had beaten his wife regularly for many years, although he had stopped several years earlier when, drunk, he had slapped her in the stomach and she, pregnant, had drawn a gun and threatened to kill him. Thereafter, he stopped approaching her aggressively or sexually, turning his attention sexually to each of his three daughters and one son. The murderous attack occurred when the father, in a violent rage, began to strangle one of his daughters. The 15-year-old, observing the attack on her sister, ran for the gun she had hidden earlier (to avoid anyone finding it in the midst of an argument). When she threatened to shoot unless he stopped, he ignored her, and as she saw her sister turning cold and blue, she shot her father. Later, she expressed surprise that her family responded in a hostile way toward her action, when they had seemed in agreement at the time it occurred. She believed that because she was nervous and impulsive, the family always used her when they wanted some "dirty business" done.

To begin with, then, a particular family climate or atmosphere must exist for homicide to occur. Gorney (1971) has suggested, after investigating some aspects of interpersonal bonding in widely different species and human cultures, that those societies which give rise to the most intense interpersonal relationships often display not only the highest level of achievement, but also the highest levels of intrapsychic conflict and violent aggression. That is, he maintains that high-intensity interpersonal bonding is prerequisite for various human behaviors, including violence and aggression.

Within a high-intensity emotional family atmosphere, children who kill may be unwittingly acting out an unconscious *family conspiracy*

(Sargent 1962), in which they, as scapegoats, are simultaneously killer and victim. Sargent (1971) has employed the concept of a *lethal situation* to explain the transmission of the urge to kill from adult family member to child. He contends that a necessary factor in a murder within a family is the occurrence of a lethal situation in which a combination of social and interpersonal elements exist. These, he concluded, were every bit as important in understanding the violence as the usual considerations of motives, opportunity, and the availability of a lethal weapon. Within a family context, the child who kills had received both overt and covert "commands" to commit murder. Thus, one parent may play upon the inevitable latent hostilities the child feels toward the victim. However susceptible, under ordinary circumstances the child would control his or her murderous behavior except for the unconscious prompting of the adult.

In one poignant example, Sargent (1971) describes a case of Freddie, a nine-year-old boy who smothered his six-month-old half-brother when the baby's crying distracted him from watching a television murder story. Left in charge of the infant, Jack, and another half-brother, George, age two, Freddie held a pillow over Jack's face until he was dead, then fell asleep beside the dead body, a position the parents found them in when they returned home. As his stepfather attempted to resuscitate the baby, Freddie later recalled, his mother shook him awake, demanding of him, "Why didn't you kill George instead?" The mother, apparently filled with many sadomasochistic fantasies, had herself grown up in a violent home with a drunkard father who eventually deserted the family. She did report one incident, occurring when she was 11. As she showed off a party dress her father had bought her, her jealous younger sister set the dress ablaze. Only her screams attracted her father's attention, and he put out the flames. George, her wished-for victim, was an illegitimate son whom she beat savagely, sometimes near to death. Freddie, as her favorite, was deeply entwined with his mother in a symbiotic relationship, and often acted out her impulses as if they were his own. Sargent hypothesizes that the mother, whose emotional life was dominated by the wish to regain her lost father-rescuer, was driven to place her children in dangerous situations in the unconscious hope that a father-rescuer would be attracted to her by their plight.

Family theorists are interested in the process by which a particular child is selected as the lethal agent as well as the manner in which destructive impulses get communicated within the family. Murder is an intensely emotional act occurring within a close and intense set of interpersonal relationships. In some families, parents may encourage and condone (and even vicariously enjoy) destructive expressions of aggression, as though the child were acting out the parent's repressed fantasies. Some children grow up in a climate of brutality, where aggressive behavior among family members requires only the slightest provocation. Some families, unable or unwilling to verbalize anger, act out with physical attack. Not surprisingly, the child may be carrying out the family-wide homicidal wishes.

Family therapists use the concept of *enmeshment* (Minuchin 1974) to describe the extreme form of proximity and intensity in family interactions in which members are overconcerned and overinvolved in each other's lives. In some cases, the family's lack of differentiation of roles and responsibilities and lack of clear boundaries makes any separation from the family an act of betrayal. Belonging to the family dominates all experiences, at the expense of each member developing a separate sense of self. Whatever happens to one family member reverberates throughout the system. Excessive togetherness and sharing may lead to a lack of privacy, as members intrude on each other's thoughts and feelings. Family members caught up in such a family system rarely have an opportunity to explore new relationships or develop competencies outside of the safety of the family.

Another relevant family concept in regard to homicide is Bowen's (1976) notion of a *multigenerational transmission process*. Developed originally to explain how schizophrenia is a process that requires three or more generations to develop, Bowen's formulations are equally applicable to various forms of disordered behavior. He proposes that one offspring, most fused or enmeshed into the dysfunctional family system, will emerge with a poorer level of functioning than his or her parents or siblings. He or she in turn is likely to find a spouse at about the same functioning level ("most people choose mates at more or less their own level of differentiation," to use Bowen's words), probably producing another generation of low-level functioning children, one of whom is even less mature than the others. How is such a child "selected" by parents in the first place? Bowen believes immature parents will consciously or unconsciously choose the most infantile of all the children, regardless of birth order in the family. Most emotionally attached to the parents of all the children within the family, that child will end up with the lowest level of functioning or sense of self and will have the most difficult time separating from the family. Such a child is most vulnerable, most susceptible, often most scapegoated by the family; tied into a symbiotic relationship, he or she may ultimately become a killer-victim carrying out a family conspiracy to kill a family member.

As Tanay (1976) reminds us, killing of a parent may have a large element of self-preservation. In what he calls *reactive parricide*, the murder may be a last-resort effort to protect the psychic integrity of the perpetrator. In families caught in a catastrophic conflict, one that exceeds the adaptive capacity of an individual (and of the family), Tanay reasons that the conflict can only be resolved by structural changes. These may include changes in the structure of reality (divorce, truancy, homicide) or changes in the structure of the person (psychosis or suicide). Killing the parent viewed as responsible for the catastrophic conflict may be seen by one or more family members as leading to a resolution. Either directly encouraged or done so tacitly, the child-perpetrator kills the adult person seen as the major irritant and culprit.

Sadoff (1971) appears to confirm these same psychodynamics and family dynamics in adolescents who have killed a parent. He reports a cruel and unusual relationship between victim and assassin. Ambivalence—fear and hatred on the one hand and a seemingly inexplicable loyalty and yearning on the other—was an outstanding characteristic in the murderer. It is as if the young person cannot leave the family or free himself or herself voluntarily and without explosive violence. The adolescent is pushed to the point of explosive violence. A sense of relief, rather than remorse or guilt, is felt following the matricide or patricide. The assassin no longer feels entrapped. Sadoff suggests that one reason for this sense of relief from the bond is that the killer often blames the victim for setting up the circumstances for his or her own demise. From this perspective, the parents have killed themselves, using their children as weapons. Support and confirmation from other family members, who were witnesses to the cruelty perpetrated upon the killer by the victim, serve to release guilt and allow the return of the feeling of freedom and relief.

Family theorists would refer to this return to a previous balance or equilibrium as the family's effort to achieve *homeostasis*. In family terms, homeostasis—a term borrowed from physiologists who study the human body as a self-regulating system—refers to the inclination of the family system to maintain a dynamic equilibrium, undertaking all necessary operations to restore that equilibrium whenever it is threatened. Through a process of feedback, information about the state of the system is fed back through the system, automatically triggering any necessary changes to keep the system "on track" and operating smoothly. Families communicate through such feedback loops, since the behavior of each affects and is affected by each other person's behavior (Watzlawick, et al. 1967).

Thus, it becomes meaningless to speak of causality in linear terms (A causes B), as though the trouble resides in one person and is imposed on the other. Rather, we look at the behavior of an individual within a context in which another person or persons is present and exchanges information with that individual, each influencing the other. Within a system, a single event such as violent behavior by the father toward the mother is both effect and cause. There is a circular movement of parts that affect each other, but no beginning or end to the circle. Each person's behavior is simultaneously caused by and causative of behavior in another part of the system. It is that entire system which the family therapist tries to help them change or overhaul.

We believe that the family systems framework provides us with at least three levels where we might make effective interventions. *Diagnostically*, workers in the fields of medicine, psychology, law, and allied professions are provided with a broader outlook of what has transpired during a homicidal act. Rather than a simple classification label of schizophrenia or sociopathy, the entire family context must be assessed for clues as to the multiple factors operating between persons and culminating in the homicidal act. More than seeing the killing as the irrational act of a disturbed person, it would seem more reasonable to look at the entire family context and the homicidal behavior as a family-wide phenomenon.

Therapeutically, as we have indicated earlier, the focus of treatment should be the entire family. All members need to recognize their roles in the phenomenon and to see the act itself as one final step in a process in which each has participated. Finally, and perhaps most important, we may begin to make some significant inroads in *preventing* homicide. Adopting the family systems framework, existing local agencies, such as those concerned with child abuse cases or with battered wives, can be sensitized to the potential family violence. They are early warning system stations and are in an excellent position to recognize potential trouble. However, rather than concerning themselves only with victims, they need to look at dysfunctional families—families at a high risk of future violence. Early identification of such families, along with early intervention, may save many lives. From our point of view, if the family problem in not attended to in this generation, it may very well spring up in the next.

REFERENCES

Anthony, E. J. and A. Rizzo. 1973. "Adolescent Girls Who Kill or Try to Kill Their Fathers." In E. J. Anthony and C. Koupernik, eds. *The Child in His Family, II: The Impact of Disease and Death*. New York: Wiley.

Bowen, M. 1976. "Theory in the Practice of Psychotherapy." In P. J. Guerin Jr., ed. *Family Therapy: Theory and Practice*. New York: Gardner Press.

Gorney, R. 1971. "Interpersonal Intensity, Competition, and Synergy: Determinants of Achievement, Aggression, and Mental Illness," *American Journal of Psychiatry* 128:436–45.

Grinker, R. R. Sr. 1971. "What is the Cause of Violence?" In J. Fawcett, ed. *Dynamics of Violence*. Chicago: American Medical Association.

Minuchin, S. 1974. *Families and Family Therapy*. Cambridge: Harvard University Press.

Minuchin, S., B. L. Rosman, and L. Baker. 1978. *Psychosomatic Families: Anorexia Nervosa in Context*. Cambridge: Harvard University Press.

Sadoff, R. L. 1971. "Clinical Observations on Parricide." *Psychiatric Quarterly* 45:65–69.

Sadoff, R. L. 1976. "Violence in Families: An Overview." *Bulletin of the American Academy of Psychiatry and Law* 4:292–96.

Sargent, D. A. 1962. "Children Who Kill—A Family Conspiracy?" *Journal of Social Work* 7:35–42.

Sargent, D. A. 1971. "The Lethal Situation: Transmission of the Urge to Kill from Patient to Child." In J. Fawcett, ed., *Dynamics of Violence*. Chicago: American Medical Association.

Tanay, E. 1976. "Reactive Parricide." *Journal of Forensic Sciences* 21:76–82.

Watzlawick, P., J. H. Beavin, and D. D. Jackson. 1967. *Pragmatics of Human Communication*. New York: Norton.

PART THREE

LAW AND
JUSTICE

15

GUN CONTROL TO PREVENT HOMICIDE AND SUICIDE

Bruce L. Danto

◇

Aside from the Vietnam war, few issues have polarized citizens in the United States like the fight between those who want firearms either banned or controlled and those who want freedom of firearm ownership without restrictions. Few objective studies have been done and even fewer published papers have rested on a dispassionate base. In 1971, Danto presented some research findings based on his study of firearm death in Detroit and concluded that the use of firearms in homicide and suicide involves different groups of people. He questioned whether availability of firearms themselves was a significant contributing factor and advocated screening, training in firearm use, and other measures as a way of encouraging safe use of firearms. In addition, he questioned the Second Amendment position of those defending the possession of firearms as an absolute right.

While the battle between those favoring banning and control and those advocating the uninfringed right to keep and bear arms rages, more people are dying. From 1900 to 1970, 800 persons were killed each day by firearms in the United States (Newsletter 1970).* Browning

---

* A Task Force of the National Commission on the Causes and Prevention of Violence estimates that the number of privately owned firearms in this country is around 90 million; other authorities put the figure as high as 200 million. The report of that group, *Firearms and Violence in American Life*, contains much systematic information on this general topic.

(1976) revealed that the lethal use of the handgun increased 127.4 percent between 1970 and 1974, and that as of 1974, handgun homicide was 3.5 to 10 times greater in the United States than in 13 other countries. European countries were used for the comparison as well as New Zealand, Japan, and Australia. Unfortunately, the strength of his argument is considerably diminished when knowledgeable people compare the United States homicide rates in terms of firearm ownership and use with Israel, Canada, or Switzerland where, despite sizeable ownership of firearms, the homicide and suicide rates are relatively low. Furthermore, Browning failed to note that in countries like Great Britain, where legal handguns are at a minimum, there is a higher incidence of homicide by bombing and poisoning than in the United States.

Those who are passionate about banning handguns, especially, fail to understand that rifles are far more lethal. The shooter can achieve better protection for himself—he can also escape detection with greater ease, because he can put greater distance between himself and his target. Furthermore, as DiMaio and Zumwalt (1977) observed, compared with handgun injuries, wound tracts are more extensive and lethal when high velocity, center fire ammunition is fired from a rifle. Such wounds produce significantly more disintegration of internal organs than handgun wounds.

Canada has experienced a rather modest problem regarding homicide which involves the use of firearms. Government officials there have pointed out that murders committed by firearms rose from 178 in 1970 to 272 in 1974 (Department of Justice and Solicitor General 1976). Because of this increase in homicide, laws were amended to add authority to the police. Before 1974, the police were able only to confiscate weapons used in crimes. Under new measures, it was proposed that persons owning handguns would have to justify having them for protection of life, lawful occupation, target shooting, or bona fide collection. Legislators thought that registration of all firearms would not work and that some form of control would be possible with age restrictions (owners of firearms would have to be older than 18 and be licensed for five years). Sellers of firearms and ammunition would have to acquire permits and keep records of transactions.

The Canadian plan is not harsh and does not advocate confiscation of firearms. Surprisingly, the pamphlet outlining the amendments states that many of the 10 million long guns owned by Canadians have no apparent use. Aside from how that conclusion was reached, one wonders why everyone is so upset about homicides caused by firearms in a country which has more than 10 million long guns, when the deaths in 1974 from such firearms were only 272. In Canada and other countries with similar size populations and geographical areas, there are more automobile fatalities in ratio to automobile ownership and use than there are deaths from firearms. Certainly this is true for Israel, where automobile fatalities far exceed firearm deaths in a population which has a high concentration of rifles, handguns, and machine guns in countryside and city homes.

Experts have approached the study of firearms and their use from many different directions. Some have studied individual cases of murder and suicide; others have employed personality inventories and have compared different variables. Some have compared sociological variables. Thus far, no one has studied firearm sportsmen who have handled guns and kept them in their homes without mishap or violence.

In a study conducted in Detroit from July through September 1969 (*Task Force on Gun Control*, 1970), a 90-person sample (57 homicide victims, 29 suicide victims, and 4 accident victims) was studied. The entire sample consisted of cases as they came to the attention of the medical examiner's office. Only 47 killers in the homicide group were actually known at the time of the study. In each case, the cause of death by firearms had been legally established.

The largest proportion of homicide perpetrators were young black men from lower socioeconomic areas. By far, handguns were the most common type of firearm used. These weapons were frequently stolen or rented from one of the black markets in gun trade. In all, there were 36 handguns; only eight were registered. The other weapons among the 57 homicides were long guns of various types. In the suicide group, where 18 handguns were used (in 29 gunshot cases) 14 were registered. The suicide group thus had a proportionately higher number of registered handguns (78 percent) than did the homicide group (22 percent).

The 57 killers and victims had characteristic demographic profiles that distinguished them from members of the suicide group. Those who made up the accident death group more closely resembled the homicide, rather than the suicide, group. Both low educational level and elevated rate of unemployment were significantly higher for the homicide group than for the suicide group. These data were consistent with the observations of Wolfgang (1958) and Kendell (1970). However, the present study found fewer family members to be victims than did these previous studies. In the present study, firearms were kept in the home ostensibly to protect and defend the family. Such an assertion is in marked contrast to statements made in the report of the Task Force on Gun Control:

Psychiatric study of homicide indicates that a majority of homicides are committed by law-abiding citizens, perpetrating the act in a state of altered consciousness against some emotionally significant person. The presence of a firearm during such a state is usually the most significant factor, since in the absence of a lethal weapon, a less destructive discharge of aggression can take place.

The latter statement is particularly not true in the absolute sense, as Wolfgang has reflected the fact that more men are killed in the kitchen because a knife is handier to the woman. A woman, however, stands more chance of being killed by a firearm in her bedroom. The Detroit study shows that the majority of firearms used were kept in the bedroom. It would seem that during a state of anger and frustration, any instrument can be used to express rage.

In Detroit, the victim is usually not a "significant other"; a majority of the homicides involve murder of a neighbor, stranger, or holdup victim. In the holdup and "business-type crimes," narcotics and drugs were almost invariably involved. Typically, the acts are not those of a law-abiding citizen.

Another notion concerning people who use and keep firearms handy is that weapons are used as symbols of masculinity. In the Detroit study, the killers used firearms of small caliber, like .22 or .25. If the firearm or its caliber were an expression of masculinity, it might be expected that larger bores—.357 or .30 caliber—would be sought. Complementing the latter finding, shooting as a sport has become extremely popular with women throughout the country. One would have to speculate about the role of penis envy, assuming that a firearm is a penis symbol. Some of the psychoanalytic group, such as Leon Salzman (1967), question whether this concept can be verified by present-day observations in terms of the changing position of women throughout the world. Again, the sportswoman does not seem to have the same type of demographic profile as does the woman who uses a firearm to kill. The latter finding is based on the author's experience over many years of direct use and contact with firearms, contacts with owners of firearms, and research on homicide and suicide.

One finding of investigations of homicide versus suicide concerns the age distinction (Kendell, 1970). In both the United States and Europe, suicide rates rise steadily with age, even up to the ninth decade. Criminal homicide, however, reaches its peak in the third decade, and fewer than 10 percent of the murderers are over 50 (Wolfgang, 1958). Such figures—along with observations of lower socioeconomic factors among the homicides as compared with suicides—point to multifaceted causation rather than whether or not the firearm is available. One must look at the abuser, not the object alone.

In his study of 588 homicides in Philadelphia over a five-year period, Wolfgang (1959) found that when a man kills a man, he is likely to do it away from home, but 75 percent of the time, women murder at home. Such information might well explain why it was that in the Detroit study most of the homicide victims were not primary family members. Interesting to any suicidologist or student of violence is the observation of how many homicide victims precipitate their own deaths in terms of suicide. Thus, the other person becomes the vehicle; the fact that the murderer has a gun or knife is of secondary significance except for the certainty of the outcome. However, the attitude of the killer is a necessary prerequisite at the time *because* if the person will not kill, the lethality of the gun is reduced or lowered.

Attention focused on the homicide victim further reflects the fact that most are of the same sex, race, ethnic identity, and socioeconomic strata as the killer. The suicide group in the Detroit study reflects the opposite picture in that the better-educated, more Caucasion group with a higher employment rate and better jobs tended to commit suicide. Also, the latter group was older and had registered its handguns with greater frequency than the homicide group. Thus, handgun registration served as one additional index of identification with society and socialization.

In suicide, the availability and the choice of firearms as a method for committing suicide seem to be evident, independent of the issue of whether or not the handguns are registered. One can raise the question about whether mortality or morbidity would be reduced if firearms were removed. For example, Farberow (1969) compared suicides in Vienna with those in Los Angeles and found that guns were used in 42 percent of the suicides in Los Angeles, compared with 8 percent in Vienna. Obviously, the use of firearms varies from country to country. Nonetheless, suicide remains high in countries like Japan and Sweden where firearms are not held in great numbers by citizens. Thus, it would be fair to doubt whether firearms "cause" suicide when data show that people will find a way to kill themselves regardless of the availability of firearms. As another example, in Vienna domestic gas was involved in 28 percent of the suicides, whereas in Los Angeles the figure was zero.

Richard Drooz (1977) takes issue with Browning (1976) on several points. He cites Bruce-Briggs (1976) who said that gun control has nothing to do with crime control. He acknowledged that the gun is a deadly weapon but needs a person to pull the trigger. He cited Murray's study (1975) which concluded that gun control laws have no effect on rates of violence, that such laws do not effectively limit access to guns by violent persons, and that firearm availability has nothing to do with rates of crime and firearm accidents. He took Browning to task because Browning had cited FBI figures about homicide but pointed out that the Uniform Crime Reports have never listed handguns or other firearms as among the substantial variables that influence crime rates. First, he felt that Browning's views fail to account for important variables such as demographic distinctions between close groups like families where homicide runs high and frequently is related to firearms. Second, he said that Browning failed to account for the role of alcohol in the commission of homicide, a rate which, like suicide, involves about 50 percent of the cases. Third, criminals sometimes direct violence toward their families, and this is a reflection of their lifestyles, rather than the presence of a firearm. He also thought that family members and others should not include enemies of the criminal because that infers a different kind of intimate relationship than with friends. Drooz attacked Browning's own cited study and pointed out that in June 1976, the New York *Times* reported that in 1975, intrafamilial killings made up 5.5 percent of the killing, and that 91.9 percent of the time the killer and victim were unrelated.

In 1968 the Dodd Subcommittee (U.S. Senate 1968) showed that

80 percent of those who used a gun had a prior criminal record and that in 78 percent of the homicides, there was a criminal record with an average of six prior arrests.

Although Browning thought that guns at home were not useful for protection, Drooz pointed out that there is no risk of accidentally killing a family member, as most persons who collect them or shoot for sport keep the gun unloaded at home. Furthermore, he thought that many persons might use the gun to scare away intruders or to capture them without shooting. Or, for example, a shot might be fired into the air. In the reported 23 instances of unlawful intruders being killed by a firearm, as cited by Browning, there was not one instance of accidental injury to a member of that household. Finally, Drooz points out where one of the supporters of Browning's position, Frank Zimring, wrote in another section of the article quoted by Browning, that his idea that gun ownership and homicide go together might have to be revised in areas where firearm crimes have increased but where there is a lower-than-average rate of firearm ownership.

According to Drooz (1977), the established figure of 2.5 million handguns sold in the United States includes these purchased by armed guards, watchmen, armed investigators, messengers, peace officers, and citizens who either collect them or have them for self-defense. This rate of handgun purchase occurs in context with a population of 210 million people. He points out that target shooters wear out the precision of their firearms and must replace them. New models are a must for peace officers and collectors.

One of the chief experts on the sociology of homicide, Marvin Wolfgang (1958), wrote:

Several students of homicide have tried to show that the high number of, or easy access to, firearms in this country is causally related to our relatively high homicide rate. Such a conclusion cannot be drawn from the Philadelphia data. . . . It is the contention of this observer that few homicides due to shooting could be avoided merely if a firearm were not immediately present, and that the offender would select some other weapon to achieve the same destructive goal.

On the other hand, Fisher (1976) expressed strong anti-firearm views. He studied homicide in Detroit from 1961–73, which were also the only years for which statistics for handgun registration were available. He found that assaults among blacks were higher than for whites.

During the period described, homicide by handgun increased seven times, while those involving a long gun increased by a factor of 13. Murder and assault by knife doubled and tripled during the same period. He thought that murder by handgun rose significantly despite an increase in all weapons employed to kill. However, he found that violence as a means of coping with conflict accounted for more than three-quarters of the yearly variation in homicide, while the availability of firearms accounted for one-quarter. He demonstrated in his study that mental set for violence was more significant than availability of firearms and that murder by firearms will be higher in cities where there are high rates of murder.

Marks and Stokes (1976) studied firearm use in suicide and found that children were introduced to firearms by their fathers at an early age, and boys had them introduced more often than girls. Southern men had more exposure to firearms than Southern women or men elsewhere. They felt that Southerners were reared in homes with firearms, and therefore used them more when committing suicide. They concluded that use of firearms to commit suicide was probably a function of normative patterns of socialization with firearms that differ for males and females. They felt that the reasons for suicide method are totally different from the reasons for committing suicide, and are basically the product of socialization patterns. They found out about socialization patterns with firearms but did not interview groups of suicidal persons; rather, they took suicide statistics from those regions and inferred that nonsuicidal groups with firearm socialization could offer insight into firearm suicide data. It would seem that much was lacking in their basic assumption or research design.

Because homicide has risen, regardless of method, almost everyone agrees that something significant needs to be done to control such deaths. The big problem rests with the kind of control plan that can be devised, one which will be effective and will satisfy most persons with vested interests in regard to firearm possession and use for lawful purposes. At this point, some discussion about control issues will be presented.

Perhaps one of the basic approaches to gun control has involved whether or not there is a right to own one. This issue in terms of constitutional issues has been significant in the United States.

One of the most important determinants of possession of firearms for the purpose of personal, home, or business defense has been the tremendous increase of crime against the law-abiding citizen. In the Detroit area, requests for handgun purchase permits and concealed weapons permits began to rise significantly in 1965. At that time, one of the issues in the mayoral campaign was that one of the candidates was conducting and supporting firearm instruction for grocers whose stores were being robbed at an alarming rate. Police were unable to stem the tide of attacks against innocent citizens. The courts and mental health centers were equally helpless. Such factors make attempts to abolish possession of firearms difficult—probably impossible. To some it would be almost irrational to deprive people of a reasonable defense in light of the helplessness of police and other community agencies.

Debate about the Second Amendment has been approached by both sides of the firearms issue. In general, it would appear to be an issue overworked by the pro-firearm group. Unless a constitutional right can be interpreted to involve an inherent responsibility, the argument is unrealistic. If a constitutional *right* to bear arms cannot be established by legal argument or if, because of rising levels of violence, that right needs reexamination, then, without abolishing the use of firearms for the law-abiding citizen, the *privilege* of having guns could be emphasized. Such a maneuver would restrict the notion that one can possess guns without responsibility. Further, such a position might make it possible to introduce reasonable legislation to control safety in the use of firearms, particularly handguns. For example, since handguns can easily be concealed, it is reasonable to ask any handgun owner to submit to some screening procedures (such as suitable psychological tests, ones that could be administered in a matter of minutes). Such tests could be devised to pick up signs of impulsivity in relation to aggressiveness, as well as danger signs of homicidal and/or suicidal impulses. Secondly, applications from persons with known criminal or mental hospitalization records could be turned down. Thirdly, before any approved applicant could purchase a firearm, he would have to produce a training certificate received from an approved program. Such a course would teach safe and proper use of firearms. Perhaps a refresher course could be required before each license renewal. The emphasis on safety in itself encourages the maintenance of control, because it promotes it as a positive value in the way that those who belong to shooting clubs learn to use their firearms.

If people want to use firearms for sport or safety, they ought to be willing to prevent dangerous and irresponsible individuals from obtaining guns. Such measures would appear to be a reasonable alternative to the hysterical cries of those who are basically frightened of firearms and their use. Criteria for those who might not be entitled to possess or handle firearms are contained in Rotenberg and Sadoff's recommendations (1968): the seriously mentally ill (the psychotic individual), criminals, the impulsive character, and drug addicts. The authors further proposed that automatic weapons should be barred, as well as telescopic sights. However, as many gun owners know, telescopic sights are used for hunting and targetry. Those frightened of firearms should not be forced to use them, but others should not be kept from using them. On one occasion, the author noticed two outspoken critics of firearms examining some guns, and upon picking them up, they squeezed the trigger several times. They failed to check if the guns were loaded; further, no shooter would damage the firing pin or hammer by dry-firing the firearm.

With respect to the positive sporting aspect of firearms, a very definite appreciation for the control over danger is involved, along with the training and teaching of the individual to develop control and coordination of reflexes. To excel at targetry, absolute control is necessary, and such a concept is in direct opposition to the notion that only the impulsive person uses firearms or has interest in them. Discipline and control are determinants, in part, of the law-abiding citizen, not the dangerous one. The framework of competing against oneself or others is an emotionally healthy type of sporting activity, and the sublimation of aggressive energy onto the target of paper or clay is an emotionally healthy type of outlet.

Drooz (1977) cited some reasons why he feels that gun control is not practical or has been based upon some erroneous conclusions from loosely designed research. Questions about gun control by legislation can be seen from another example.

In 1974, in Jamaica, civilian-owned firearms of all kinds were banned and severe penalties were mandated for offenders. Gun scenes were banned from movies and television programs. Research conducted one year later (Diener and Crandall) revealed that homicides were reduced by 14 percent and other crimes were similarly reduced, e.g., rape 32 percent, robberies 25 percent, and non-fatal shootings 37 percent. There was an increase in non-firearm homicide, but the study did not reveal the actual number of these deaths. Concerning the banning of firearms, after the initial turning in of 500, the number of guns surrendered dwindled. It was thought that crime was reduced more because of extra police who were hired and kept visible than picking up the firearms. Finally, as happens in many dictatorships where firearms are banned and confiscated, the civil rights of people are abused; this happened politically in Jamaica. The researchers who viewed the effects of banning firearms there concluded:

These data demonstrate that even outlawing guns with strict enforcement of the gun ban will not eliminate crime, nor reduce crime so that it is no longer a serious concern. While the 14% reduction in homicides may represent a substantial number of lives saved, the present data indicate that there will still be a large number of killings after gun bans are enacted. In other words, a ban on guns and concurrent enforcement measures reduces crime, but does not eliminate it. It is important to note that crime levels were still substantial after the anticrime measures were in effect, indicating that crime reduction is a multifaceted process that cannot be attained solely by strict law-and-order legislation. Were the reductions in crime worth the price? The cost of the gun control measures was in liberty lost, the opportunity for hunting and sport shooting gone, and the cost in police and prison manpower to enforce the law (Diener and Crandall).

Some homicidal deaths appear to be triggered by the behavior of the victim. As recounted by Wolfgang (1959) and MacDonald (1968), the victim frequently acts in such a manner as to provoke the murderer with dares and taunts. Additionally, inaction by the victim as well as the family or friends of the murderer may be instrumental or provocative of the murder. Many times the murderer clearly communicates his future course of behavior in, for example, his history of assaultive arrests. Aggressive behavior while drinking is a predisposing factor common among those who threaten and commit homicide. Although MacDonald disagrees, Hellman and Blackman (1966), believe that a history of cruelty to animals, fire-setting, and enuresis is highly related to committing homicide. Families often know of these elements in the background of the murderers. Thus, the cast of characters enlarges with respect to those playing a role in the murder: the murderer, the victim, and his family, as well as neighbors, friends, and co-workers. Illustrative of this aspect of the homicide was a case called into the Detroit Suicide Prevention Center. A doctor telephoned about her brother-in-law, whose alcoholism, violence, and homicidal threats against his wife were becoming more frequent. On advice, the local prosecuting attorney was called, and he referred the case and wife to the police for investigation. The police, not knowing the history, decided the situation involved marital problems and dropped the man off at a bar near his home. Later, he went home and killed his wife.

Another example concerns a young woman whose husband had repeatedly beaten her and one of their two children. She had been seen by two different social workers for several weeks, but at Thanksgiving time they were too busy to help her arrange for emergency hospitalization for her homicidal husband. The same reaction occurred with the others to whom she turned desperately for help, namely, her father, the police, her minister, and the Salvation Army. Everybody was too busy. When her baby son ran a fever of 105 degrees, he was taken to the hospital, and a doctor innocently asked if the mother had considered the possibility of meningitis. To the mother, who had been a nursing student, this meant her baby would die. Irrationally, she decided to kill her other son and herself so as to join the dead baby in a reunion in heaven, where all three would be safe, protected, and removed from an indifferent world. Only the son whom she stabbed 10 times died.

Although it is undeniably true that firearms are used as the method of killing in suicide and homicide, it is not true that the resulting homicides or suicides can be directly blamed on the firearms. Were they not available, other methods would be chosen. It is true that firearms are used predominantly for suicide in the United States, but in other countries, like Czechoslovakia and Hungary, which have higher suicide rates per hundred thousand population, hanging, gas, or poison are involved.

In my opinion, we are blaming the tool rather than the user. Perhaps we hope that by banning the tool, we shall also ban this type of death. I suggest that this kind of thinking is simplistic and expresses the influence of our valuing things or tools beyond the limits by which these items can be used by death seekers.

REFERENCES

Browning, C. H. 1976. "Handguns and Homicide." *Journal of the American Medical Association* 236(19):2198–2220.

Bruce-Briggs, B. 1976. "The Greatest American Gun War." *Public Interest* 45:37–62.

Danto, B. L. 1971. "Firearms and Their Role in Homicide and Suicide." *Life Threatening Behavior* (Spring) 1(1):10–17.

Department of Justice and Solicitor General of Canada. 1976. The Highlights of the Peace and Security Program: The Criminal Law Amendment Act (1) and (2).

Diener, E. and R. Crandall. "Impact of the Jamaican Gun Control Laws." Psychology Department, University of Illinois, Champaign, Illinois (personal communication).

DiMaio, V. J. and R. E. Zumwalt. 1977. "Rifle Wounds from High Velocity Center Fire Hunting Ammunition." *Journal of Forensic Sciences* (January) 22(1):132–40.

Drooz, R. B. 1977. "Handguns and Hokum." *Journal of the American Medical Association* 238(1):43–45.

Farberow, N. L. 1969. "Suicide in Los Angeles and Vienna." *Public Health Reprints* 84:389–403.

Fisher, J. C. 1976. "Homicide in Detroit." *Criminology* (November) 14(3):387–99.

Hellman, D. S. and N. Blackman. 1966. "Enuresis, Fire Setting, and Cruelty to Animals." *American Journal of Psychiatry* 122:1431–35.

Kendell, R. E. 1970. "Relationship Between Aggression and Depression." *Archives of General Psychiatry* 22:308–18.

MacDonald, J. M. 1968. *Homicidal Threats.* Springfield, Illinois: Charles C Thomas.

Marks, A. and C. S. Strokes. 1976. "Socialization, Firearms, and Suicide." Presented at the Annual Meeting of the American Association of Suicidology in Los Angeles, California, April 29.

Rotenberg, L. A. and R. L. Sadoff. 1968. "Who Should Have a Gun? Some Preliminary Psychiatric Thoughts." *American Journal of Psychiatry* 123:841–43.

Salzman, L. 1967. "Psychology of the Female: A New Look." *Archives of General Psychiatry* 17:195–203.

Task Force on Gun Control. 1970. *Newsletter.* Michigan Society of Psychiatry and Neurology. No. 6, p. 12.

United States Senate. 1968. Hearings Before the Subcommittee to Investigate Juvenile Delinquency of the Committee on the Judiciary. June 26–28; July 8–10. Washington, D.C.: U.S. Government Printing Office.

Wolfgang, M. E. 1958. *Patterns in Criminal Homicide.* Philadelphia: University of Pennsylvania Press.

——. 1959. "Suicide by Means of Victim Precipitated Homicide." *Journal of Clinical and Experimental Psychopathology and Quarterly Review of Psychiatry and Neurology* 20:335–49.

16

POLICE AND HOMICIDES

John Bruhns

◇

Officer Joseph Brown, a recent graduate from the Police Academy who is still motivated by his high ideals of helping people, receives a call. Upon arriving at the location, he finds a victim with multiple gunshot wounds, obviously dead. Officer Brown feels the hastily eaten lunch he finished less than an hour ago about to come up, and everything seems to be closing in on him. Added to this is the morbid thought running through his mind: "My God, my first homicide case and I just know that I'm going to screw it up!" Then his mind begins to focus in on what the homicide instructor covered in the academy.

Death is never pleasant. Homicide is often called the classic crime. Certainly it can be the most terrible and gruesome of crimes. Some people think that homicide and murder are synonymous terms. They are not. Some homicides are criminal in nature, while others are justifiable or excusable. Justifiable homicides are self-defense situations and would include police officers having to shoot someone in the performance of duty. An excusable homicide, in Michigan, is a killing done by misadventure. It is done without any intent, without any criminal negligence, and without any justification under circumstances that would constitute an excuse.

The perpetrator of a homicide may attempt to conceal his crime by making it appear as a suicide, an accident, or even a death due to natural causes. The police, because of their role in society, are called upon to investigate and make reports on all types of deaths. In some cases, it may also be the responsibility of the police through their investigation to determine if, in fact, the death was a homicide.

When a death comes to the attention of the police, it is usually telephoned in. Whoever answers that telephone call needs to find out where it happened, what happened, and who is there. On all incoming emergency calls to the police, the most important piece of information is, where did it happen? If for any reason the call is cut off, at least a patrol car could be dispatched to the location to see what the trouble or nature of the call is. A most important factor, if that call concerns a homicide, is the officer or officers responding to that call. Their first responsibility is to verify if indeed there has been a homicide. If so, then every effort should be made to protect the scene of that homicide. In protecting it, the police officers must not turn off or frighten away any potential witnesses. Telling everyone to "get back" or "you're not needed or wanted here," as they do on television detective stories, may run off a potential witness or, in some cases, a prime suspect (they have, in some cases, stayed in the area).

Media people monitor police calls, and often they will respond to a homicide scene. Lately, the TV camera crews have taken up stations a block or two away. They rely on telephoto lenses for their pictures. And with the advent of infra-red cameras, even darkness is no longer a problem for them. They will often get the entire scene onto a videotape and will, in some cases have as much as the police do.

The investigation of a homicide receives more attention and criticism than any other crime. The police officer frequently faces pressures from many sources: a demanding news media, the emotional storm of relatives and friends of the deceased, and often inquiries from insurance companies that don't want to pay off on double indemnity policies. Even elected politicians, who want to show the voters they have some power over the police, will make all types of demands and suggestions on what should be done. It seems everyone knows how police work should be done better then the police. If you add to this confusion on the scarcity of facts and witnesses, you can see some of the problems facing the police in homicide case investigations.

The police officer is also a person who, at the scene and during the investigation, must deal with his own personal feelings. Most police officers were attracted to law enforcement because they were looking for something meaningful to do with their lives. None that I know of became cops because of the financial inducements. In surveys done at the police academy in Macomb County, Michigan, over half of the trainees stated they wanted a job that helped other people. It is not unusual to hear a trainee claim to have taken a pay cut to become a police officer. This desire to help people was also seen in air disasters in Chicago and San Diego. Many of the officers who responded to those disasters had to seek professional help because they could not cope with their frustrations—frustrations, resulting from the absence of any survivors to be helped: everyone at the crash scenes was dead. Even veteran police officers, who have been exposed to the harsh realities of life and who were looked upon as cynical, hardened, une-motional individuals, felt frustrated and welcomed the opportunity to obtain stress counseling.

Police in any type of an investigation draw on many resources such as *Res Gestae* witnesses, chemists, fingerprint technicians, firearms experts, photographers, and various public as well as private agencies. By coordinating these resources and then objectively sifting the evidence collected, they can generally bring an investigation to a satisfactory solution. Therefore, the most important principle in any investigation is to remain objective in the search for a solution. The temptation to jump to conclusions is found to be present in all cases. Premature assumptions on what happened can close the mind to facts or evidence that does not fit into a preconceived theory of how something occurred. Theories reached or jumped to without all of the facts are not proof of what happened—only speculations. Finding out the truth of what happened is the sole purpose of an investigation. Police must be objective if during their investigation they expect to learn the truth.

It is very common for a police officer during a homicide investigation to sympathize with the victim. It is also necessary to empathize with suspects during interrogations. Where it is not immediately obvious who the perpetrator is, the pattern followed to find the solution is to learn as much as possible about the victim. The officer must get to "know" the deceased more than he does members of his own family. Getting to know as much as possible about the victim and possible suspects makes it easy to become involved personally, and trying to remain objective sometimes becomes extremely difficult. The police officer, however, must be objective if he expects to learn the truth.

Many homicide investigators claim that they are the only ones protecting the rights of the deceased. Others feel they are the victim's avenger; they are the only ones interested enough to see that the perpetrator is brought to justice and punished. In Michigan, as in many other states, the complainant in a homicide case is the officer who investigated it. The officer signs the complaint on information and belief because the real complainant would have been the victim. As the complainant, the officer must appear for all the various court hearings. The officer has, in fact, become the accuser who may be responsible for sending a person to jail for life and maybe even to death by execution. He shoulders a great deal of responsibility—responsibility which rests on a person who, in many cases, has had only a high school education, who may not have been properly trained, who feels that he is under paid and stuck into a profession which is not held in high esteem by the citizens of the community he serves.

The first few hours in any investigation are the most critical. This is the time when suspects, witnesses, and evidence are often still readily available. Since every crime scene may at times involve any given type of evidence, it is clear that that investigator is the key in making sure that evidence is effectively used. The investigator must know how to collect and preserve physical evidence. He must also know what to collect and why it should be collected. To this end, he must understand what can be done with it and how, and know to what extent it will benefit him. Thus, he has to have a sound motive in intelligently cooperating with the crime lab, the medical examiner, the prosecutor, and others. However careful a suspect may be to avoid being seen or heard, he will leave some trace behind. Not only his fingerprints or footprints, but his hair, fibers from his clothes, toolmarks, paint scrapings, and numerous other things. All these, and more, bear mute witness to what he did and to who he is. This is evidence unlike eyewitness evidence. It does not forget, does not become confused by the excitement of the moment, and it is not prejudiced for or against the suspect. This is factual evidence, physical evidence that cannot be wrong, cannot perjure itself, nor can it be wholly absent. Only when it is misinterpreted does it lie. Only human failure in not finding it or failing to understand and study it can diminish its value.

The scene of any crime is in itself evidence, and the testimony of a trained officer concerning his observations and findings at an unchanged crime scene are vitally important to the successful clearance of a case. Improper protection of a crime scene will usually result in contamination and permit unnecessary movement of physical evidence that may render such evidence useless. Therefore, the first officer to arrive on the scene of a crime automatically incurs the serious and critical responsibility of securing the scene from unauthorized persons or any type of intrusions. Even though the officer who arrived first will also search for evidence, the necessity to immediately take precautions to protect and preserve evidence remains unchanged.

There is no definite set of rules that can be applied to defining what actually is the scene of the crime. The best physical evidence is normally found at or near the site of the most critical action taken by the criminal against his victim. Thus, it is more likely to find important physical evidence in the area surrounding the body in a homicide case than at some distance away.

Officers assigned to patrol cars are usually the first to arrive at a scene of homicide, suicide, or accidental death. Frequently, upon arrival, the officers will find the victim critically injured and possibly dead. As the primary function of the police officer is to preserve life, a highly erroneous procedure which many officers follow is to immediately load the victim into an ambulance and drive off to the nearest hospital; then left at the scene are the witnesses, and possibly the assailant, who leave when they see the officers drive off. When faced with this type of a situation, the officer should come into an ambulance, radio for extra help at the scene, and if there is no immediate response, have one man stay at the scene while the other goes to the hospital with the victim. Usually, the police dispatcher will send extra cars to assist or provide backup. The police officer accompanying a seriously injured victim to the hospital should avail himself of the opportunity to question that victim as closely as his condition allows. Quite often after arrival at the hospital the doctors take over, and investigating officers are unable to question the victim. Sometimes death ensues, and valuable testimony is lost forever.

When the first officer arrives at the scene, he is likely to be met by hysterical members of the family, sympathetic neighbors, and curiosity seekers. Conditions will probably be in a state of chaos owing to the noise and the confusion. The officer must observe tact in ushering the family into another room and excluding all others from the premises (after first ascertaining that they do not have any valuable information pertaining to the case). It is very important that the officer, when he arrives at the scene, display a good professional attitude, because the bystanders, among whom may be witnesses, have a tendency to make an estimate of whether or not they can trust or can talk to that particular officer by their first impression of him.

A good golden rule for that officer to follow is to never touch, change, or alter anything until it has been identified, photographed, and checked out by evidence technicians, lab people, or whoever is going to be in charge of collecting evidence. When a body or an article has been moved, it can never be restored to its original position. The officers should notify the station as soon as possible, giving as many details as possible concerning the particular crime. If an assailant is in custody, or if the assailant has escaped, the officer should give a description of him and the method of escape for teletype purposes. The scene, as already mentioned, should be left exactly as it was when the officer arrived. Investigating officers have one chance only to make a good crime scene search. By moving nothing, that first officer on the scene does not have to make the search and does not have to be responsible for it. The best way to keep from touching or moving anything at a scene is to close the doors of the house, apartment, or business place and remain outside until the investigators and the evidence technicians or lab people arrive and finish processing that particular scene.

Photographs are used not only as evidence in court, but also they have often been found useful in researching a scene later for evidence that may have been overlooked. The officer, while waiting for the arrival of the investigators and the medical examiner, should pick that time to start making notes as to what he found when he arrived at the scene. Also, by taking notes and a sketch he will get his mind off that particular corpse and will also reinforce the importance of not touching anything. Notes are especially important in homicide cases because there is usually a long lapse of time between a homicide and a trial date. Notes, in addition to aiding the memory, have also been impressive to a jury. For example, in a recent Detroit case, several officers, while testifying, became so confused they seemingly turned the body around in circles in attempting to tell the court and the jury in what position the body was when they arrived on the scene. When the jury hears poor testimony from several officers who were at the scene of a homicide, they may discount the testimony of an investigator to whom a confession was made. They cannot reconcile the fact that one officer can remember nothing while another can recall exactly a conversation he had with the defendant. As noted, the officer should prepare a small sketch of the scene, indicating the location and position of the body in relation to other objects in that room. Locate the position of the weapon, shells, slugs, bloodstains, or anything else that may be important.

One reason why the first officer at the scene should use great care in not moving objects or altering a scene is that investigators use what is known as the association method to determine, or attempt to determine, the time of death. The time of death is important information needed to check out alibis. Many people are under the impression which has been created by detective stories and television that a doctor, upon examining a body, can place the time of death within minutes of its occurrence. Unfortunately, this is not the case. In many cases, a medical examiner can give you hours, and then again, sometimes only days. An illustration of the association method, as is found in the manual for Detroit homicide officers, is the case of a man found dead on the kitchen table of his home. The remains of a breakfast are on the table and the milk, which was left by the milkman at 7:00 A.M., is in the refrigerator. The morning paper, which the deceased is in the habit of picking up from his front porch on its arrival at 8:00 A.M., is still on the porch. We then can surmise through association that the deceased man was killed some time between 7:00 A.M. and 8:00 A.M.—unless, of course, some unthinking police officer arrived at the scene and decided to pick up the paper from that front porch, glanced at the headlines, and tossed the paper into a room inside the house. If, when that first officer arrives at the scene, the perpetrator is still there, an arrest is made. The officer should not allow the perpetrator to talk with any bystanders or with witnesses, and an officer should always stay with the perpetrator. Even though he might be handcuffed, he is still going to be able to destroy evidence. No attempt to antagonize or argue with him in any way should be made as this may affect the interrogation later. The officer should not discuss the case in front of the perpetrator, as this may bring the realization of the seriousness of what he has done and give him time to think up a defense to any questions put to him later. He should not be taken directly to the station and registered, because prisoners are usually fingerprinted and then wash the ink from their fingers after. In doing this, they destroy the effectiveness of many types of tests; for example, the thermal nitrate test which is used in shooting cases. He may wash and clean his fingernails, thereby eliminating fingernail scrapings, and this can give the suspect an additional opportunity to destroy incriminating evidence. If the prisoner does talk, then the arresting officer should give the Miranda warnings and make notes as to what that person tells him since that officer may have to repeat his statement in court.

At an outdoor crime scene, although the same general rules are to be observed, the officer will encounter different circumstances. There may be adverse weather conditions, greater crowds of curious on-lookers, and a greater area to cover. It may become necessary to block off the area by using ropes; if ropes cannot be found, patrol cars can be used to block off that particular area. One way to save a lot of time, and avoid much legwork, in an outdoor crime scene—if it covers a large area—is through aerial photography.

If footprints are found by the officer upon arrival, they should be covered with a piece of carboard, garbage can lids, or whatever. If this is not done right away, and the officer finds it necessary to leave the scene for a few minutes, the next officer at the scene may destroy the footprints which were there. If it is raining or snowing, bloodstains should also be covered and protected, as the water will dilute them, and usually render them unfit for any type of identification. The deceased person may also be covered with a blanket, a plastic raincoat, or anything available for this purpose. If the body is covered for any reason with any kind of material, the material should stay with the body and be taken to the morgue, and then the lab for processing, as it has contaminated the body. The importance of protecting the scene of the crime can be illustrated in the following actual Detroit case.

A wife told the responding officers that a prowler had entered the house through a side door, robbed, fatally shot her husband, and then escaped out the front door. Intensive and prolonged investigation was necessary to prove the woman had lied to the officers and that she was the one who had killed her husband. This work could have been avoided if the first officer at the scene had protected the area. There had been a fresh snowfall during the night, and one of the first things done by the investigators who responded to the scene to check out the wife's story was to examine the snow beside the side door to see if a prowler had entered. They found that the responding officers had trampled all the snow around the house. A clean untrampled side yard would have solved this case in a much shorter period of time.

The responding officer should not search an unconscious or dead person. This is the responsibility of the medical examiner or of the hospital attendants, but it should be done in the presence of the police officer. This is a rule which police violate many times. For example, an officer calls the station with information that he is sending an unconscious person to a hospital. When asked the person's name, the officer is able to give it. When asked how he obtained the name, he will state that he looked into the unconscious person's wallet. This is definitely wrong. Often, a citizen observing an officer looking through an unconscious person's wallet will claim the officer took money out of the wallet. If, at a later date, it is claimed that money is missing from that wallet, the officer will be unjustly accused.

A drunk, who apparently fell in an alley and suffered a fractured skull, was dead upon admission to a hospital. It was observed there that his pockets had been turned inside out. This first led the investigators to believe he had been assaulted and robbed. Later, it was discovered that the first officer at the scene had turned the subject's pockets inside out seeking identification and then failed to notify anybody about what he had done.

The day of the super sleuth is done—if it ever existed. Although investigators take advantage of the latest scientific developments to combat crime, there is no real-life Sherlock Holmes. The modern investigator must evaluate evidence, interrogate suspects, interview witnesses, and coordinate the efforts of the people involved in the process of a particular homicide case. In order to function properly, an investigator is going to have to enlist the aid of many different agencies. The investigator should be the one taking full charge. He should have the responsibility of seeing that the necessary links in the chain of evidence and in the chain of events are fulfilled to provide an efficient investigation.

Often, investigators must conduct a painstaking investigation to determine the cause of the death and generally have to depend on an autopsy to get the answer. This is one of the primary factors necessitating the attendance of the investigating officer at the postmortem and hearings. The investigator pools his knowledge of the police aspects of the case with the medical knowledge of the pathologist or medical examiner to arrive at the exact cause of death. The investigator, by attending the postmortem, also gets firsthand information on the nature of wounds, possible weapons used, and the course of blows or bullets. This information is important in subsequent interrogations of suspects and later on in court. The autopsy may reveal a previously unsuspected homicide, as is illustrated in the following case.

A downstairs tenant complained of a strong odor emanating from an upstairs apartment. The officers found a dead woman. She had lived alone and apparently had suffered a heart seizure. Fully clothed, she had apparently just entered her apartment several days before and had collapsed, scattering groceries she had been carrying on the floor. The morgue autopsy, however, revealed a bullet was lodged in her brain. The wound had been hidden under her hair. Only a cursory examination had been made at the scene by the officers and the medical examiner owing to the decomposition of the body and the strong stench. The deceased's foster stepson was later arrested in Arizona with the victim's car. The motive in this case turned out to be robbery.

Autopsies can also ascertain, by the nature of the wound, if it is compatible with a fall or a blow. For example, an elderly man was found unconscious with a head injury. His head rested on a blood-stained curb, giving the impression that he might have fallen. The man died in the hospital without making a statement. The autopsy eliminated the possibility of accidental fall by the nature and course of the blow. It was properly classified as a murder and after three months of intensive investigation, five youths were arrested and later confessed to assaulting the man in an attempt to rob him.

Sometimes an autopsy can even clear a murder suspect. Signs of trauma on a victim after a fight which ends fatally usually finds the winner of the fight in custody awaiting the outcome of the postmortem. Quite often the medical examiner may find that death was due to natural causes and was not related to the fight, so then the prisoner is released.

Search of a victim before he is sent to the hospital will be very limited. This usually consists of a quick observation of dress, general condition, and the nature of the wounds or injuries. In some situations, even this much cannot be done. In the case of an obviously dead victim, the search is going to be much more detailed before the body is moved even slightly. Its position and all pertinent information about its discovery have to be recorded in detail. It is photographed to show its relative position and then photographed in closeup to show details of wounds or injuries. Photographs and measurements, the scene, and the position of apparent items of evidence with respect to that body are also going to have to be taken.

To illustrate the importance of taking these types of photographs, Dr. Bruce L. Danto was able to determine that a suicide was, in fact, a homicide just by studying the photographs taken at an undisturbed crime scene. Investigators in the city of Southfield, Michigan, also by checking over the photographs from a bizarre homicide, observed impressions made in a snowbank by a car bumper. Working from those photographs, officers were able to identify the make of the car. That car may have been used to transport the victim to the lonely spot where he was found. This was done months after the snow had melted, and it was done by the officers reviewing the photographs. It was necessary to work from the photographs because the officers first at the scene had never measured the height or the depth of the bumper impressions.

After the details have been taken care of and recorded, a careful search should be made of the body. It should be examined for traces of evidence—such as hair and fibers, paint, or glass chips. It is best to start at the top of the head and then proceed down one side of the body as if the officer were conducting a search of a live suspect. The soles of the shoes or the feet should be checked on the dead body. Particular care should be taken to find hairs or fibers clinging to clothing or attached to fingernails. Sometimes, in order to see these hairs or fibers, it may be necessary to view the silhouette of the body against a light. The position of any evidence found on a body must be recorded precisely. Often the location is as important as what that evidence happens to be. Paper bags, rather than plastic bags, should be placed over the hands and tied securely at the wrists, plastic bags tend to cause condensation which can destroy some forms of trace evidence. Upon the completion of the detailed search of the body, it is then removed to the morgue for further examination. The area under the body should also be examined immediately after the body is removed.

When the investigator has to interview a hospitalized victim, he should collect all the items of physical evidence. He should be concerned with anything that came into physical contact between the victim and the suspect. The victim's clothing should be recovered, and each item of clothing should be wrapped separately and marked by the investigator. If the victim reported having clutched or grabbed the suspect, fingernail scrapings should be collected. If the victim has been injured in such a way as to cause bleeding, a sample of the victim's blood should be obtained for typing by the lab. This should be done even if the pathologist runs extensive blood tests. If blood is involved, the crime lab will want to run its own tests. The nature and the exact location of the victim's wounds or injuries should be ascertained by the examining physician. An arrangement should be made to photograph the victim's wounds as soon as possible, for the appearance of bruises changes rapidly. Before removing the body from the scene, it should be placed in a disposable body bag to ensure that the physical evidence around that body is not lost in a cross-contamination of the evidence during transportation to the morgue. The search of the body is continued at the morgue with the assistance of the pathologist performing the autopsy. An investigator should be present during the autopsy to make notes of any cause of death, and the depth and general nature of the wounds, as well as other contributing factors described by the doctor. Before undressing the victim, the clothing should be examined for trace material. Lighting is usually better at the morgue and quite often material missed in the field is discovered in this additional search. The deceased is then undressed. Cutting of garments should be avoided. Bloody or other stained areas and points of entry of bullets or other weapons should be left intact, and the garment should not be shaken out. If the garment is wet or blood soaked, it should be laid out flat to dry in a ventilated place at room temperature. Warm wet areas should never be allowed to come in contact with any other surface of the garment, as each item of clothing will be wrapped separately; damp garments should never be put into a plastic bag, because rapid biological changes will almost certainly result.

Once the body is undressed, it is again examined, and all the marks and wounds are recorded on a wound chart. Closeup photographs of wounds should be taken, and a ruler should be placed in the picture to indicate the scale. Head and pubic hair samples are collected if the nature of the case requires it, and these are placed in clean pieces of paper, folded carefully and then sealed in a clean envelope marked with the necessary information. If a rape is suspected, vaginal smears should be obtained by the medical examiner to be forwarded to the lab, and the swabs used should also be submitted. Ink elimination finger and palm prints of the deceased victim should be taken at the morgue, and if the hands are to be swabbed for firearms residue, this has to be done before the fingerprinting.

Officer Joe Brown, remembering everything covered in the academy by the homicide inspector, decides to call his station and the homicide investigator. While he is talking to him on the phone, the homicide investigator asks where the phone is located. Officer Brown says, "Right here in the room with the body." The homicide investigator says, "Did you ever stop to think that the phone may have been used by the perpetrator to call for a taxi?" Officer Brown drops the phone and a short time later calls back from the house next door. Apparently he did not learn all he should have in the basic academy class.

17

SOME ASPECTS OF
THE PROSECUTION OF
CRIMINAL HOMICIDE

Peter E. Deegan

◇

If people lived in isolation, no law would exist for them nor would it be necessary. But as individuals come into frequent contact with their fellows, differences arise. Might is often substituted for right, and the will of the strong prevails. . . .

In some of the early societies, the community as a whole was not always greatly concerned with persons whom we, today, treat as dangerous criminals. Even murder was sometimes recognized as nothing more than a private matter to be settled between the killer and the close kin of the victim. While at times the family of the victim might feel obliged to kill the murderer, on some occasions they even settled for the payment of substantial quantity of goods or money. Regardless of how detestable the offense, the act was of little concern to the community as a whole: but as people become more civilized, new ideas developed regarding each individual's responsibility to all his fellow humans. No longer was a crime an offense against one single individual. Rather, it was a revolt against all society, an attack against all people.

In the final analysis, criminal law is effective only to the extent that it represents the will of the majority of the people it serves. People must exchange a small part of their freedom to gain the protection of the law. Society is held together by the invisible bonds of common regulation. Since people need society, they must pay society's price. That price is the law and punishment imposed for disobeying it (Gammage and Hemphill 1974).

The Decision To Charge

In most countries of the world, the investigating agency, be it the domestic police or the military, determines what crime has been committed and who is to be charged. This is not so in the United States, where the investigating agency must bring its report to a prosecutor who is an attorney not a part of, or answerable to, the investigation agency. Rather, he is answerable only to the people who elect him. By law, it is the prosecutor only who has the power to decide who is to be charged with a crime, and with what crime; this gives to the people the power and the right to retain in office or to replace the elected prosecutor who enforces the peoples' state criminal law.

Homicide is the killing of one human being by another. But not every homicide is a crime. Homicides which are excusable, or justifiable, might include a police officer killing an armed escaping felon or a soldier killing an enemy during combat. Other homicides are not criminal because of legal defenses: the defendant who was legally insane at the time he committed the homicide, or the person who, while the victim of an armed robbery, in true self-defense overcame and killed his assailant.

The responsibility to decide whether a homicide is justified or chargeable rests with the prosecutor. It is an awesome responsibility which is classified as a "quasi-judicial" determination. This means that, at some times, the decisions made by a prosecuting attorney are equivalent in nature to the final decisions rendered by a judge or jury.

In order for homicide to be criminal in nature, it must be covered by existing criminal law. All chargeable criminal homicides embody the intentional taking of a human life on the part of the perpetrator, or at least require demonstrating a form of negligence by the defendant that directly results in the death of the victim. Thus, "negligent homicide with an automobile" contemplates the holding of a negligent driver criminally responsible for a death, even though there never was a direct intent by him to kill. A lifeguard at a school pool who intentionally sits by and watches a student drown could be guilty of manslaughter because of his failure to perform his duties. Compare this to a bystander, who has no direct *legal* duty toward such a drowning student, and who refuses to get involved; he could probably not be criminally chargeable.

"Michigan law classifies all murders which are perpetrated by means of poisoning, or laying in wait, or any other kind of willful, deliberate and premeditated killing, or, which are committed in the perpetration (or attempted perpetration) of any arson, rape, robbery, burglary, larceny, extortion, or kidnapping, as murder in the first degree" (Michigan Statutes Annotated).

To establish murder in the first degree, it must be shown that the killing was deliberate and premeditated, or was perpetrated by the means mentioned in the statute; in addition, if a second degree murder occurs during the commission of certain felonies it becomes first degree murder (People v. Aaron 409 Mich. 627 1980).

The Michigan statutes designate all of the kinds of murder not specifically designated as murder in the first degree as murder in the second degree. In both degrees of murder there is a design and intent to take human life, but with murder in the second degree, deliberation and premeditation are not present. "To constitute murder in the second degree, there must be an unlawful killing and a purpose to kill preceding and accompanying the act, but not as a result of a sudden provocation and stirring of passions that precluded the exercise of reason. This provocation would operate to reduce the crime to manslaughter" (People v. Bryant 1972).

Preparation and Proof

When a homicide occurs in any community, headlines scream the gory details. An anxious public, accustomed to television programs in which the crime is committed, the investigation takes place, and the culprit is apprehended and brought to justice—all within the course of an hour's time—expects similar speed and drama in real life.

The prosecutor's job begins with the discovery of the homicide. While a *quick* solution of the crime is certainly desirable, a *correct* solution is more important. His every move must be made with the ultimate objective of a proper prosecution in mind.

When the prosecutor has exercised his "quasi-judicial" discretion and charged a person with murder, he then is put in a position where he represents "the people" in attempting to hold the defendant accountable for violating a law of the state. Because the prosecutor brings the charges against the defendant, it is his responsibility to bear the burden of proving (beyond a reasonable doubt) that the crime was committed, and that the person charged is the one who committed it.

In proper preparation of his case, the prosecutor will rely upon good police investigation. The coordination and cooperation between the police and the prosecutor is of paramount importance. If they do not work as a team and prepare their case together before getting into the courtroom, they will find it is too late. The prosecutor cannot successfully discharge his duty simply by being a clever, flamboyant lawyer, capable of spinning out unsurpassed rhetoric in court at the drop of a hat.

To be sure, imagination and a sense of theatrics are useful tools in the forceful presentation of evidence. However, in most murder trials, a just result is achieved not because the prosecutor has a superior sense of theatrics; instead, murderers are most often held responsible for their crimes because of careful, thorough, and methodical investigation and preparation of the case for trial.

The need for thorough investigation and preparation is always important, but it tends to be even more so in murder cases. This is true not only because society views murder as a very serious offense, but also because in all murder trials the key "participant," the victim, is dead.

There are other reasons why gathering evidence carefully is particularly important in murder cases. First, the defense will scrutinize the method used to gather physical evidence in a murder case more closely than in other cases. Second, by the time the case comes to trial, the press may well have cast the accused in the role of an underdog, and the prosecutor will need strong evidence in order to overcome "underdog sympathy." Third, the very seriousness of the charge and punishment attached would tend to make a jury very unforgiving of any "human error" in the gathering of evidence by the state and its agents. Fourth, frequently a juror will be so awed by the responsibility of passing judgment on a case that may result in the imposition of a life sentence (or, in some states, the death penalty), that he will acquit if he harbors any doubt whatsoever about the nature of the prosecutor's evidence. Also, the prosecutor owes himself a duty to his sense of justice. A prosecutor must never forget that the consequences of convicting the innocent in a murder prosecution are perhaps even more tragic than seeing the guilty acquitted (Condit and Nicholson, 1970).

The Jury

The trial of a murder case is different from other criminal trials. Tensions are greater, courts are more exacting in their rulings, and juries in their requirement of proofs. These create both legal and psychological pressures which successful prosecutors must recognize and be prepared to meet at trial. Public revulsion, which frequently prevails at the time the crime is committed, may shift to sympathy for the defendant at the time of trial. The public likes to imagine a contest. Jurors who have few qualms about the performance of their duties in run-of-the-mill criminal cases tighten up when the crime is murder. They are mindful of their awsome responsibility. It is a new experience for the jurors, and one they do not relish. They will find an escape from the unpleasant duty by voting to acquit if they can.

Though the law requires but one measure of proof, jurors in murder cases do in fact require more. It is not uncommon to find prospective jurors who state on being questioned that they would never convict on "circumstantial evidence." Occasionally, a juror will state that he could only convict if someone saw the crime committed. This same juror would have little difficulty with other cases.

The solemnity of the trial is perceived also by the trial court. The judge is acutely aware of the fact that an appeal is nearly always taken from a conviction in a homicide case. He is reluctant to rule in favor of the people on a challenging legal interpretation because of the possibility of reversal. Appellate courts closely scrutinize possible errors that have been missed by the defendant's trial lawyer. The entire record is before the court whether an objection has been made at trial or not. They may, and do, consider issues that have been neglected by either counsel.

Evidence

The evidence upon which the prosecutor relies for getting a conviction, and the only evidence the jury will be allowed to consider, is the sworn testimony from the witness stand, or physical exhibits properly identified and admitted into evidence by the court.

Evidence is of two different types. *Direct evidence* is, for example, a statement by a witness about something he actually saw or heard himself. An exhibit is also direct evidence. If believed, direct evidence establishes a fact. Thus, if a witness were to say that he saw a cow in a field, that, if believed, would directly establish that there was a cow on that property. This kind of evidence describes the murder case in which everything is witnessed by some third person, including the killing itself as well as previously uttered statements by the defendant clearly showing that he intended to kill the victim, and had thought about his plan (1 Wharton's Criminal Evidence).

Circumstantial evidence does not directly prove a fact, but points to the existence of that fact. If, for example, a witness were to tell you that he saw fresh cow tracks, this, if believed, would point to the presence of a cow or cows on that property (Michigan Criminal Jury Instructions). It is not necessary that every fact be proven directly by a witness or an exhibit. A fact may be proven indirectly by other facts or circumstances from which it usually and reasonably follows according to common experience. Such evidence is proof which can be used to show that a certain fact existed. It therefore follows that in every murder case the evidence will be direct evidence, circumstantial evidence, or a combination of the two.

The Trial

The outcome of a murder case will frequently depend upon the extent to which the accused's account of what happened is supported or refuted by the physical evidence gathered: the physical items gathered are classified as "circumstantial evidence." An example is People of the State of Michigan v. Robert E. Taylor (Michigan Court of Appeals [no. 77-481]).

On December 5, 1975, the victim, Valerie Mills, age 19, went to work at her job as desk clerk at the Howard Johnson's Motor Lodge in Port Huron. Shortly before 9:00 P.M., a curious citizen, intending to transact business at the desk, called the police. The citizen reported that something suspicious had happened at the office. When the Port Huron police arrived at about 9:00 P.M., they were not at all sure what type of crime they were investigating: The cash register was empty and the drawer was open; Mills was gone but her coat was there; her car was parked in the Lodge's parking lot. Her purse was missing. The police found the waxpaper wrapper from a hamburger and a paper cup half-filled with 7-UP that still had ice cubes in it. (It was later learned that this food had been delivered to her about 7:30 P.M. by her boyfriend.) There was absolutely no indication of a struggle, and therefore the officers at that time could not rule out the possibility that she was a participant in a crime of larceny. Over the past two years there had been four unsolved murders of young women or girls in the Port Huron area. Port Huron is the largest community (40,000 population) in St. Clair County (130,000 population), and there existed a certain amount of understandable concern and fear among the area residents.

On December 10, 1975, Mills's nude body was found in a desolate field approximately 14 miles northeast from Port Huron. A neighbor said that he heard what sounded like six rapid shots being fired at approximately 9:30 P.M. December 5, when he was doing his chores, and then an auto sped away from the entrance of the field where the body later was found. Because illegally hunting deer at night is common in that area, the neighbor did not investigate.

The morning after Mills's body was found, I, as county prosecutor, met with the chief of the Port Huron Police Department, Charles Gentry, to see if a coordinated police investigation could be put together. Chief Gentry, one of the most qualified and dedicated professional police officers I have ever met, agreed to lead a team of six detectives (two from his department, two from St. Clair County Sheriff's Department, and two from the state police) who would work exclusively on the Valerie Mills murder.

This crack team of detectives worked night and day chasing down leads under Gentry's direction from December 10, 1975, when the body was found, until January 28, 1976. (They took a half day off on Christmas and a half day off on New Years.) Every day, the officers would meet at 7:45 A.M. in Gentry's office and debrief each other on the previous day's work. Chief Gentry would then assign them in teams of two to work the various assignments of that day. I would be called in from time to time to give legal advice. Other than that, complete secrecy was kept. The only news-media contact was done through me.

Because leads were scarce, we agreed to allow some local businessmen to put up a secret tip fund amounting to close to $15,000 to go to anyone having information that would lead to the apprehension and conviction of the murderer.

Physical evidence at the place where the body was found indicated Mills was murdered there: the body was nude; a man's belt was found 30 feet away, knotted in a way that indicated her hands had been tied. Her hands had clasped grass and dirt; two or three gunshots had gone through her body at close range; there was blood on the ground under her body. In the dirt under her body, two spent bullets were found. Tests by the state police crime lab ballistics and firearm expert, Trooper Berglund, showed that the spent bullets were Hornady Carbine ammunition, most likely fired from a Blackhawk Rugger; certainly they were fired from the same weapon.

On January 20, the investigating team had exhausted all available leads and were considering disbanding until possible new information came forth. Instead, they got their first break. Don Taylor, seeking the reward, advised the police through a news reporter that he thought his brother Robert might be involved. Don Taylor stated that a few days after Mills had disappeared, his brother had asked him to help get a bullet removed from his foot. Robert Taylor claimed that a girlfriend had shot him accidentally. Don Taylor drove his brother to a neighboring town, where a doctor removed the bullet; they told the doctor that he had gotten shot in a hunting accident. Don Taylor said his brother had never confessed to the murder. But Robert had told Don that he had retrieved and destroyed a gun he had left at another brother's; and he had said that he had broken into the doctor's office to steal the bullet which had been removed from his foot. On the testimony of Don Taylor alone, we would never have hoped for a conviction; but by coupling it with the circumstantial evidence, it ultimately put us in a position where we were able to focus on Bob Taylor, and then charge him with the murder.

After Bob Taylor was charged, some key circumstantial evidence came to our attention. A friend of Taylor's said that he knew that a year previously Taylor had a .30 caliber carbine Blackhawk Rugger. He had been with Taylor when he fired it in an old dump a few miles outside of Port Huron. The witness took our detectives to the dump and pointed out a small sandhill that the rugger had been fired into. The detectives discovered a .30 caliber carbine spent casing lying on the ground in that area, and by digging into the sandhill found two spent .30 caliber carbine bullets. Trooper Berglund, from the state police crime lab, was able to confirm that the .30 caliber bullets removed from under Mills's body, and one .30 caliber carbine bullet dug out of the sandy hill had been fired from the same weapon. When we arrested Bob Taylor, I got a search warrant for the car we believed he had used to transport Mills. Under the carpeting in his Lincoln Continental, the detectives found two spent .30 caliber carbine shells.

Trooper Berglund was able to confirm that the spent casings found in the car were fired from the same weapon (most likely a .30 caliber carbine Blackhawk Rugger) as the spent .30 caliber carbine casing the detectives had recovered from the dump. Trooper Berglund had spent more than 80 hours looking into a dual comparative microscope matching the bullets and casings in preparation for testifying. After hours of firearm research, he was able to testify that, in his opinion, a .30 caliber carbine seven-shot Blackhawk Rugger was the murder weapon. This was the same as Taylor was known to have previously owned. The FBI has told us that, as far as they know, there never has been a successful comparison of this nature in a case in which the murder weapon had been destroyed.

It was our theory that Bob Taylor, while shooting Valerie Mills to death, had been shot in the toe when one of his bullets passed through her body into his foot.

Though Taylor had been successful in breaking into the doctor's office and stealing and destroying both the .30 caliber bullet removed from his toe and the x-ray of his foot showing the bullet, we were able to have the radiologist, who had x-rayed Taylor's foot with the bullet in it, testify that he had "miked" or measured the bullet on the x-ray, and that its dimensions on length and width were consistent with the dimensions of a .30 caliber carbine bullet.

We also found that shortly after the killing, Taylor went to a brother's and had his brother's wife wrap the injured foot, claiming it had been injured by a forklift at work. Taylor left the murder weapon at the brother's home. This information came from Taylor's family members, and represented a story which conflicted with what Bob later told his brother Don.

At the time when Bob Taylor was arrested and charged with Valerie Mills's murder, he was 31, and held a good supervisory job at one of the auto plants. He was a member of the local Jaycees and lived in a $48,000 home. He was active in scouting with his children and well thought of by his neighbors and fellow workers. He had been captain of his high school football team and a former state weightlifting champion. At the time of the trial, sitting next to his attorney, his demeanor and appearance were such that many spectators could not decide who was the accused and who was the lawyer. He had become the darling of the news media.

Bob Taylor chose as his defense attorney Charles Campbell, who specialized in defense of murder cases. A recent Detroit newspaper article claimed Campbell had successfully defended over 60 persons charged with murder and had had only two convicted of first degree murder. He arrived in Port Huron for what would be a six-week trial, claiming that his client was innocent and could not lose. He advised the local press he had never represented a defendant who had been convicted of a felony based on circumstantial evidence.

I knew that Campbell had a reputation for being very pushy and great at intimidating jurors and witnesses. Therefore, on questioning prospective jurors, I looked for jurors who were above average in intelligence—jurors who had strong, stable roots in the community (they tend to accept and uphold the law), but most of all, jurors whom I could not push around (and believe me, I tried). My theory was if I could not push them around or browbeat them, there would be less of a chance that Campbell could. I was sure that before the case was over, Campbell would surely try. I feel we got a good, sensible jury.

The theory that we presented to the jury was that sometime shortly after 8:00 P.M., the defendant, Robert Taylor, entered Howard Johnson's armed with a .30 caliber handgun. Taylor robbed the motel, abducted Valerie Mills, and drove her to the "Beard's Hills" area, about 14 miles from Port Huron, where he stripped her, sexually attacked her, and shot her to death in that field. In the process of killing Mills, Taylor accidentally shot himself in the right big toe. Later he made up several stories to tell his family to help explain his injury.

The circumstantial evidence, which had been so carefully gathered by some very capable and dedicated police officers, when properly presented to the jury, convinced them beyond a reasonable doubt of Taylor's guilt. The jury handed down its verdict on October 16, 1976. Taylor was sentenced to Southern Michigan Prison at Jackson for life.

Even after the jury convicted him, the newspapers seemed more concerned with the fact that he was planning to write a book about himself and wanted to go to law school than the fact that he had murdered a young woman in cold blood.

What the public did not know about Taylor (and in order not to prejudice our case we were not allowed to let the potential jurors know) is that Bob Taylor as a youth had often been in serious trouble and had to be placed in a reform school. At age 14, he had tried to rape a young girl and was involved in so much trouble with the law that, at age 19, he was sentenced to four to fourteen years in state prison on a forgery charge. He was later charged with raping a babysitter he had hired for his children (the case was dropped when he allegedly paid her $1,200 and she then refused to testify). None of these facts, under our legal system, could be brought to the jury's attention.

Taylor escaped from Jackson Prison in June 1977. He remained at large until January 5, 1978, when he held up a massage parlor in Seattle, and took two of the women hostage. While he was trying to rape one of them, the other wrestled his .22 caliber handgun from him and shot him in the stomach. (When he was captured, he had on him the personal identification of a saleswoman who had disappeared from a store in Seattle in December 1977. When that store's owner returned, he found the woman gone, the cash register empty and some .22 caliber bullets on the floor. Her body has never been found.) He was convicted in May 1978 on the Seattle kidnappings, assault, and robbery and was given 60 years. On February 9, 1979, Taylor was stabbed to death outside his prison cell in Walla Walla, Washington.

Most legal authorities believe that it is harder to convict with circumstantial evidence than with direct evidence. My own experience of this is quite different. I have found that jurors do not like to convict just because they have been told what happened by an eyewitness. They tend to realize that an eyewitness will give only his version as to what he thought he heard or what he thought he saw. The way our senses perceive things must then be translated into a personal interpretation, which leaves the jury having to accept the witnesses' interpretation, as opposed to being able to perceive the truth of the facts on their own.

Bear in mind that the duty of jurors is to decide the facts and, as fact finders, they like to do so on their own without having to accept someone else's interpretation.

On the other hand, it has been my experience that jurors like to work with circumstantial evidence to find facts. Though it usually takes more circumstantial evidence than direct evidence to convince a jury of a defendant's guilt, I have observed that once a juror is convinced of a fact by circumstantial evidence, he tends to remain unshaken, because he has concluded it on his own. I believe most jurors would rather rely on their own findings of fact. In a word, it has been my experience as a trial attorney that it takes more circumstantial evidence than direct evidence to convince a jury of a fact, but once the jury is convinced, it tends to remain more steadfast in that belief.

Many times when one relies upon direct evidence to prove a case, one is confronted with having to overcome the credibility problem presented by eyewitnesses offering direct evidence. This is most often the case when the prosecutor relies upon an accomplice's testimony to convict. Jurors have not just the right but the duty to test the credibility of any witness, and they tend to be very hesitant at accepting the testimony of a codefendant who is getting a favor from the prosecutor, such as a reduced charge, in order to get him to testify against another codefendant. When this happens, the prosecutor will generally be looking for circumstantial evidence that tends to bolster the credibility of the accomplice witness.

Many times I have found myself telling juries in murder cases that the key witness we shall produce was involved in the crime himself; but truth is truth, no matter from what source it comes. We are not asking that jurors like the witness, but only that they keep an open mind, evaluate the witness's testimony properly, and determine its truthfulness. I have many times pointed out to jurors that I would like nothing better than to be able to produce the local rabbi, minister, or priest as an eyewitness; but most likely if one had been present, a crime would not have been committed. When we deal with accomplices, in other words, we are dealing with less than impressive witnesses.

An example is People of the State of Michigan v. Jim Noel Nave and Danny Beckwith Stoots (Court of Appeals, nos. 77-3518 [Stoots] and 30688 [Nave]). In this case, three persons from the Detroit area came to a farm located in St. Clair County on March 25, 1974, in an attempt to rob a cocaine distribution house. The three people shot the two male occupants of the "drug pad" to death and then set fire to the house with the victims' bodies in it. The bodies were so badly burned that their sex could only be determined by examination of internal organs.

In the process of committing the crime, one of the victims-to-be grabbed a .38 caliber handgun and shot the defendant Welker in the back twice; Welker ran from the house and collapsed in a field where Danny Stoots and Jim Nave left him for dead. When the firemen arrived, they found Welker and rushed him by ambulance to the Port Huron Hospital. After three days in intensive care, he was interviewed and confessed to our sheriff's department detectives that Stoots, Nave, and he had commited this crime. I immediately went to the hospital and videotaped his confession.

Welker, an unemployed bum with long hair and a beard, had been involved in one previous armed robbery. Instead of a gold earring through his earlobe, he wore a small hypodermic needle. In his motorcycle gang, he went by the nickname "Jesus." I charged Welker with first degree murder, and on April 12, 1974 (which happened to be Good Friday), I met with his defense attorney to view his videotaped confession. The attorney after seeing this tape, became convinced that I had Welker wrapped up tight on first degree murder. He wanted to know what plea considerations we would give Welker in exchange for his testimony against Stoots and Nave. I reminded him that it *was* Good Friday, and that his client was known as "Jesus," and that I would have to have a plea to second degree murder from him. His agreement was to testify against Nave and Stoots and to submit to a polygraph on any issue of fact arising out of this crime. I made it very clear that the agreement did not include any sentencing agreement and that he would have to take his chances with the sentencing judge.

I was aware that, without Welker's cooperation, we could not even charge Nave and Stoots, and therefore if I were not willing to concede something to him, two murderers would never be held accountable for their acts. This, in my opinion, is one reason why responsible plea bargaining should not be abolished. After Welker pleaded guilty, we charged Nave and Stoots with first degree murder. Even with Welker's direct evidence testimony, we had barely enough to hold the defendants to stand trial. The detectives and I started scouring around to find circumstantial evidence that tended to support the credibility of Welker, an ex-felon, admittedly involved in a murder and who was being allowed to plead to a lesser degree of homicide in exchange for his testimony against the others. Nave was a husband and father who was gainfully employed, and had no previous contacts with the law. Stoots had one previous possession of marijuana conviction; Welker did not even know him by his correct name, having met him for the first time the night of the murder.

The main break in the case came when the police found a jeweler who had, two years earlier, bought a stolen diamond on the street and put it in a gold ring which he made and sold to one of the victims. The jeweler had a description of the cut and carat weight of the diamond and he had a photograph of the ring which he had taken before selling it to the victim. We had witnesses who would testify that the victim was wearing the ring the day of the murder and witnesses to the fact that no ring was found on or near the body when it was removed from the fire.

The police also found a reputable jeweler who would testify that a few weeks after the murder, Stoots sold him a diamond for $1,000, claiming he and his wife were getting a divorce, and that he had originally bought the diamond for her, but wanted cash for it now. This jeweler had put the diamond in a ring setting and sold it, but was able to retrieve it for us. The original jeweler who had made up the victim's ring years before could positively identify the diamond as the one he had sold to the victim. The crime lab was able to testify that the diamond was the same weight and shape as the original receipt indicated.

This circumstantial evidence, which tended to support the direct evidence and credibility of Welker, put Stoots in quite a bind. On the day of trial, Stoots and Nave decided that pleading guilty to second degree murder was better than running the risk of first degree conviction. I allowed them to enter that plea.

The case of People of the State of Michigan v. Arthur Lee Anderson (Court of Appeals no. 18988) affords another example of the use of circumstantial evidence to support direct evidence. Arthur Lee Anderson, with his face covered, broke into the house of Margaret Lyon, a widow living alone in Marine City. He tied her and blindfolded her. While Anderson was ransacking Lyon's home, she was able to untie herself and run next door to the neighbor's house, and there she called the police. Anderson discovered Mrs. Lyon gone, pursued her to the neighbor's house and cut his right ring finger breaking the glass in the door to gain entrance there.

About this time, two police officers arrived and Anderson shot both (one has recovered, but the other still carries a bullet in his brain and will never recover beyond about 40 percent of his speech or motor control). Anderson then shot Mrs. Lyon through the leg and shot the neighbor in the back, killing him. Anderson then jumped in the police car and drove it about three blocks where he left it in the middle of the road with its motor running and its top lights flashing.

Anderson got in his own station wagon and made his escape. He was captured three weeks later, and none of the people he victimized that night could identify him. They never had a look at his face.

The key circumstantial evidence we had to use in the murder trial against Anderson was a fingerprint, in blood, on the steering wheel of the police car. When the lab arrived approximately an hour after the murder, they examined the police car which had been secured and not touched except to turn the ignition off. The lab removed the steering wheel and lifted a latent print made in fresh blood which had not yet completely dried. The blood was analyzed as being the same type as Anderson's. When he was captured, he was observed to have a cut on his right ring finger which was still healing. The latent fingerprint lifted from the police car steering wheel was identified as being made by Anderson's right ring finger. A fingerprint, in and of itself, shows nothing more than at some time previously, the person has touched the object. But, because Anderson's print was in fresh blood, the jury knew that the print was of recent origin. He is now serving life in prison.

Conclusion

The terms "murder" and "mystery" have become inseparably joined in the public's imagination. Yet perhaps only the police and prosecutors, who deal with murder regularly, and the friends and relatives of the dead fully appreciate the tragic finality manifested by the untimely and unwarranted end of a human life. Killing another human being with malice aforethought represents a nearly complete rejection of those values that make a society civilized. The prosecutor who undertakes to fully, fairly, and persuasively present the evidence of a culpable homicide undertakes a grave task indeed.

The prosecutor must neutralize the appeal that has been made to the emotions of the jury and is being used by the defense. His appeal must be to reason. He must analyze the defense and meet it with fair and legitimate argument. He should deal with the heart of the matter and not dwell upon insignificant details. His reliance should be on the strength of his own case rather than the weaknesses of the defense, and always with recognition that strong preparation and fair presentation will stand him in good stead.

A prosecutor owes a special duty to his conscience and his sense of justice. The adequate protection of society and the accused alike demand a great deal of a prosecutor in a murder trial. They demand not that he always be successful, but that, instead, he always be right. A prosecutor must never forget that the consequences of being wrong and successful in a murder prosecution are every bit as tragic as the consequences of being right and unsuccessful (Condit and Nicholson 1970).

REFERENCES

Gammage, A. Z. and C. F. Hemphill, 1974. *Basic Criminal Law*. New York: McGraw-Hill.

3 Gillespie 1973. *Michigan Criminal Law and Procedure*, (2d ed), 1636 et seq, p. 644; *People v. Allen*, 390 Mich 383, 212 NW 2d 21.

Michigan Criminal Jury Instructions (CJI) 3:1:10.

Michigan Statutes Annotated 28.548; 28.549 Michigan Compiled Laws Annotated 750.316; 750.317.

People v. Allen, 390 Mich 383, 212 NW 2d 21 (1973).

People v. Bryant 43 Mich App 659, 204 NW 2d 746 (1972).

Condit and Nicholson. 1970. *Murder: A Methodical Approach*, CDAA National Homicide Symposium Handbook.

Strauss. 1970. *The Prosecutor Prepares for a Murder Trial*, The Prosecutor's Deskbook, Practicing Law Institute.

1 Wharton's Criminal Evidence, 13th ed., 6:4;

ADDITIONAL BIBLIOGRAPHY

Block, R. 1975. "Homicide in Chicago, a Nine-Year Study (1965–1974)." *Journal of Criminal Law and Criminology* 66:496.

Bourdouris, J. 1974. "Classification of Homicides." Criminology (February) 11:525.

Kadish, S. H. 1976. *"Respect for Life and Regard for Rights in the Criminal Law." California Law Review* 64:871.

Lunde, D. T. 1975. "Our Murder Boom." *Psychology Today* (July).

O'Leary, M. E. 1974. *Evidence of Prior Similar Incidents Is Admissible to Show the Corpus Delicti of Murder*. United States v. Woods, 484 F2d 127 (4th Cir 1973) 43 Cincinnati L. Rev 437

Sidney, K. M. 1978. "The Felony Murder Doctrine in Michigan." *Wisconsin Law Review* 25:69.

18

THE LEGAL DEFENSE
OF HOMICIDE

Neil H. Fink

<>

Murder is defined as the unlawful killing of one human being by another with malice aforethought. Malice aforethought may be expressed when death is caused by an act which discloses such an abandoned state of mind as to be equivalent to an actual intent to kill.

For first degree murder, there must be evidence of premeditation. This may be shown by acts prior to the killing that show planning (such as the making of a map of the victim's home and purchasing rope to tie the deceased up) or by a manner of killing indicative of preconceived design. In this regard, consider an execution style murder, such as the planting of a bomb in the victim's car, or look to facts about the deceased's and defendant's relationship that show a motive. Motive is evidenced by facts which indicate, for example, that the deceased had cheated the defendant out of a large sum of money and that the defendant had wanted to get even.

Motive alone, however, is not enough to sustain a finding of premeditation. First degree murder also includes murder during inherently dangerous felonies such as arson, rape, kidnapping, and armed robbery. Under this doctrine the Michigan Court of Appeals upheld the conviction of Bonnie Warren, Jr., in a case involving a stickup and subsequent killing. The facts indicated that on April 21, 1970, the defendant and two others went to the home of a third party ostensibly to buy a bottle of cough syrup. After the defendant entered the house he announced a stickup. The intended victim and one of the defendant's companions began to struggle, and the defendant produced a revolver and shot at the two men. Warren's companion died as a result of the wounds suffered in this incident. This defendant was properly charged, tried, and convicted of first degree murder although it was clear that he never intended to kill his companion.

Murder by poison, lying in wait, and torture are also first degree murders because premeditation is inherent in these methods. In fact, in a very tragic case, where the defendant placed a poison within reach of his wife to enable her to put an end to her sufferings, he was guilty of murder by poison within the definition of first degree murder, even though she requested him to do the act. The furnishing of the poison to his wife for the purpose and with the intent that she would commit suicide (and her use of it for that purpose) was sufficient to support a conviction.

The division of murder into first and second degrees had its origin in Pennsylvania, at a time when death was the penalty for murder. Its objective was to diminish the area of cases to which the death penalty was applicable. The lesser charge of second degree murder consists of a killing with malice aforethought but without premeditation. It also includes murder during felonies that are not inherently dangerous—for example, larceny, grand theft, or possession of a firearm by an ex-convict. As previously mentioned, second degree murder carries a lesser penalty than first degree murder, and even if a life sentence is imposed, the possibility of parole exists for this offense.

Voluntary manslaughter is the intentional killing of a human being without malice aforethought under circumstances that mitigate but do not excuse or justify the killing. Generally, such a killing occurs when a defendant is moved by intense passion induced by adequate provocation. The standard for applying this test is that defendant must be so provoked that a reasonable person in defendant's condition would lose his self-control. In addition, once it has been determined that adequate provocation exists, it must be shown that the killing took place before a reasonable person would have "cooled off." If these standards are met, the charge may be reduced to manslaughter. Courts have held that adequate provocation is shown when the accused or a close relative has been violently attacked by the deceased, during mutual combat unsought by the accused, and when the accused actually *sees* (mere words are not enough) his or her spouse committing adultery and kills either adulterer or both.

While in most jurisdictions mere words are not enough to establish adequate provocation, in some jurisdictions words will be sufficient if: (1) they are informational as opposed to merely insulting; and (2) if the fact conveyed would be sufficient provocation if the event were actually seen instead of merely being described. This exception would encompass the situation where a concerned friend informs the defendant that his wife is, at that instant, committing adultery with the defendant's closest friend. The defendant, incensed with anger, runs toward his home whereupon he meets his best friend running away from the scene of the adultery. If adequate cooling time has not yet elapsed and our defendant kills his friend, he may raise the defense of provocation and have the crime reduced to voluntary manslaughter.

Another partial defense, which, like the provocation defense, does not excuse or justify the taking of human life, is diminished capacity. It provides a compromise between guilt and exculpation and serves to mitigate the punishment. This defense allows evidence of mental incapacity to disprove or negate evidence of premeditation or malice, thus reducing the crime to second degree murder or manslaughter. The partial defense of diminished capacity may be distinguished from the complete defense of insanity, which will be explained more fully below, in that the mental capacity involved in diminished capacity is not as serious and may have been self-induced, as in voluntary intoxication. In addition, the test for diminished capacity is less stringent than for that of insanity. It asks only if the defendant could maturely and meaningfully act on the gravity of the intended act (People v Wolff).

Some courts, however, do not recognize this defense. The District of Columbia Circuit Court rejected evidence of diminished intellect saying "the problem of classifying, assessing and analyzing the results of the application of modern psychiatry to administration of criminal law as it relates to gradations of punishment according to the relative intelligence of the defendant is beyond the competence of the judiciary. Courts are neither trained nor equipped for this delicate task" (Stewart v United States).

Diminished capacity is at best a fairly ambiguous defense with no sharp delineations or definitions, but, if applicable, it should not be overlooked as it may increase jury sympathy and thus decrease what would otherwise be a heavy sentence.

Unintentional Homicide

Unintentional homicide includes involuntary manslaughter and criminal negligence. Involuntary manslaughter is the killing of another human being, without malice and unintentionally, but in the doing of some unlawful act not amounting to a felony nor naturally tending to cause death or great bodily harm. Involuntary manslaughter can also be shown where the accused has negligently done some act lawful in itself, or by the negligent omission to perform a legal duty. Not every degree of carelessness or negligence, if death ensues, renders the party guilty of involuntary manslaughter. The act must amount to wanton or willful misconduct.

Such misconduct was described in People v Clark. That case involved a manslaughter prosecution against a physician for the death of his patient from an injection of Sodium Pentothal. The requisite wrongful conduct was evident from the fact that the physician did not follow well-known procedures, that he failed to maintain adequate resuscitative equipment, and that he disregarded the manufacturer's instructions and left the patient alone during infusion.

Another case demonstrating involuntary manslaughter was People v Ogg. The defendant was properly judged guilty when she left her retarded child with his brother in a windowless room of an empty house which mysteriously caught fire, killing both children. The jury found that the mother had failed to adequately supervise and care for the retarded child and his brother. The lack of such care amounted to a negligent omission to perform a legal duty and thus constituted involuntary manslaughter.

In contrast, negligent homicide was enacted by the legislature to deal with a negligent killing caused by the operation of any vehicle. The negligence required here need not be wanton nor willful, nor must it be of such a character as to evidence a criminal intent. The vehicle must only be driven in a careless, reckless, or negligent manner to sustain a conviction under this statute. Recklessness and negligence may be differentiated as follows: if a defendant exhibits a conscious disregard of the risk he has undertaken, he is reckless; if he should have been aware of the risks but was not consciously aware of them at the time of the act, he is negligent.

Excusable Homicide

The law recognizes that a homicide may be excusable. For instance, insanity, involuntary intoxication, and automatism may be complete defenses to a charge of homicide.

INSANITY

The law permits insane individuals to escape the jaws of criminal justice because, absent minimal elements of rationality, condemnation and punishment are obviously futile and unjust: the accused could not have employed reason to restrain the act he is accused of. The husband who chokes his wife in the belief that he is squeezing lemons, or the young man who believes that homicide is the command of God is well beyond the restraining influences of law; he needs restraint, but condemnation is entirely meaningless.

The American system of jurisprudence is fundamentally concerned with protecting a person charged with crime at all stages of the proceedings. In keeping with this basic tenet, in Michigan, once the defendant has raised the defense of insanity by some evidence, it is the prosecution's burden to prove that the defendant was sane beyond a reasonable doubt at the time of the act.

The law in relation to legal insanity has been undergoing subtle but continuous change since 1843 when the landmark M'Naughton's case was decided. The rule set forth in that case is that to establish a defense on the ground of insanity, it must be clearly proved that "at the time of the committing of the act the party accused was laboring under such a defective reason, from disease of the mind, as not to know the nature and quality of the act he was doing; or, if he did know it, that he did not know he was doing what was wrong."

This rule is still followed in about half of the states, but it has been severely criticized for merely recognizing cognition and ignoring the emotional level of response. In answer to this criticism about one-third of the states adopted what is known as the irresistible impulse plus M'Naughton test. This supplements M'Naughton's right-wrong standard by adding acts resulting from irresistible impulses. Under this rule a legally insane individual may have knowledge of what is right but because of mental disease cannot adhere to that right.

Another twist to the doctrine of insanity occurred when a federal court of appeals in 1954 adopted the Durham product test which was intended to elicit increased expert testimony on the issue of insanity. This test provided that the accused may be found not guilty by reason of insanity if: (1) he was suffering from a mental disease or defect, and (2) his act was a product of that disease or defect. A mental disease or defect is defined as any abnormal condition of mind which substantially affects mental or emotional processes and substantially impairs behavior control. This same court, however, in the case of U.S. v Brawner rejected the rule as distorting the role of the expert. The Court stated that moral issues, such as insanity, are to be handled by the jury. In response to this, the federal courts, as well as the State of Michigan, have adopted the compromise position set forth in the Model Penal Code.

This test is one of substantial capacity. That is, a person is legally insane if, as a result of mental illness—or as a result of mental retardation—that person lacks substantial capacity either to appreciate the wrongfulness of his conduct or to conform his conduct to the requirement of law (MCLA §768.21[a]). The definitions of mental illness and retardation are also of a legal nature. Mental illness is a substantial disorder of thought or mood which significantly impairs judgment, behavior, capacity to recognize reality, or ability to cope with the ordinary demands of life (MCLA §330.1400[a]). Mental retardation is defined as significantly sub-average general intellectual function which originates during the developmental period and is associated with impairment and adaptive behavior (MCLA §330.1500). This test broadens the previous standard for insanity by encompassing not only sudden overpowering, irresistible impulses but any situation or condition in which the defendant's will is insufficient to restrain commission of the homicide (People v Martin).

Michigan courts have emphasized that this rule requires a causal relationship between the mental condition and the homicide (Committee Commentary on Proposed Michigan Revised Criminal Code, §705). Thus, an individual commonly known as a kleptomaniac may use the defense of insanity for a larceny charge, but not for homicide.

The preceding comments, of course, deal with the definition of legal insanity insofar as insanity at the time of the act is raised as a defense at the trial. The law, however, attributes significance to the insanity of the accused for other purposes as well. A person who is insane may not be tried, convicted, or sentenced. Nor may he be executed if he is convicted of a capital offense. In each instance, however, the definition and focus of legal insanity differ.

Regarding insanity for the purposes of determining whether an accused may be tried and sentenced, the Model Penal Code states the generally accepted rule that if a person is not able to understand the proceedings against him or to assist in his own defense he may not be tried or sentenced so long as that incapacity endures (TENT, Draft No. 4 [1955 §4.04]).

Basically, then, it can be seen that American courts have found that legally insane people, much like young children, cannot be held responsible for their criminal acts. Thus, any homicide committed by them will be excused.

INTOXICATION

Involuntary intoxication is a complete defense and can excuse a homicide. Only under narrow circumstances can voluntary intoxication serve as even a partial defense. Voluntary intoxication is recognized as a defense only to the extent that it negates a specific intent. Because voluntary drunkenness has its own wrongful intent, general intent is not negated. To illustrate this, consider a charge of assault with intent to murder. The prosecution does not have to prove a specific intent to assault; it is a crime of general intent. But the prosecution will have to prove that beyond intending to commit an act, the defendant specifically intended to murder the victim of the assault. If, however, the defendant was so drunk that he could not have intended any such thing, the defense of intoxication will be available. He will, however, still be guilty of the general intent crime of assault. In addition, it should be noted that even in cases of specific intent crimes, if the intent is formed before intoxication, there will be no defense.

AUTOMATISM

A rather unconventional but effective defense is automatism. Used in the legal sense, an automatism is a state of unconsciousness which is not caused by mental disease or defect but by some external factor.

Examples of this are epilepsy, diabetes, and hypoglycemia. If believed, automatism will operate as a complete defense. It results in complete exculpation with no civil commitment; thus, it is preferable to an insanity plea. The defense of automatism, however, is very rarely used, and although the burden of proof is technically on the state, the defendant, practically speaking, must prove he was in a state of automatism at the time of the homicide.

Justifiable Homicide

Certain homicides are done under circumstances which justify the taking of human life. Killing in self defense, in defense of third parties, and of necessity are each examples of justification.

Michigan courts have stated that the rules which make it justifiable under certain conditions to take human life in self defense are really meant to ensure protection to life. Although this at first seems contradictory, the rules are designed to prevent "reckless and wicked men" from attacking others by exposing them to the danger of fatal resistance at the hands of those they may attack (*Pond* v *People*).

The rules governing self defense dictate that one may use a reasonable amount of force if there is an honest belief that one is in present and imminent danger of death or serious bodily harm, if that belief is based on reasonable grounds and if the use of such force is necessary to avoid the danger. Thus, if the deceased approaches the accused with his hand in his pocket, threatening to shoot him, and the accused then kills his would-be assailant, even though in reality there was no gun in the victim's hand this defense is applicable (1) if the defendant actually believed there was a gun in the deceased's pocket and (2) that it was reasonable for him to believe that. In other words, if the defendant knew his assailant was a practical joker and an extreme pacifist, it would be unreasonable for him to think that there had really been a gun in the deceased's pocket. On the other hand, if the defendant had never seen him before and met him in a dark inner city alley, it would certainly be reasonable for him to believe that the gun did exist. If the defendant unreasonably believed that defense was necessary, self defense will not be a valid justification. However, such belief may serve to mitigate the punishment.

Some jurisdictions require retreat before defending with force. Two exceptions to this rule are widely recognized. First, in keeping with the principle that a man's home is his castle and he is lord therein, there is no duty to retreat from one's own home; second, the defendant need not retreat unless he can do so in complete safety. Michigan courts have interpreted the first exception to hold true even when the accused is the spouse of the deceased. For example, a wife has no duty to retreat from her own home when assaulted by her husband and in case of his death she may still assert a plea of self defense, provided she had cause to reasonably believe that there was a necessity to act to prevent the infliction of death or great bodily harm.

In this context, recent cases have indicated that expert testimony on wife battering may be admissible to show the ordinary lay opinion, that the battered wife should have left her husband earlier, is not entirely accurate. Such experts may testify as to why battered women may react differently from what one would expect, showing that, for a woman in such circumstances, she acted reasonably.

When coming to the defense of third parties, a majority of courts hold that the intervenor/defendant has the same rights as the person being defended. Under old common law this defense was allowed only where the parties stood in a special relationship, e.g., parent and child or husband and wife. Currently, however, the rule is that if the third party had the right to use reasonable force to fend off an attack, then so does someone coming to his aid. The defendant, however, intervenes at his own risk. If, for example, the third party is resisting a lawful arrest employing reasonable force and the defendant mistakenly thinks the third party is being unlawfully attacked, then he has no right to use force against the police officers. A few jurisdictions depart from this general rule and merely require an actual belief that the third party is being unlawfully assaulted.

Necessity is a very limited defense which generally applies to situations where the compulsion to act comes from some physical force of nature. Take, for example, the case of a tremendous rainstorm flooding a small town. The only way to save the town is to open the floodgates of the dam, but to do so would cause one individual to be swept away. The defendant who opens the dam to save the lives of the townspeople but kills that one person may raise the defense of necessity and, if believed, it will justify the homicide. This principle is subject to two vital limitations: (1) the necessity must be avoidance of an evil greater than the evil sought to be avoided by the law defining the offense charged (in this case murder), and (2) the defendant must not have been reckless and negligent in bringing about the situation requiring the choice of evils. Thus, under the first limitation necessity will not provide justification for the defendant who killed an innocent person to save his own life (Regina v Dudley). An exception to this last rule is that if two men are floating on a rubber raft after their boat has been swamped in a storm and one kills the other to save his own life, then, even if otherwise it is clear that both would have died, the defense is unavailable.

Circumstantial and Direct Evidence

While certain homicides may be justifiable or excusable, the fact nonetheless remains that the defendant did kill someone. The most complete defense is one in which the defendant claims to have never killed the victim. In other words the defendant maintains that he is innocent.

In making such a defense the crucial interplay of circumstantial and direct evidence plays an important role. Generally, the lay person believes that a conviction for homicide based on circumstantial evidence is harder to obtain than one based on direct evidence. Many times in my experience the opposite has been true. An example illustrating this proposition is known as the smoking gun case in which two hypothetical situations are considered. In the first, defendant is seen by an eyewitness robbing a jewelry store and killing the proprietor. This eyewitness, however, may be discredited by showing that he really does not have very good eyesight or that he is no longer positive that the defendant was the man he saw. In this manner the damaging nature of direct evidence can be minimized. In the second, instead of an eyewitness, we have the defendant found with a recently fired gun and a bag of jewels. This evidence, although circumstantial, cannot be as easily disputed. Questionable perceptions of eyewitnesses will not come into play. A scientific report matches the bullet found in the proprietor's body to one fired from that gun and the jewels are easily and unequivocally identified as being part of the jewelry store's inventory. This is a story which is much less likely to be discredited.

In fact, in a murder case I handled a few years ago only direct evidence was presented. No less than six eyewitnesses claimed to have seen the defendant commit the murder. Yet the stories of all six were discredited and the client was acquitted.

I have explained, rather simply, some of the problems a defense attorney in a homicide case faces, as well as certain options for solving these problems. While it can in no way convey the extreme excitement of handling a murder case, the heightened challenge involved should be clearly evident.

19

MURDER IN THE COURT

Justin C. Ravitz

◇

Every lawyer remembers his or her first murder trial well. I am no exception. Soon after I was admitted to the bar, I represented a man who, while serving a murder sentence, killed the prison's athletic director. The prosecutor knew my client was not criminally responsible, but in the county with the largest walled prison in the world, prison killings are prosecuted—especially when the victim is a member of the administration.

My senior partner had handled pre-trial matters in the case before turning it over to me. He had carefully set the stage for my Murder I debut, assuring me that everyone understood that the verdict had to be not guilty by reason of insanity.

I was still very scared. My client was not. After a ritualistic bench trial, the expected verdict was returned, and that was the first of a string of unforgettable murder trials where I would appear for the defense.

Some years later I learned that murder trials are also something special for lawyers who become judges, but less so. I doubtless remember all the murder trials I defended as a criminal lawyer. I do not recall all of the murder trials I have presided over. I do not even recall the first one. But a number of memories are vivid. Perhaps the following discussion will provide some flavor of the view from at least one bench in the city that used to be known, unfairly, as Murder City.

Here Comes the Jury

When jurors file into the courtroom, they hurriedly check us all out. Some seem emotionless, if not downright bored; but all are wondering, I think: "What's this about? Is it a murder case? A rape? How long is this going to take? Might there be some danger—any hit men around?"

"This is file no. 196970, State of Michigan vs Spiro Nixon," I intone, "the charge is murder in the first degree, and the matter is before the court today for purposes of trial. Counsel, are both sides ready?"

I gaze intently out, looking for jurors to wince, postures to abruptly straighten. It happens, sometimes. Women tend to show their feelings much more openly than men. But despite some of these predictable occurrences, surprisingly few Detroit jurors try to avoid service on murder cases. Only rarely do prospective jurors say they are unable to face the magnitude of such a heavy responsibility as a murder trial. But then, how often are people in our country called upon to represent their entire community and to decide extremely important matters? Unfortunately, the answer is very rarely, if ever. Jurors exercise one of the highest forms of genuine citizen involvement in this country. Jurors know the seriousness of their task, and they will nearly always respond appropriately.

All Rise: Here Comes the Judge

The courtroom's atmosphere is designed to be serious, and properly so. However, I remain a critic of the usual courtroom milieu. I believe most people find courtrooms intimidating and alienating. This is in keeping with the apparent game plan: They place some people on high, in funny looking robes, and you are to stand and bow when they enter. They call these begowned figures "Your Honor" and people speak in all that funny talk that requires citizens to pay professional mouthpieces (a/k/a attorneys) to speak on their behalf and interpret these foreign proceedings for them.

While the electronic media will generally glamorize trials, they do not always depict reality. In the real world, I believe most people have a healthy suspicion of the judicial process.

Jurors are no exception. They are serious, and they are somewhat suspicious. Jurors are also generally curious and uncertain. They are center-stage in an unfamiliar setting which they do not control, and they feel unprepared for their difficult task.

A judge wields considerable influence over the atmosphere that affects all participants to a trial, including jurors. So jurors are given respect. We stand for the jury in our courtroom. And they are explained a number of groundrules to enable them to understand the vital process that they are about. Further, I try to emphasize to jurors that they should not hesitate to ask questions if there is something they do not understand; and, they are firmly and often told that it is their responsibility to judge the case solely on the evidence, to apply the law given to them, and to report any possible improprieties to the court. One tries to establish an atmosphere that will enable the jurors to be properly serious, but not overly tense.

The McCoys vs. the Hatfields

In murder cases, there are other variables that wield a considerable influence over the court proceedings and atmosphere. While the atmosphere in many cases involving parties hostile to one another is often charged and tense, this is particularly true in murder cases. As a colleague of mine recently stated, the area between the family of the decedent and of the defendant is often a "no-man's land." There are occasional cases where actual assaults break out in or just outside court. Such situations simply highlight the added drama and pressure that often accompany a murder trial.

Ready for the Prosecution

After jury selection and opening statements, the first witness is often a family member called to testify to the identification of the decedent. After establishing the identification of the decedent at the morgue, the pathologist will often follow.

One gets squeamish when family members testify. I generally get anxious, myself, and hope that maybe the parties will stipulate to the identification of the decedent so that the family member will not have to testify. If not, I hope the defense lawyer will not have any questions to ask the identification witness. And, if these two hopes are to no avail, I hope the still bereaved family member will not break down while on the stand.

The problem I have just described obviously becomes compounded when the family member is also an important eyewitness. In these situations, all we can do is grit our teeth and push on. Usually, it is advantageous to the defense to avoid having the witness display a broken heart on the stand; most witnesses do not want to do this either. In these situations, a judge can try to move things along while setting a sensitive though resolute atmosphere. This pain has to be endured, so let us proceed and get it over with.

Other unusual circumstances sometimes arise. The bereaved family may seem to engage in tactical displays of emotion. This is always painful, too, but it requires another form of judicial firmness. For example, one might be quick to declare a recess and minimize the impact of outbursts; or, one might, after excusing the jury, suggest that the spectator will have to wait outside until he or she is able to regain composure.

Sometimes the saddest of all cases are those where no one seems to even care that the deceased is no longer with us. "Unidentified John Doe No. ——" may be the appellation used by the Coroner's Office; and the identification may ultimately be made by a disinterested near stranger.

But missed or not, every murder trial does indeed involve a corpse. Prosecutors, of course, will remind jurors of this, and hardly a closing argument goes by when the jury is not told that "there is one witness you have not heard from." This emotional appeal, though sometimes overdone, is tolerable. However, it is the court's responsibility to ensure that a jury's judgment is not clouded by overly inflammatory evidence or arguments.

Photographic exhibits can be especially troublesome. At the morgue they lay folks out on a cold, hard slab, stripped of even a modicum of warmth, and they photograph the subject of the autopsy. Worse yet, there are often gruesome photographs taken of a victim at the crime scene. Judges have to determine the admissibility of such exhibits.

My reactions to such an evidentiary question are several. First, I appreciate the wisdom of relatively recent appellate decisions that require trial judges to exercise discretion and exclude from jury viewing exhibits that are more prejudicial than probative. Secondly, I am grateful to prosecutors who spare me the burden of looking at photos which they know I will rule to be more prejudicial than probative. Third, I have a level of disdain for prosecutors who disingenuously try to suggest that gruesome, inflammatory exhibits are more probative than prejudicial in cases where the nature and cause of death are uncontested. Finally, it must be said, that there are many times when a criminal court judge or jury cannot and should not avoid the inherent sadness and stark realities that are a part of a homicide case; and, occasions certainly arise where very awful evidence is necessarily received.

The public probably has the view that especially talented police officers and prosecutors handle murder cases. In Detroit, this is not the case. Many murder trials are handled by regular prosecutors who are not especially skilled, nor are they usually very well prepared. Similarly, while it may be the case that the homicide bureau of the police department is a cut above other bureaus, the truly capable homicide officer is hard to find.

There are outstanding prosecutors and police investigators, but they are few in number. The problem of incompetence is a serious one in murder cases and in less serious cases as well. Moreover, incompetence is by now endemic to the system itself, especially in a large urban area that has a huge volume of crime.

Police and prosecutors, defense attorneys and judges, are mere cogs in a wheel that turns too rapidly through a vicious cycle that is too impersonal to offer any real assurance that justice will be done. No cure is in sight for this troubled institution; government has no program or plan for exercising the sort of preventive measures that would help to combat the causes of crime in general, and murder in particular.

Sometimes the worst job is done in the biggest murder cases. This may be attributable to the pressure generated by the massive publicity that may be given to such cases. The police feel the heat and in order to bust the case will too often cut corners and either overlook important leads or constitutional safeguards. When evidence is unconstitutionally secured, it often becomes the responsibility of the court to exclude the evidence so that the government will come to understand that if we are going to respect the laws that we seek to enforce, it is essential that they be enforced in a lawful manner.

In a number of major cases in recent years the government has hurried to solve a crime through the testimony of a participant in the crime who in return for his or her cooperation has been given immunity from prosecution. Too often, the grant of immunity has been given too hurriedly and later trials result in acquittals because the star witness is found to be unreliable or because the jury or judge may conclude that the prime criminal is the party with immunity and not the party charged.

While these problems are serious and need to be combatted, and while the government in all criminal cases has the very heavy burden of proving guilt beyond a reasonable doubt, the deck is definitely not stacked.

Ready for the Defense

In truth, the defense is often not ready and suffers in noncapital and murder cases alike from the same problems that confront the prosecution: attorneys who are often unprepared, uncommitted, and less than competent.

Over the years a friend and I have often grimaced at the thought of a person being locked in the horror chamber known as the Wayne County Jail, without bond, charged with first degree murder, indigent and—let us presume—innocent; and this person, we imagine, is called from his or her cell, led down a narrow corridor to a tiny interview room to meet Attorney X, or Attorney Y, or Attorney Z, who says, often with liquor-slurred speech, "I've been appointed by the court to represent you." The scene is Kafkaesque.

There are a variety of defenses advanced in murder cases, and it may be useful to speak to some of them.

IDENTIFICATION

In many homicide trials the murder itself is not in issue, but there are questions of identification, which may or may not be supplemented by an alibi defense—i.e., the defense asserts that the prosecution wrongly identified the defendant as the murderer, and also that the accused was at another location (with alibi witnesses) at the time of the killing.

These cases often turn on the preparedness and projection of witnesses called by both sides, the skill of respective counsel, and the quality of police investigation. The answer to two questions is often decisive: (1) Is the identification made by a single witness alone, or is there additional, corroborative testimony? (2) Was there a lineup conducted, and, if so, was it a fair lineup or was its composition such as to be unfairly suggestive?

Where an identification case pits but a single identifying witness against a lone defendant who tells the jury he or she did not do it, an acquittal is often the result. And for good reason, too, since the government has the burden of proving guilt beyond a reasonable doubt and to a moral certainty. The jury knows neither party; the offense often occurs hurriedly, at night, and under emotional circumstances. Where there is no corroborating evidence and the real criminal was a stranger to the witness, you can see how hard it can be to convict. The issue is not whether the witness is consciously lying, but whether or not it is a case of mistaken identification.

You can see too, in these one-on-one situations, how a good lineup helps the government if the defendant is truly guilty. This is so because where the defendant is picked out from a group of people whose characteristics favor the description of the real offender, then the identification can truly fortify the prosecution's case. A good lineup is, of course, also consistent with the best interests of innocent people, who will be less likely to be wrongly identified in a fair lineup than in one that is suggestive—say, where only the defendant has facial hair similar to that of the offender, or is the only person obese, like the offender, etc. Obviously, an identification from an unfairly suggestive lineup is a powerful weapon in the hands of a minimally competent defense attorney who will use this evidence alone to create a reasonable doubt. The prosecution would do much to help itself by conducting excellent lineups and by photographing them so that they can be proudly displayed to jurors. Efforts to persuade the Detroit police department to do just this have not met with success.

Too often the prosecution's case is hurt by what it fails to do, especially in these one-on-one cases where defense counsel, very properly, is often heard to argue: "Why didn't the government, with their vast resources and their heavy burden of proof, bring you scientific evidence, such as fingerprints? Why didn't the government secure a search warrant and seek out the murder weapon or search for trace evidence such as bloodstains, fibers, etc?"

The reader can see how these issues are joined in ID cases, where the contest is "whodunit" and both sides try to carry the jury down trails leading in opposite directions.

SELF-DEFENSE

Self-defense cases are joined in a totally different way. Here, the parties come to the center of the ring and do battle in what is often a much more emotionally charged atmosphere. In these cases the killing is often admitted, but the defense claims that the accused had an honest and reasonable belief—under the tense circumstances of that heated moment—that he or she had to use deadly force to protect self, or another, from immediate death or great bodily harm.

In self-defense cases, the competing lines and decisive factors are fairly obvious. When the decedent had a bullying history, this is brought out, and properly so: it can show the likelihood that the decedent was the aggressor, and if the defendant knew of this history, then his claim that he honestly believed that he had to resort to force to defend himself is strengthened.

The formula for success by the defendant may include calling character witnesses to attest to the defendant's reputation for being a peaceful and law-abiding citizen. Local clergy—of enormous varieties—dutifully take the stand and add that the accused also enjoys a reputation for truth and veracity.

While the law given to the jury instructs that "good character may be a person's greatest asset when charged with a criminal offense" and that "good character alone may create a reasonable doubt," this testimony rarely seems to be of decisive value to a defendant. Perhaps this is because character witnesses are often unprepared and because the law is structured in such a way that the jury hears very little from a character witness. For example, character witnesses cannot flesh out the reasons and examples for their opinion as to a defendant's excellent character.

But character witnesses who are unprepared can be made to look foolish by the prosecutor. Sometimes you find a close church friend of the defendant's mother who will religiously vow that the defendant is of superior character, only to learn on cross-examination that the witness hardly even knows the accused, does not know his peers and those in a position to best know his "reputation." In these situations I do not fault the witnesses, but rather the attorneys who fail to properly investigate and prepare their cases.

While the character of the defendant and that of the decedent may meet headon at center ring, sometimes the match is strictly no contest. In some one-sided cases, self-defense is advanced in a most incredible manner. The line might be that the poor defendant mistakenly thought that the vicious decedent was armed with a weapon at the time that he opened fire, striking the decedent six times in the back. This type of defense usually gets what it deserves, a Guilty Verdict. There are exceptions, however, and they are the subject of substantial documentation in Detroit, where some years back Detroit police officers were consistently murdering citizens and getting away with it. (Millions of taxpayers' dollars have been paid out in civil lawsuits for the vicious assaults and outright murders committed by the police decoy unit known as STRESS, an acronym for Stop the Robberies Enjoy Safe Streets.)

There is another kind of self-defense case which has surfaced repeatedly in recent years. Cases abound where women have been driven to killing their brutal men. I do not mean by this loaded statement to suggest that all such claimed defenses are legitimate; but surely in many cases a history of brutality coupled with the failure of the criminal justice system to intercede in time has offered women very few choices. If the vicious and brutal bully cannot be restrained short of killing him, and if the relationship necessarily leads to regular contact and brutality, there really are not very many options available to one who cannot afford to escape to California, Hawaii, or Cyprus.

I have often thought that it would be a worthy graduate study for one to analyze over several years how many prior assaults graduated to later homicides; and to study the action or inaction of the criminal justice system at the earlier, prehomicide stages. This would not only demonstrate how irresponsible the criminal justice system often has been, especially in the area of domestic violence, but it would also demonstrate how earlier intercession could save human life. I have actually seen cases where women have been shot and men should have been charged with assault with intent to murder, but were instead charged with the misdemeanor of assault and battery.

The prosecution's response to accusations of undercharging is usually this: "So often when Eve charges Adam, by the time it gets to trial they have reconciled, and she wants to dismiss charges." The inadequacy of this rationalization is obvious, despite the fact that it is true that in a certain percentage of cases Eve does renege.

More often than not the prosecutor is accused of overcharging rather than undercharging. This is particularly serious business where a first degree murder conviction carries a life sentence. In many cases the defense goal is to get the charge reduced at the preliminary examination to second degree murder so as to pave the way to a guilty plea to the even less serious charge of manslaughter. Second degree murder can carry a prison sentence of life or any terms of years. Manslaughter carries a maximum sentence of 15 years in prison.

The "brutal man" is not the only type of vilified decedent. In a jurisdiction like Detroit, where drug wars continuously take their toll, the decedent may have been a budding entrepreneur in the profitable heroin import business. In other cases, the family of the decedent might all but concede that "he had it coming." In situations like this, the defendant is rarely convicted of first degree murder.

These practical accommodations are no doubt a part of the real world, but it does seem terribly presumptuous for one to judge whether another person deserved to live or be murdered. But experience has taught me, at least in Detroit, that 12 jurors from the community have a wonderful ability for doing justice.

The Jury's Verdict

When I preside over a jury trial, I consciously try to avoid emotional involvement in the outcome. I am usually quite successful, but not always. My ability to stay somewhat aloof is based in part on the great confidence I have in the jury. I recall only one occasion where a jury found a defendant guilty of murder where I would have returned a not guilty verdict; and in that case I ultimately concluded that they were right and my thoughts were wrong.

In seven years I recall only one occasion when I disagreed with a jury acquittal in a murder case, My staff makes for a pretty good jury itself, and in that case we were all convinced that the verdict was the fault of the prosecutor. Over an eight-month period this prosecutor managed to lose 11 of 12 jury cases he tried in my courtroom. His attitudes and outlook were so revolting that jurors would favor Attila the Hun over him. This same dynamic can be created by a partisan judge who may abuse a defense attorney during the course of the trial and, in the process, alienate the jury. I am sure that in many cases the defendant is better off in a courtroom where it is manifest that he or she is receiving an unfair trial, than in a courtroom that does not allow the creation of that dynamic.

The same type of judge I have described will also engage in a practice which seems most incredible, namely that of chastising jurors who acquit. Sadly, this has become a rather routine practice in Detroit Recorder's Court. Such judges all but say they hope the next time the defendant commits such an atrocious crime it will be committed against the jurors or their mothers.

To me it is utter hypocrisy to tell the jury that the decision is for them and them alone to make, and to tell them that you have not at any time tried to influence their decision, and then attack them for their decision.

The Judge's Verdict

In any jurisdiction with a huge case volume and serious docket problems, bench trials are preferable to jury trials because they are quicker, much easier to administer, and less subject to appellate reversal. This preference can vanish rapidly as the weight of deciding a close case develops.

Also, in a non-jury case, I can take a much more active role with no need to worry about a jury's questioning my impartiality. There certainly is every incentive to learn as much as I can about the facts; and where counsel fail to pursue matters that I think important, I will not hesitate to question witnesses.

In the majority of the non-jury cases I hear, the decision is reached with ease and announced from the bench at the very end of closing arguments. In maybe 40 percent of the cases, I will retire to the jury room or chambers to deliberate. Sometimes, I pretty well know what the result will be, but want to reflect on it briefly and to organize the delivery of my verdict.

On occasion, however, the decision is an agonizing one. One of the best Recorder's Court accounts of this began to circulate shortly after I took the bench. A colleague, a young woman elected when I was, was said to have gone into the jury room to deliberate a verdict. People became concerned when hours passed and she failed to emerge. At long last, she reentered the courtroom, took the bench and announced that the jury was hung. (I never verified the accuracy of what remains to me no more than court lore.)

The simple answer is that if one cannot decide a case there exists no proof beyond a reasonable doubt and to a moral certainty, and the defendant should therefore be acquitted. But I confess, that over the years, I have laughed while deliberating, not at my allegedly hung colleague's indecision but at my own.

The toughest cases are murder cases and cases that may take on a special community importance, or those that involve the greatest emotional intensity. As you sit up there listening to the evidence, you see the anguish and pleas of a number of very involved parties and spectators. They watch you intently, trying desperately to transmit their support or rejection of testimony. Eyes dart from a witness to the court, and back. No matter. If someone truly has something to communicate, the way to do so is by testifying.

For the verdict is based upon the evidence, and in every case someone will win and someone will lose. Sometimes you acquit, not because you believe the defendant to be innocent, but because the government has not proven guilt beyond a reasonable doubt. In these cases one tries to explain this clearly while realizing that some people will probably not understand.

This problem is compounded in those occasional cases where the court has suppressed evidence useful to the prosecution but secured in violation of the exclusionary rule fashioned to try to pressure law enforcement into following the law, the constitution, the Bill of Rights.

In such cases I explain as best I can the logic of my verdict and how no verdict can bring back the decedent whose life was so sadly extinguished. "But the law requires," I piously state, "a not guilty verdict, because. . . ." You hear the bereaved family screaming, silently. It hurts. It can be even more uncomfortable when they yell not so silently. But if that is a healthy release, a jurist should be able to withstand such an occasional occupational hazard.

Murder cases are difficult, for everybody. They are especially difficult for the accused. Guilty or not, there is a special pressure on the defendant charged with first degree murder, namely a mandatory life sentence. This serves as a special hammer to persuade defendants to relinquish their rights to trial and to plead guilty to a lesser charge. As with other charges, the greatest percentage of murder cases are disposed of not by trial, but by guilty pleas.

For years many pretended the U.S. criminal justice system was just. Youngsters learned of the cherished right to a trial by jury, but did not learn how or why it is most often abandoned. In recent years, however, the true character of the system has become so apparent that many apologists are now quick to concede that the system would suffocate under its own caseload if deals were not cut to dispose of cases by way of guilty pleas.

This is not to suggest that there is emerging a better understanding of criminal justice. Rather than moving to combat the causes of crime and cut down the relentless stream of new cases, greater emphasis is being placed on creating a more efficient railroad and in imposing harsher penalties, including capital punishment. It is in this area of sentencing where I have had to evaluate the question of compromise and principles.

Sentencing

Sentencing: a sordid subject often exploited by demagogic politicians. For years, liberals pretended rehabilitation efforts were underway in the prison warehouses of this country. Instead, the "Department of Corrections" was offering advanced degrees in crime.

When the pretense could no longer be maintained, rather than pursuing the difficult task of organizing real alternatives to crime, many seized on simple and stale nonsolutions, like capital punishment or minimum mandatory sentences.

While I know I would not order an execution because the "law" told me to, would I sentence someone to prison for life only because the "law" told me I must? The answer was, and is, yes.

In an odd but understandable way, the pressure on a judge may be most pronounced when there is no choice as to the sentence to be imposed. This is the case in Michigan where the mandatory sentence for murder in the first degree is life in prison, without parole.

I feel downright dumb adjourning the sentencing date until I get a pre-sentence report. What good can the pre-sentence do when I have no choice? But the wait only underscores the seeming finality of a life sentence. Twice, over the last seven years, I have sentenced people to life in prison only because the law so required. Both times I did my duty, threw away the key, imposed a life sentence which I thought to be stupid and unfair.

In both cases, I made the best record I could, stating my objection to the mandated sentence and why I thought another sentence would better serve the interests of both society and the convict. I then assigned the best appellate attorneys I could in the hope that they would successfully challenge this rather mindless, though probably popular, statute. One appeal failed. The other is still pending.

Other times, when required to impose natural life sentences, I have done so without opposition in the form of a better, viable alternative. While I can imagine, frankly, some satisfaction in sentencing some (unindicted) criminals to life or some unfathomable number of years, I have never imposed such a sentence with any satisfaction or without real regret. Every person I have so sentenced is a living and dying victim of some horrible abuses inflicted upon large numbers of people in our society.

What does one do with a 16-year-old, illiterate defendant who broke into the home of an 83-year-old woman, raped her, robbed her, bound her to a chair, wrapped a bedspread around her head and left her there to die, suffocating and choking on her own blood? At age 10, he had been made a state ward and placed in what is euphemistically called the Child Development Center, where he was evaluated as having "an intellectual deficiency" and being "emotionally disturbed," and regarded "as being highly aggressive, impulsive, and having a poor capacity to relate to others." He went on to have 36 juvenile contacts with the law and 12 admissions to the Youth Home.

What do you do to the 17-year-old who at age 7 had dominant household responsibilities for his younger siblings because "mother" habitually slept out? He no doubt wishes she had slept out more. At 12 he was hospitalized after being severely beaten by mom's boyfriend.

At 16 he was shot four times by mom's boyfriend. No prosecution followed his lengthy stay in the hospital; mom told the police and others she'd "take care of it." She didn't; he did—returning the favor of near mortal wounds and two days later was arrested on a charge of felony murder. There were many other crimes, assaultive in nature.

The probation officer who interviewed the defendant before he was sentenced said he exhibited no remorse and had none; the psychiatric clinic personnel, however, detected under this cold façade an insecure and frightened youngster.

What does it say that people facing years and years in prison are asked if they have anything to say on their own behalf before the court imposes sentence and the usual response is no. Would it matter? What does matter? What does one make of this madness called murder?

Conclusion

In 1979, there were 451 recorded homicides in Detroit. It was good that there were 47 less than the year before. But this improvement meant precious little to the 451 people killed and to those scarred by their deaths.

There is no simple answer to murder, or to crime in general. Surely the answer cannot begin after the case gets to court; after someone has already been victimized.

The crime problem cannot be significantly reduced unless we purposefully attack the conditions that breed crime. These conditions should be fought, not simply because we want to win a war against crime, but because the problems themselves are crying out for human attention and resolution.

The system we live under teaches children to be out for themselves, to be competitive, materialistic, and violent. "Nice guys finish last," and gals apparently don't even start.

By the time a child reaches adolescence he or she has seen thousands and thousands of vicious assaults and murders, by way of a little video box that could so easily educate and humanize, but which instead deadens the mind and hardens the heart.

Life is cheap.

Many more people die in auto accidents than by murder. Thousands are slaughtered in a country that produces cars that go 150 m.p.h.

with 55 m.p.h. speed limits; in cars that are obsolete just about the time they're paid for; and we go bumper-to-bumper on the expressways, inhaling carcinogenic fumes, on highways built with our hard-earned money while subsidized millionaires reap record profits.

Life is cheap.

People die in plants and shops laboring under unsafe working conditions because many owners place profits above people.

Nuclear reactors are built to protect us against war and sustain us in life, but more Three Mile Islands loom on the horizon.

Black lung disease, 10 million alcoholics, a half-million drug addicts and countless people addicted to pills; advertisers spend billions creating ridiculous wants; 100,000 Detroiters go to bed hungry, each night; and 25 million people in the U.S. live in poverty, unable to meet basic needs; people are frustrated, angry, and alienated, one from the other.

There will be crime, and plenty of it, unless and until we organize and make some fundamental changes.

There will be no peace until we focus our attention, energy, and resources on solving our human problems, on developing healthy human beings in a healthy society where all people will be entitled to a meaningful and enriching education, to dignified labor, decent housing, food, shelter, health care, transportation, and recreational activity.

New generations, some day, will be raised with values and attitudes that sanctify human life and potential.

20

CAPITAL PUNISHMENT
Are We For It or Against It?

Jonas R. Rappeport

◇

The end of the process of justice when homicide is involved is punishment, and the ultimate punishment is capital punishment, death to the perpetrator. Are we for it or against it? This question has been asked over and over again throughout our history. "And the Lord spoke unto Moses saying, 'and he that killeth any man shall surely be put to death. And if any man cause a blemish in his neighbour; as he hath done, so shall it be done to him; breach for breach, eye for eye, tooth for tooth'" (Leviticus).

However, Charles Black in a book on capital punishment writes,

> The law of Moses is full of the death penalty. But as time went on, the court in ancient Jerusalem, without, of course, touching one syllable of this law, devised *procedural* safeguards so refined, so difficult of satisfying, that the penalty of death could only very rarely be exacted. So approved was this process that it is said in the Talmud that when one rabbi called "destructive" a Sanhedrin that imposed one death sentence in seven years, another said, "once in seventy years" and two others said that, had they been on that great court, *no* death sentence would ever have been carried out (Black 1974).

We must ask ourselves whether the establishment of extremely rigid procedural safeguards indicates ambivalence.

The debate over capital punishment is not a recent phenomenon in the United States. Michigan abolished it in 1847, Rhode Island in 1852, Wisconsin in 1853, and Maine in 1887. At present, in addition to those states, capital punishment has been abolished in Alaska, Hawaii, Iowa, Kansas, Minnesota, New Jersey, New York, North Dakota, West Virginia, and the District of Columbia. After 1967, there were no executions until Gary Gilmore went to the firing squad in Utah on January 17, 1977. In the interval, a struggle ensued between the abolitionists and the retentionists.

The criminal law supposedly has four major goals—punishment, retribution, deterrence, and rehabilitation. Why are people *for* capital punishment? Certainly the concept of punishment is an inherent part of humanity. Death is the ultimate punishment for the transgressor.

Then there is retribution, the Talion principle, also seemingly inherent in mankind at a very primitive, instinctual level. Are there any who have not had a passing fantasy of getting back at someone who did them wrong?

Next, of course, are deterrents. Supposedly the death penalty, as a possible punishment, will deter those who think about committing a crime before they act. If not, then it will certainly deter those who have committed a crime from ever again doing so. In this manner we hope to deter present and future crime and thus protect society.

As a retentionist, Frank Carrington (1978) writes in the introduction to his book, *Neither Cruel Nor Unusual*:

This book is written from the point of the proponents. It is not objective. It is a defense of the death penalty. In a prior book, *The Victims*, I took the position that it is high time that the rights of the victims of crime were recognized in our criminal justice system. Nowhere is this more true than in the area of capital punishment. Richard Franklin Speck is today contentedly watching television in an Illinois penitentiary at the taxpayers' expense. The eight student nurses whom he murdered have been in their graves for ten years, all but forgotten. There is an imbalance here that must be corrected, one that this book will address. (p. 14)

Carrington's position may seem strong and emotional. However, that is the aura around most discussions about capital punishment, whether involving abolitionists or retentionists. Carrington writes further,

Some—the abolitionists—swear that society has no right to take the life of any murderer, no matter how villainous he may be; others—proponents of the death penalty—contend with equal fervor that society has not only the right, but the affirmative duty, to exact the supreme penalty from foul and vicious killers (p. 18).

Carrington then describes several gruesome murders. He cites chilling statements made by Salt Lake City murderers Myron Lance and Walter Kelbach in a television interview:

As the program opened, Lance and Kelbach mused about how much fun it would be to take a machine gun (or tank) out into a street and shoot people at random, Kelbach said, "You could see people scattering all over, windows breaking, people just falling down, blood running all over. It would be exciting." (pp. 27–30)

With reference to deterrents, Carrington writes:

The question whether future murderers will be deterred by the statutory availability and the application of the death penalty is far and away the most important argument in the entire controversy. No airtight mathematical proof for or against the deterrent value of capital punishment is available to us now although scientists on either side of the question have come up with their own analyses and a lively, if rather arcane, debate is raging today.

The basic reason for the lack of certainty in the statistical battle is obvious; it is very difficult to prove a negative conclusively. And that is precisely what the proponents, at least, would have to do. By looking at the number of murders committed while the death penalty was on the books and enforced, we can gain some indication of how many killers were obviously not deterred (because they committed murders).

However, there is absolutely no way that we can ever know, with any certainty, how many would-be murderers were, in fact, deterred and, therefore, we can never know what numbers to enter on that side of the statistical equations." (pp. 82–83)

He cites the amicus brief filed in Gregg v. Georgia:

There is an inherent logic to the belief that the death penalty deters at least some people from committing crimes. Belief in the deterrent efficacy of penal sanctions is as old as the criminal law itself. Just as some penalty deters a prospective offender by making the prospect of crime less attractive, so does a more severe penalty make crime still less attractive, and so less likely to occur. (1976:193)

In my opinion, Carrington's point is correct; proof is beyond our scientific capabilities. Yet abolitionists say there is no proof that capital punishment deters. We might concur with this when we read about continuing crimes in those countries adhering to strict Islamic law with its cruel punishments (*Newsweek* 1979).

In a law review article Forst (1977) writes:

The findings do not support the hypothesis that capital punishment deters homicide. The 53 percent increase in the homicide rate in the United States

from 1960 to 1970 appears to be the product of factors other than the elimination of capital punishment. Foremost among these is a decline in the rate
at which homicide offenses resulted in imprisonment (from 41.3 percent in
1960 to 34.6 percent in 1970 for the states that reported in both years and
increasing affluence during the 1960's). (p. 762)

In summary he writes,

Capital punishment may be a justly deserved and appropriate sanction in some
instances. It is certainly an effective way to ensure that a person convicted of
murder will not commit further crimes. The results of this analysis suggest,
however, that it is erroneous to view capital punishment as a means of reducing
the homicide rate. (p. 764)

Jayewardene (1977), a respected Canadian sociologist, has concluded that the validity of the research designs and the accuracy of
the data employed could not be considered conclusive (p. 79). According to him:

The debate on capital punishment has always proceeded on the assumption
that if the penalty is on the statute books, every single homicide offender
would suffer an inevitable fate. But nothing is further from the truth. Even
when the homicide offender is convicted of murder—the offense which carries
the penalty of death—the royal prerogative of mercy remains to prevent the
execution. The trend the world over has been fewer and fewer executions (p.
85).

He writes that there are two expectancies, death as punishment or
imprisonment as punishment.

The data suggest that punishment does have a deterrent effect. It compels
one to conclude that there is a minimum threshold value below which punishment is both meaningless and useless—a hypothesis that has support in the
experimental work of Bandura in which it was found that children are deterred
from indulging in behavior perceived by them as unsuccessful or punishable
only to the point that reward for such behavior becomes too valuable to pass
up. (p. 28)

We know that while the arrest rate for murders is high, the conviction
rate for first degree murder is low. There are many variables that affect
the outcome of a trial. Only about one in 500 crimes committed ever
results in punishment for the perpetrator, although the incidence of
arrest and conviction in murder is quite a bit higher.

What is capital punishment for? Many believe that capital punishment should be limited to certain heinous crimes. The Supreme Court
has made that relatively clear. Some crimes—particularly multiple

murders, bombing, treason, and murder of police officers, jail, or prison guards—are considered of such a nature as to require capital punishment. Rapes had previously been included in this category. However, the Supreme Court in Coker v. Georgia held "that the infliction of capital punishment was disproportionate to the offense of rape where no life had been taken."

In these arguments it is understandable that the majority of police officers, and others involved in law enforcement are people who are in favor of capital punishment. This is probably as it should be. These are the individuals who are on the front line, who see the bodies of the victims. They have an opportunity to speak with the offenders and have strong feelings about them. They seem to believe that capital punishment is needed for their own protection. The Supreme Court appears to agree. Nevertheless, there are no data to support the contention that in those jurisdictions which have capital punishment there are fewer murders of police officers in the line of duty than in those that do not have capital punishment. Data would seem to indicate the opposite.

Jayewardene (1977) writes:

One of the earliest studies in this connection [murder of police officers] was made by Campion (1956). He studied 24 American police forces of which 18 were in states retaining the death penalty and 6 in states that had abolished it. The study covered a period of 50 years and led to the conclusion that the data: "do not lend empirical support to the claim that the existence of the death penalty in the statutes of the state provides a greater protection to the police than exists where the penalty has been abolished." Sellin studied homicide of police in 183 cities and 11 states with capital punishment and 82 cities and 6 states without it over a period of 25 years. His analysis of the data led him to contend that, "It is impossible to conclude that the states which had no death penalty had thereby made the policeman's lot more hazardous" (p. 63). . . . The analysis of police officers killed and wounded in Chicago, 1919 to 1954, has shown that most of them were killed in the encounter and that in all but 26 of the 1968 killings, the killing occurred when police interfered with holdups, were trying to arrest or search a person, or were investigating some complaint—all of which tends to give the impression that the police officer's job is a highly hazardous one. (p. 64)

On the other hand, there are anecdotes such as one presented to the legislature of the State of Maryland when it was hearing testimony on the death penalty. It is reported that the Governor told some rioting prisoners that he would see that the death penalty was invoked if they murdered the guard whom they were holding at knife point. They chatted with each other for a few moments and then released the guard. Is this a good example of a crime being deterred because of the death penalty? The prisoners believed the Governor. This raises the question of assurance, an important factor in deterrents.

Why are people opposed to the death penalty? Quite clearly, a large majority of people are opposed to the death penalty because they cannot tolerate the thought of killing for any reason. I have been told that no prosecutor, judge, or member of a jury that has imposed a death penalty has witnessed an execution. If this statement is true, then we need to give serious thought to why this is so. McLendon (1977) describes the horrors of electrocution and the personality characteristics of those who are able to participate. Camus (1957) wrote:

Shortly before World War I a murderer whose crime was particularly shocking [he had killed a farmer's family, children and all] was condemned to death in Algiers. He was an agricultural worker who had slaughtered in a bloody delirium and had rendered his offense still more serious by robbing his victims. The case was widely publicized, and it was generally agreed that decapitation was altogether too mild a punishment for such a monster. I have been told that this was the opinion of my father who was particularly outraged by the murder of the children. One of the few things that I know about him is that this was the first time in his life that he wanted to attend an execution. . . . He never told what he saw that morning. My mother could only report that he rushed wildly into the house and refused to speak, threw himself on the bed, and suddenly began to vomit.

Is capital punishment cruel and unusual?

There is a serious question whether capital punishment is indiscriminately distributed. More of the poor and the black have been executed than the wealthy and white. Statistics support this fact not only in the United States but supposedly in other countries as well. It is my understanding that these data have been corrected for the possibly higher incidence of capital crimes among these groups so that it is a true statistic indicating discrimination.

Black (1974), in speaking of cruelty, states:

When we turn from the two usual arguments in favor of capital punishment—retribution and deterrence—to the other side, we find above all that the *cruelty* of it is what its opponents hate—the cruelty of death, the cruelty of the manner of death, the cruelty of waiting for death, and the cruelty to the innocent persons attached by affection to the condemned—unless, of course, he has no relatives and no friends, a fairly common condition on death row. (p. 27)

Black describes the arbitrariness of the entire procedure, from the arrest to the prosecutor's plea bargaining; then the actual trial; the presentation by competent defense attorneys and prosecutors; the decision of the judge and jury. The jury, of course, or the judge, must decide in terms of first degree murder, from the basis of the physical facts as well as the psychological facts. Also taken into consideration is the insanity plea. Then, of course, comes the sentencing following which are appeals and, perhaps finally, the request for clemency from the Governor. Black writes, "our criminal justice concepts and institutions cannot administer the punishment of death without a measure of our arbitrariness and a measure of susceptibility to mistake, unacceptable when life or death is the issue" (p. 35).

He continues, "To put it in terms they [the rabbis] might naturally have used, I think they were saying at last, 'Though the justice of God may indeed ordain that some should die, the justice of man is altogether and always insufficient for saying who these may be'" (p. 95).

However, Lewis Richmond, a psychiatrist, has written (1976, p. 19):

> For capital punishment to be effective and, in fact to exist, there should be the consistent execution of all perpetrators of certain criminal acts. It would remain for society to define those crimes for which the death penalty is mandatory. This certainly should include at least those crimes in which the murdered is chosen indiscriminately. Thus, society and not the capriciousness of the judge and/or jury would decide the fate of the murderer. Only under these circumstances should capital punishment be an effective deterrent for future criminal behavior. At worst, capital punishment certainly eliminates the possibility of the same person committing a similar crime in the future.

Should we make capital punishment mandatory in our criminal justice system? This would be totally impossible, and attempts to do it could not produce the desired results. It is cheaper to house a man in prison for his entire life than to allow him to go through the expensive processes of appeals, etc. It is estimated that each case of murder for which a death penalty has been ordered costs one million dollars in appeals before the execution occurs. Even in a model (expensive) prison it would be cheaper to keep a man living for 30 years or longer.

The legal issues in the capital punishment argument were presented in the case of Furman v. Georgia (1972). The Supreme Court found that the Georgia capital punishment law constituted cruel and unusual punishment in violation of the Eighth and Fourteenth Amendments. They felt that the imposition of the death penalty was done in an arbitrary, capricious, and random manner. They suggested ways in which legislatures might overcome these defects. Several determined legislatures went to work and produced new capital punishment laws. In 1976, the Supreme Court reviewed six of these new statutes. The court found that three met the constitutional test, those of Georgia (Gregg v. Georgia 1976), Florida (Proffitt v. Florida 1976), and Texas (Jurek v. Texas 1976). Three failed to meet the test, those of North Carolina (Woodson v. North Carolina 1976), Louisiana (Roberts v. Louisiana 1976), and Oklahoma (Green v. Oklahoma 1976). Of the three acceptable states the Court said, "The death penalty statutes in each of these states limited imposition of the death penalty to those cases in which certain aggravating circumstances were shown and perhaps more significantly required the sentencing authority to consider the existence of mitigating circumstances." These procedures, while not constituting an absolute requirement in every case, permitted the sentencing authority to be guided by and to focus on an "objective consideration of the particularized circumstances of the individual offense and the individual offender before it can impose the sentence of death" (Jurek v. Texas 1976:2957). In the three that were rejected the court claimed that they omitted, "the fundamental respect for humanity underlying the 8th Amendment. . . . which requires consideration of the character and record of the individual offender and the circumstances of the particular offense as a constitutionally indispensable part of the process of inflicting the penalty of death" (Woodson v. North Carolina 1976:2991).

In Gregg, they explained:

In summary the concerns expressed in *Furman*, that the penalty of death not be imposed in an arbitrary or capricious manner, can be met by a carefully drafted statute that insures that the sentencing authority is given adequate information and guidance. As a general proposition these concerns are best met by a system that provides for a bifurcated proceeding at which the sentencing authority is apprised of the information relevant to the imposition of sentence and provided with standards to guide its use of the information. We do not intend to suggest that only the above-described procedures would be permissible under *Furman* or that any sentencing system constructed along these general lines would inevitably satisfy the concerns of Furman. For each distinct system must be examined on an individual basis, if, rather, we have embarked upon this general exposition to make clear that it is possible to construct capital-sentencing systems capable of meeting Furman's constitutional concerns. (Gregg v. Georgia 1976:2935)

To resolve this problem Texas has devised a procedure in which there is a separate trial for the defendant found guilty of a capital crime to determine whether he is so dangerous that he can never be rehabilitated by currently available correctional techniques. If the decision is that he will continue to be a danger to the community, he can be sentenced to death. In order to assist the jury, psychiatrists have been called upon to examine such defendants and render an opinion. Although the ability of anyone to predict distant future behavior is questionable, there are a few professionals trying to do this. The reliability of such testimony is highly questionable.

Can we be for or against capital punishment? There are no really clear-cut, accurate statistics to guide us. There is no proof that capital punishment deters individuals, other than the person so punished, from committing crimes. Yet even he is not deterred. He is incapacitated. One fact is true: no one, or practically no one, wants to witness or participate in an execution. For that, as well as other reasons, the Supreme Court has established complicated procedural safeguards similar to those the Sanhedrin established a few thousand years ago.

Although we ourselves may not be personally involved and, therefore, need not make a decision, those who do deal with homicide should come to an intelligent, thoughtful, unemotional decision as to their position on capital punishment. And we, as citizens in a democracy, should give careful consideration to our own philosophy of what is just.

REFERENCES

Black, C. L., Jr. 1974. "Capital Punishment." In *The Inevitability of Caprice and Mistake*. New York: W. W. Norton.

Camus, A. 1957. "Reflections on the Guillotine," *Evergreen Review*, 1:3.

Carrington, F. G. 1978. *Neither Cruel nor Unusual*. Westport, Connecticut: Arlington House.

Cohen v. Georgia 97 S.C. 2861.

Ehrlich, Isaac. 1965. "The Deterrent Effect of Capital Punishment: A Question of Life or Death," *American Economics Review* 65:367.

Forst, B. E. 1977. "The Deterrent Effect of Capital Punishment: A Cross-State Analysis of the 1960's," *Minnesota Law Review* 61:743–67.

Furman v. Georgia 408 U.S. 238 (1972).

Green v. Oklahoma Mem. 96 S.Ct 3216 (1976).

Gregg v. Georgia 96 S.Ct 2909 (1976).

Jaywardene, C. H. S. 1977. *The Penalty of Death.* New York: Lexington Books.

Jurek v. Texas 96 S.Ct 2950 (1976).

Leviticus 24: 1, 17, 19.

McLendon, J. 1977. *Deathwork.* New York: Lippincott.

Proffitt v. Florida 96 S.Ct 2960 (1976).

Richmond, L. 1976. "Point of View on Capital Punishment," *Corrective and Social Psychiatry*, 22(4):19.

Roberts v. Louisiana 96 S.Ct 3216 (1976).

Woodson v. North Carolina 96 S.Ct 2978 (1976).

21

RECOGNITION OF THE RESCUE FANTASY IN THE PREVENTION OF HOMICIDE

Irwin S. Finkelstein

◇

Reviews of literature on the subject of murder are replete with examples of methods, detailed historical accounts, criminological discourses on punishment, and comparatively unsophisticated "psychological theories" as to causation. On the other hand, because much of this information is obtained from criminology studies rather than from psychiatric investigation, there is a dearth of information concerning the psychological motivation of the act of homicide. This information in turn might contribute to homicide prevention, since psychological clues are ordinarily found prior to the act. In addition to this, homicide is primarily described in the psychiatric literature in connection with suicide, or included in the general category of violent acting out behavior. It is quite evident that knowledge and experience do not allow separation of these two, and, indeed, we find that one often replaces the other, or both suicide and homicide occur together.

But the hope still exists and the question arises as to whether it would be possible to be as sensitive to clues concerning homicide as we are toward suicide, and if so what are the possibilities of homicide prevention, utilizing this information. I propose that the "rescue fantasy" can be applied to violent acting out and offer as illustrations cases where this is in evidence. These cases consist of homicidal actions either in fantasy or in reality.

Jensen and Petty (1958) illustrated clearly that the "wish to be saved is an element in every attempted suicide." Further, they went on to describe how the rescuer is chosen consciously from among those having the capacity and interest to save the victim. In addition, Jensen and Petty emphasized that the psychotic individual makes his choice as an expression of primary process thinking—one that is symbolic and less clear. These authors give excellent examples of potential rescuers who fail, despite recognition, to perform the rescue. These are individuals who, by allowing the suicidal persons to destroy themselves, are in effect relieving their own latent homicidal fantasies. The reverse may also be true—that is, the person who commits suicide, and thus puts his death at his partner's door, fails to rescue his partner from homicide.

This principle is illustrated by the reader of the mystery story who enjoys predicting how and when homicidal acts are preventable by detecting these clues along the way. To expand the thought of Menninger, where he draws attention to the paradox "one who wishes to kill himself does not wish to die," I propose that psychotic individuals who wish to kill really wish to be stopped. In other words, within the very act of violence is a plea to be rescued from the fantasies and terror that are responsible for it. Thus, one recalls the case of William Heirens, the murderer who was diagnosed by Roy Grinker, as being psychotic and uncontrollable. He wrote on mirror walls: "Please stop me before I kill another." Evidence in case records shows that this plea is not limited to that one famous example, but is quite common. A similar, more recent example, of this phenomenon is found in the writings of psychotic killer David Berkowitz ("Son of Sam").

If there is no outside rescuer, how does the individual make his choice to kill or not to kill? Does he harbor aggressive acts repressed in fantasy (often associated with masturbation) or suppressed superficially? He could express them in oral sadistic fixations, either in fantasy or during the sexual act, thus further fusing the two drives (sexual and aggressive). He could burst out into violent, erratic, temperamental acts that are destructive to inanimate objects and avoid personal contact. He could sublimate them in scientific research, as through vivisection, through police or guard work, or in creating the violent plays of TV and movies.

What stops any given person or collective from ultimate expression of aggression? We have to ask ourselves if there have been significant signs of such attempts to stop. Given the direction of aggression upon his own species as an ever-present historical phenomenon, we must answer in the negative. There are the countless battles, wars, and even aggressive acts upon those who peacefully protest man's inhumanity to himself.

The failure of people to attempt rescue when a violent act is being perpetrated in their very presence is another example of the failure to rescue on a group basis. So frequent has this phenomenon occurred in recent years that the phrase "not wanting to get involved" has become specific to this kind of failure. Many satisfy voyeuristic impulses by observing but remaining detached, as do "viewers" of potential suicides. They plead that they do not become involved out of fear of retaliation, but perhaps this lack of action is a direct result of their own fantasy in the violent act. After all, they have long become accustomed to the passive viewing of violent acts on television and motion picture screens.

In 1964, Catherine Genovese was stabbed in several separate attacks over a 35-minute period by her assailant. Thirty-eight of her neighbors in Queens, New York, heard her repeated screams and pleas for help but not one of the 38 phoned the police until after she had died.

It is not surprising that failures to rescue either victim or aggressor occur. I suggest that the plea for rescue is not only from the victim, but from the aggressor as well, the individual who is acting out the homicide fantasy.

The rescue has often been described, not only in literature but in general clinical presentation, as related to the defensive processes of the patient. For example, the patient may deal with his or her murderous aggressive impulse in a variety of ways, unconsciously. These defenses may be displacements or projective resultants; they may reach a distorted level and become compromised into a symptom, with or without the presence of anxiety. The patient may, therefore, have a symptom the direct function of which is a defense against the need to destroy an object. The symptom may take a variety of forms: denial, undoing, and reaction formation.

The following clinical description illustrates rescue obtained through a symptom-defense structure.

A woman in her 30s, married with three children, came into therapy extremely depressed, speaking of feelings of loneliness and inactivity because she had in recent years moved to a subdivision where her house is isolated—it was the first to have been finished. Treatment soon illustrated that the patient was obsessed with the fear that she was homosexual. This obsession soon grew to occupy her entire day in thought, and resulted in avoidance of contact with most people. She had been born and lived in Holland. Before coming to the United States after marriage, she had always been curious about the prevalence of homosexuality, especially lesbianism, in her country and the openly free way in which it was expressed. Her thoughts were in that direction. However, it soon became evident that she was utilizing this obsession as a defense against a growing murderous impulse toward her husband. He had previously worked for more than 15 years on a day shift, but had switched to a night shift, intensifying her loneliness and rejection. There was reduced sexual contact. Her only communication was with her extremely overbearing mother and a neighbor. The patient had never acted out her homosexual fantasies in recent years or in adolescence. When the patient worked through, in therapy, the pent-up aggressive strivings she had toward her husband and her denial of them, coupled with her husband's going back to the day shift, there was considerable evidence of improvement. Further expression of these impulses was markedly diminished.

Next we are more concerned with the patients whose murderous impulse is preconscious or conscious. The following are three cases of a homicidal act in the process of or actually being performed.

Mr. R. W., a young college student, whose wealthy parents were active members of a large Jewish congregation, had presented signs of incipient psychosis in his inappropriate behavior for many years. He had been hospitalized in an emergency once and had recently escaped from a state hospital. At all times he had objected to the manner in which he was hospitalized and spouted political thoughts in a paranoid manner. Although he was considered brilliant, constriction of his personality resulted from his excessive tendency to preoccupy himself intellectually. Many verbal bouts occurred between R. W. and his parents. Three nights before the tragic event, he had an argument with his father, for the last time. In his mind, his father had "kicked him out" of the house. From persons connected with R. W. one gets the impression that he had practiced target shooting in the basement of his parents' home. (The parents were thus the first potential rescuer.) He left the house to stay with friends, who are described as "intellectual hippies," in the inner city. He was taken into an apartment temporarily by one of these friends and that evening he castigated verbally all society, the Secretary of Defense, the rabbi who was counseling him, and psychiatrists. He wrote several notes giving detailed descriptions of his feelings toward society and what he was going to do. He produced his gun and took the bullets out and threw them around the couch in the living room of the apartment. His friends were quite terrified by this. They contacted his psychiatrist who, feeling that he would not harm himself at the moment, offered an appointment. R. W. refused to see him. (Thus, the psychiatrist was the second potential rescuer, following the intervention of his friends.) He left the apartment, not informing his friends specifically that he was coming back, but did return the following night. However, because of the terror of the night before, R. W. discovered the door was locked, so he waited in a bar across the street. He sent a note telling his friends where he was and asking them to let him stay the night. They did not reply, so he took a room at a hotel, where he made his final preparations. The following morning he drove to the synagogue with the loaded revolver, calmly entered the synagogue, and then fired a shot into the ceiling (thereby establishing all the members of the synagogue as the fourth group of rescuers). As he moved toward the *bima* (or pulpit), the rabbi said that he had known the boy and that he was sick and not to be interfered with. (The rabbi, therefore, prevented the fifth opportunity to rescue the boy from the act.) Subsequently, R. W. made a rather frenzied speech to the congregation, turned and fatally shot the rabbi and then himself.

This demonstrates that the fantasy of being rescued had been expressed and that five opportunities had been available to prevent the homicidal and suicidal acts within a few days.

A Chinese restaurateur, who had suffered paranoid delusions and had acted peculiarly for more than six months, demonstrated his preoccupation about being followed by members of the Communist party. He had talked about these delusions to some acquaintances, one of whom was a physician and another a lawyer. After many months, these people finally suggested he see a psychiatrist. At that time, the psychiatrist learned that the patient's delusional system was extremely fixed and that the patient could not move in any direction without feeling he was being pursued as part of some kind of fantasied spy affair. At no time was there an opportunity with this first and only contact for the psychiatrist to determine any dynamic origins of the patient's delusional makeup. The patient's family was in Hong Kong; and he had lived for several years in town, owning the restaurant with a partner. Uniquely, the partner's involvement in the delusion was completely absent, as were the physician's and lawyer's. The psychiatrist attempted hospitalization immediately, fearing that this patient would act out. Once working through the patient's delusional system from the ego side, so that the patient accepted the hospitalization as "protection from the aliens who were following him," the patient agreed. However, the patient insisted upon waiting a day and a half before he was hospitalized, because he wanted to arrange for the care of the restaurant during his working hours. The psychiatrist accepted this delay because of its rational expression and the fact that the patient seemed to be relieved that something was going to be done. The next day, the patient stabbed his partner in a minor argument at the restaurant in front of dozens of people; and the partner barely survived after months of treatment. The patient was jailed and subsequently hospitalized.

The rescuers here had failed to participate actively against the threatened danger during the months the delusional system had developed and solidified; the physician and lawyer finally sought out the means to protect this patient from his own hostile feelings. The psychiatrist, who initially had only partially recognized the immediate need for rescue, was prepared to protect him by hospitalization. However, the delay was sufficient time to allow for the acting out of the impulse, since it was later learned that the partner had indeed been at the center of the patient's delusional system.

An engineer had suspicions about his wife's infidelity that were based on more than a "kernel of truth." When discovering his wife's affair with the minister while she was "so active in the church," he became extremely depressed and had an argument in the minister's presence. He took a shotgun from his closet and proceeded to the bedroom where he fired it at his head. His wife and her lover were terrified yet made no attempt to stop him. When they heard the gun go off, they were certain of his death. As it turned out, he was only slightly burned, for the bullets did not leave the rifle's barrel. He then felt an almost religious relief of responsibility, entered the living room, obviously hurt but relieved of the affect, and without anxiety or evidence of his long-standing depression, pointed the gun at his wife, stating that now God had allowed him to destroy her. However, if she pleaded for forgiveness by getting down on her knees, accompanied by her lover, he would reconsider. He was feeling extremely comfortable, almost euphoric. She did so; and at that moment, an interruption occurred from one of the older children, which broke the "spell." The patient felt depressed and asked for help. The wife suggested going into a hospital. In the hospital, the patient made a rapid recovery, demonstrating no depressive features and minimal paranoid ideation and was resolved to rid himself of his wife, as he worked this through in supportive treatment. He, therefore, prepared for a new life, feeling that he could not return to her, and was relatively healthy upon discharge.

Here, we see that the suicide was a turning against the self of the hostile feelings that were expressed toward the wife and that the suicide itself was a rescue from the act of homicide. However, the magically futile attempts did thereby discharge the impact of the original impulse.

An interesting example of the defensive value of a symptom in the rescue of the individual from his homicidal fantasies is expressed by a 44-year-old university janitor.

The patient was a Seventh Day Adventist and extremely preoccupied with education, religion, and becoming a physician. However, because of his cultural background, financial situation, and severe religious restrictions, he was hindered from this goal during the earlier years of his life. Whenever he was held back in his educational advancement, he would have extremely hostile feelings toward his immediate superior and find some unconscious excuse for leaving the employment or the school situation. Eventually, he developed a unique symptom described as a variant of narcolepsy. This got in the way of his school work, as he would fall asleep in class whenever some interference with his unconscious impulses was expressed without his awareness. He remained close to the university setting by becoming a janitor, but exhibited grandiose fantasies. He wore a suit and white shirt and tie to arrive at work, and then changed into work clothes; he read advanced literature during his breaks; and he expressed his feelings about his future to his fellow employees—to their chagrin. Gradually, conflicts developed between him and his supervisor, and he began to fantasize harming this individual. He had gone so far as planning to obtain a gun. At this point, his narcoleptic symptoms invaded the work area. Now he was falling asleep whenever he suspected that his supervisor was coming into his presence. Eventually, he was fired from his job and went into treatment with a psychologist.

One should not ignore the relationship of this concept to the well-established idea in criminology that the criminal perceives his capture as inevitable. Uniquely, this is demonstrated in Berne (1964), where under "Underworld Crimes" he describes the game "Cops and Robbers." He refers there to Weissman (1961), who had described the case of a 23-year-old man who had shot his fiancée and then immediately turned himself in. This patient later admitted that all his life he was certain that he would end up in the electric chair. He had told everyone he knew of this. Berne concludes: "A nine-year-old boy decided that he's bound to end up in the chair. He spends the rest of his life headed toward this goal and uses his girlfriend as a target. In the end, he sets himself up." (1964: 136) Thus, we have an example of a life-long rescue fantasy from homicide that failed.

Psychiatrists are familiar with examples of displaced or substituted objects, from the patient's original object, the mother. It is not unusual to discover murderous impulses of a male patient toward his mother and see them expressed in many other areas. The following are some examples of these feelings and the means by which the patients handled them.

Several years ago, a 14-year-old boy was arrested after a great deal of searching for a sniper who had supposedly murdered his mother, the shot having entered the kitchen window and killed her instantly. A search around the neighborhood was prompted by the fact that there were two previous incidents of sniping a few weeks before the murder. No evidence was found to indicate that this was an outside situation; and police soon learned that the son was withdrawn, rather ineffectual, affectionless, but had at no time expressed hostile feelings toward his mother overtly. He soon confessed to her murder when confronted with evidence. Later, it was discovered that the maid of the family, quietly, over months or perhaps years of cleaning the boy's room, had discovered many objects of violence. What was found were not the usual magazines and books related to sadomasochistic fantasies, but objects of violence, including all sizes of knives, straight edge razors— even a saw hidden under a mattress.

We see then this boy had given indication indirectly and perhaps in other areas of his desire to be rescued from feelings that he had expressed. Perhaps if this had been discussed, the subsequent tragedy would not have occurred.

A 27-year-old pharmacist, single, without siblings, had suffered from a schizophrenic illness since adolescence. He had succeeded in college because he lived outside of his home, and at that time he experienced a relatively low period of anxiety. But, once returning to the community where his parents lived, his difficulties increased to the point where he was often hospitalized psychiatrically. In therapy, the patient had indicated how he was preoccupied with obsessions of killing his mother. These thoughts troubled him no matter what he was doing; consequently extreme feelings of panic, loss of control, and sometimes a dissociative episode resulted. The therapist became aware of times when he was free of these feelings of panic, would subsequently lose the specific object of his fantasy, and related it to all individuals in general; and thus the danger was increased. At one time, he was almost involved in the act of murdering another individual and gave himself up to the police. He was then treated psychiatrically for the second time.

Throughout his lifetime, whenever the impulse of "killing" his mother is not warded off successfully, as through displacement and generalization of the impulse, he hospitalizes himself immediately. He thus provides rescue through hospitalization.

Another patient, who was chronically paranoid but never hospitalized, had persistent fantasies that older women were seducing him, provoking him into sexual contact with them. He became convinced that the original woman responsible for this was his own mother and he was further terrified by the incestuous character of this fantasy. He soon developed murderous impulses toward her, which were displaced onto other older women. He fantasized that the woman next door was responsible for a similar action. He had voluntarily put her garbage cans out and had shoveled her walk; and when she invited him in to tea, out of gratitude, he misunderstood this as an expression of her seduction, being unaware of his own projection. He panicked and went North to visit an older aunt; but the fantasy continued. It developed such intensity that he became acutely aware of the murderous impulse. He quickly left for home to see a doctor.

This again is an example of rescue through therapy. Such movements toward therapy are excellent means by which prevention of violent acts ideally can occur. We can therefore see that the need to be rescued from performing murder is more prevalent than often described and may be a motivating force toward psychotherapy in people who previously would never have considered it.

Summarized briefly, the psychogenesis of the rescue in a homicidal fantasy can be found in a portion of that ego that, when forced to deal with extraordinary amounts of aggressive energy associated with oedipal revenge upsurgings, does not retreat to more infantalized patterns of impulsive expression but instead seeks either in reality or fantasy an external source of rescue. This external source can be individuals who witness the act and have opportunities to stop it; therapists who are capable of interpreting it and providing alternate pathways of expression; and structured areas such as hospitals or jails where such an impulse is mechanically impossible to express. Again, it should be stressed that this is not a unique interpretation of the "need to be caught," as in criminology, nor the advancing of a new theory concerning the ego methods of controlling hostility. However, its purpose is to facilitate further thought on laymen's constant question as to why the professional and the experienced people are not learning more successful methods of prevention and recognizing the precipitating events and causal factors before the tragedy is inevitable.

REFERENCES

Berne, E. 1964. *Games People Play*. New York: Grove Press, pp. 132–36.

Jensen, V. W. and T. A. Petty. 1958. "The Fantasy of Being Rescued in Suicide." *Psychoanalytic Quarterly* (July) 27:327–39.

Rosenthal, A. M. 1964. *Thirty Eight Witnesses*. New York: The New York Times Company.

Weissman, F. 1961. "Psychiatry and Law—Use and Abuse of Psychiatry in a Murder." *American Journal of Psychiatry* 118:289–99.

22

ALTERNATIVE APPROACHES TO
THE VIOLENT CRIMINAL

Bruce L. Danto

❖

In recent years there has been a gradual increase in the amount of violence, criminal and noncriminal, expressed by people all over the world. Noncriminal forms of violence include auto and other kinds of accidents, fatal and nonfatal, and suicide involving all ages, sexes, races, and socioeconomic classes. The high rates of divorce, alcohol, drug, and food abuse, and school dropouts are evidence that social disorganization is keeping pace with the growing violence.

The psychiatrist and social scientist are being called upon to study these problems and make recommendation for ameliorative steps. Here, I shall raise questions about what we have done so far to deal with the violent criminal, what the results have been, and about the demonstrated logic of continuing to proceed as we have with regard to the violent person.

Oliver Wendell Holmes wrote, "Every year, if not every day, we have to wager our salvation upon some prophecy based upon imperfect knowledge." Many authorities, including psychiatrists themselves (Holmes 1970), noting the level of disagreement among psychiatrists and the state of their knowledge about violent persons, question the wisdom of counting on the recommendations they have been making. We are sadly aware that psychiatric opinion lacks the sound substrate of hard data and laboratory results. There are different standards of judgment and competence among psychiatrists, attorneys, judges, police officers, correction officers, parole officers, and probation personnel—all of whom are supposed to be experts in their sector of the field. In spite of these limitations, the future of a defendant must often depend upon the testimony or judgment of any one of these persons.

Psychiatrists have been unable to resolve the issue of criminal responsibility or to agree on the criteria by which insanity is measured or determined. Arguments persist concerning the causes of mental illness and violence, and there is a lack of convincing evidence about the role of social factors, constitutional factors, the role of heredity, and the like. Little understanding has been obtained concerning the neuropathology of mental illness, and violence in particular has been difficult if not impossible to predict.

Many psychiatrists have remained remote from treatment of such problems and apply unrealistic and inadequate tests for the presence or predictability of violence even from the standpoint of what is known and reasonably certain. Thus, the psychiatrist must render opinions based on little certain information, clinical knowledge, or even street wisdom about violence. How can the courts accept such uncertain information and ask the jury to reach a decision about criminal responsibility, using it as the basis for arriving at a disposition?

When a defendant is convicted, he is then in the custody of the corrections system, which, it seems, does not offer a great deal more understanding than the field of psychiatry. Research covering the history of corrections shows a bleak picture of inadequate care and recidivism (Goldfarb and Singer 1973; Heffernan 1972; Blake 1971; Ohlin 1973).

The first jail in this country, Philadelphia's Walnut Street Jail, opened in 1790. It utilized a philosophy of penitence which required an inmate to live in complete isolation, without even talking with other inmates. He was given a Bible as his only book and he had to find the way himself. All of the inmates had their heads shaved, were dressed alike, and shuffled through the hall in complete silence. The conditions were so inhumane that reformers soon began to fight for changes in prison conditions and for rehabilitation rather than simple incarceration.

At the present time there are approximately 4,000 jails and 400 prisons in America. Over 71,000 people staff them for the more than 1.6 million offenders who have been placed under their control. From a mental health standpoint there is one social worker for every 350 prisoners, one psychiatrist for every 4,000 inmates, and one correctional officer for every 250 inmates. Of the total population, more than 2 percent of all males over 12 years of age are under correctional supervision, 75,000 are waiting in jail for trial, 300,000 are on parole, 300,000 are in prison, and 54,000 persons are being kept in juvenile training units. In addition, there are 242 juvenile detention homes; approximately 500,000 children have been handled by them annually since the first juvenile program in 1825 for children 8 to 12 years of age.

As of 1973, of 1,159 jails, only 13.1 percent had internal facilities for the mentally ill, even though over 50 percent of the jail population are men and women who suffer from psychiatric illness. What has been the rehabilitation effect of such a program for all these years? Approximately 30 percent of all discharged inmates return to prison within five years, and 60 percent of all discharged inmates are at least rearrested. Basically, our prisons are manned by a corrections staff which is seen as being low status, poorly educated, and of white racist rural orientation. Over 70 percent of the inmates come from urban centers, and 70 percent of them are members of minority racial groups. In addition, the prison system is asked to operate within the framework of a paradox; one day the inmate is a vicious criminal and needs to be locked up; then suddenly, once his sentence is complete, he is free to return to society.

The primary functions of prisons, as established, are to provide punishment, retribution, deterrence, protection of the public, and rehabilitation. All experts agree these purposes have not been realized. The rising rate of crime and violence attests to this failure as do the riots at Attica Prison and Indiana Reformatory. Both riots occurred because of inhumane care, and when inmates raised moderate protest, dozens were killed. Prison officials proved themselves to be the worst perpetrators of uncalled-for violence—hardly a positive example with which inmates should be asked to identify themselves.

The prison setting itself encourages a violent reaction, often in the form of suicide. I have presented a picture of this situation (Danto 1973). It has been shown that the suicide rate in jail (where the presumed offender is awaiting trial or has been remanded for a brief sentence) is 47 per 100,000 and in prison following a conviction, about

16 per 100,000. These figures suggest that incarceration claims many victims and does not offer much in the way of rehabilitation.

Thus far it would appear that both mental health and corrections approaches to the understanding and treatment of the violent criminal leave much to be desired. At this point instead of trying to explain why there have been such poor results, as those conditions do obtain regardless of the reasons, I would like to cite a recent case which I feel pinpoints the dilemma with which society is faced. It should be obvious that old approaches cannot deal with the following type of case.

Mickey is a 23-year-old, white, single male. He is 5 feet 5 inches tall, slender, has long, dark blond hair, wears a moustache, and has a light build; a pretty boy who was convicted of murder. Mickey had attempted to extort $2,500 from an older, bisexual corporation executive who had found in Mickey the innocent looking young man he had always wanted to be, and to have as a lover. When Mickey threatened to show pictures of their fellatio activities, the man was horrified and he slapped Mickey's face. Mickey pulled a .25 caliber Beretta pistol (he had stolen it from his girlfriend's mother) from his belt and fired at his victim's head, breaking out the window of the car in which they were seated. The man grabbed for the gun, asking Mickey what he was doing. Mickey fired five more times, hitting him in the head each time.

Following the murder he threw away his blood-filled clothes and hid the gun in a sewer. Seven days later he retrieved it. Ten days after the murder his girlfriend's mother caught them having intercourse. When she asked him to leave, he told her that since she was so nosey she could stay and watch them. Two weeks after the murder his girlfriend told him of her plans to leave him and he became so enraged that he stabbed her 37 times, ransacked her home, returned to her body, and finding that she was still breathing, he stabbed her another seven times. Remarkably, she lived to file a criminal complaint against him. He sneaked into the intensive-care treatment unit at the hospital and threatened to kill her if she told on him. Following his arrest he wrote letters threatening her again if she proceeded with her complaint. In jail, when his manipulative efforts failed, he slashed his wrists seriously, leaving wounds requiring sutures. At the pre-trial examination he made a grab for the police officer's gun and it took five officers to subdue him. While at the jail he was involved in several fights which resulted in injury to others.

As impulsively as he did other things in life, while in jail he blurted out to a deputy sheriff that he had killed a man. He wondered if the police would be interested in that information. He soon found that they were. He made a deal that if his girlfriend received the $5,000 secret witness reward for his information about the man he killed, he would sign a confession. It seemed that he wanted to buy her off, but in his sick fashion did not see the consequences of his confession. Up to this point the police had had no reason to suspect him of any murder. Further, after his trial began, he kept contradicting himself during his own testimony and told a deputy sheriff's officer that he fully intended to kill the girl if he ever was discharged from jail. This was reported at his trial later. Efforts to establish a defense of not guilty by reason of insanity were unsuccessful, and the jury found him guilty of murder in the first degree.

In the process of my psychiatric examination of him, I interviewed him (after administering Brevital). While being interviewed he said that he had killed four other people as well, three at another state prison and one like the one with which he had been charged. Subsequent checks by police officers revealed that inmates had been murdered while he was at the prison but none could be attributed to him.

Mickey was filled with fantasies and dreams of homicide and violence as well as suicide. He is a truly violent person whose past affirms that point.

He was born in the South. His first memory of his mother was seeing her in a casket when he was about five years of age. She had been ill with a cancer for two years after his birth, and his father had placed him, and his six siblings, in foster homes. For some reason he had been placed in an orphanage where he remained for 5½ years until his father and stepmother brought him back home. At twelve he was hanging cats from trees, placing them in plastic bags, and inserting firecrackers up their rectums and exploding them. He burned dogs alive. At thirteen he stabbed a teacher in the cheek after being corrected for fighting with another child, and finally was expelled from school because of his violence and erratic behavior.

He worked a little and enlisted in the army. Shortly after basic training he was arrested for armed robbery. By this time he was robbing to pay for his drug habit, which involved use of LSD, mescaline, marijuana, amphetamines, and downers. He was sentenced to a southern prison and served 3½ years. After returning to Detroit he learned how to extort money from homosexuals picked up at gay bars. Again he was convicted of armed robbery, sentenced, and it was while on parole that he committed the murder and stabbed his girlfriend.

Mickey is a young man who cannot relate emotionally to anyone. He holds no value for human life, including his own. He lies, is almost entirely violent, yet he does not suffer from those symptoms which would impress a jury—e.g., hallucinations, delusions, thought disorders, distant glances, etc. Most juries would see this man as a monster.

Returning to the issues raised at the beginning of this article, if psychiatry and corrections cannot offer this man anything except a parole in 15 or 20 years, what can be done? Many would advocate capital punishment for him, but research and theory suggest it is ineffective as a deterrent or protective measure.

Until the Supreme Court stopped most capital punishment, there were several executions a year in the United States. Most of those inmates who were electrocuted, gassed, hanged, or shot were members of a racial minority group, undereducated, and without enough financial support to obtain the best and most competent legal counsel. After decades of such punishment there was little or no evidence to show that crime was deterred or that violence lessened.

Expressing feelings of outrage about capital punishment, Dr. Karl Menninger wrote:

I know that there is not a particle of preventive value in the wreaking of vengeance and anger in the quick elimination of this one wretch. Putting him out of sight only puts the problem out of sight. Deterrence? Nonsense! Newspaper notices of what was done to an unknown, invisible malefactor somewhere out West is not going to have one iota of deterrent effect on another twisted mind entertaining, God forbid, similar inclinations. Then why this absurd, futile exhibition? If a violent passenger on an airplane seemed to blow it up, I can see sense in someone's taking immediate desperate measures to prevent it, even to the point of killing. But after a terrible, shocking holocaust has been accomplished and everything destroyed, why pursue an animated corpse and solemnly destroy it, like some primitive people wreaking vengeance on a ritual victim: Do courts not exist to prevent such mob action?

But, you may ask—the man was dangerous, immoral, ruthless, unpredictable—why not eliminate him?

For the reasons that I have just stated. Eliminating one offender who happens to get caught weakens public security by creating a false sense of diminished anger through a definite remedial measure. Actually, it does not remedy anything, and it bypasses completely the real and unsolved problem of how to identify, detect, and detain potentially dangerous citizens.

Dr. Menninger concluded his discourse by pointing out that capital punishment prevents us from exercising an opportunity to conduct research on the causes of violence, the ways it can be detected more accurately, and the ways it can be controlled more effectively (Menninger 1969).

Cohen (1968) pointed out that carrying out of the death penalty dropped from 81 in 1954 to 15 in 1964. The last execution occurred in 1966. Georgia had 366 executions between 1930 and 1964. By 1965 it was apparent to leaders in that state that the public was expressing a change in attitude toward capital punishment. Dr. Cohen surveyed members of the Georgia Psychiatric Association. Of the 40 percent of the members who answered the questionnaire, most had served as an expert witness in cases where capital punishment had been advocated. Thirty-four percent felt it served as a deterrent to crime and violence, but the majority felt that criminals in general do not anticipate the consequence of their actions and the small number of executions did not appear to protect society anyway. A minority of the psychiatrists in this group saw capital punishment as the only effective way of removing the violent criminal from society. Most of the members did not favor testifying before a State Senate Committee as they did not want to see psychiatrists become involved in the center of a controversy about capital punishment.

Dr. Cohen felt that psychiatrists and other physicians would not express approval of capital punishment, as their goal is the preservation of life which calls for a humanitarian perspective in situations of confronting aberrant violent thoughts and behavior. The public view seems to be changing also as in 1960 a Gallup Poll showed a decline from 68 percent to 51 percent of the survey population favoring capital punishment, and a Harris Poll in 1966 found only 38 percent in favor. Dr. Cohen remarked that prison wardens surveyed considered capital punishment nondeterrent to violence and crime. It would be interesting to see if such opinions would obtain today in light of the increasing violence and crime.

It appears that capital punishment offers little more promise of deterring violence than either mental health measures or corrections in current use. Further it appears that violence frequently begets violence, that capital punishment certainly could serve as such a model and has been ineffective during the years it has been used to cope with violence in our society.

What about a eugenic approach? What would happen if we gave a violent inmate an option to commit suicide? Suppose instead of gassing him, electrocuting him, or offering some other method of death we offered to gently put him to sleep with an overdose of sedatives or even heroin? It seems to me that an option for suicide would be simply a guise for capital punishment, offering us the rationalization that we did not kill him, he killed himself! A gentle death is still a death, and although possibly more humane, would certainly have no more effect as a preventive than methods currently in use. From a preventive point of view, there are many factors to consider.

Violent inclinations often burn out with age and in the middle years pose little if any danger. Imprisonment for that period of time at a current cost of about $7,000 per year might buy us some productive time during which we might be able to discover some effective neurosurgical, pharmacologic, or behavioral method of controlling the violent person. Further, as Menninger and others point out, it provides more time in which to learn about the causes, detection, and prevention of violence. Killing the violent offender eliminates these possibilities. In addition, certain religious groups which teach that it is wrong to kill even criminals hold the view that God will bring about change in the criminal, and if he is killed there is no time to let God work.

Robert Sherrill (1973) among others, discusses a different aspect of the problem of violence in this country. He presents the historical, hysterical, and political issues surrounding the debates over gun control and abolition of firearms as they relate to the incidence of violence. In a section entitled "The Trouble with E Pluribus Unum" he describes the sad fact that most Americans enjoy violence, as long as they are not victims. In one of many examples of how politicians often react with favor when other political and civil rights leaders are gunned down, he states: "We are like the old Wobbly who, shortly after Huey Long's assassination, told a colleague, 'I deplore the use of murder in politics, but I wouldn't give two cents to bring the son-of-a-bitch back to life.'" Later he reflects:

Ordinary murders do not really bother us as much as we sometimes pretend because, after all, only one out of every twenty-two thousand persons will go out that way in any given year, and, as we have suggested here, we can be relatively certain that the one person will be an unclean sort. Armed robbers are much more irritating because they cannot be trusted to stay on their own sides of the tracks; but even armed robbers have a place in the nation's heart because they touch, in a maverick sort of way, the theme of capitalism we love so much. Are they not, after all, simply nomadic low-overhead merchants with a kind of hard-sell? . . .

In other words, all the dark deeds that are supposed to persuade us to change our ways do not really add up to much of an influence. We will never reform. We will go on being what we are; and what we are is a people who are, in fact, much nicer and more genteel and peaceful than might be expected, considering our background. At an appropriate moment Chicago's Mayor Daley once cried, "My God, we've had the killing of a President and his brother, the assassination of an outstanding religious leader, and now we have the shooting of a Presidential candidate. . . . My God, what kind of society have we?" The answer is, the kind of society that elects Mayor Daley. We have a trashy society. Emma Lazarus's most famous lines from the poem at the base of the Statue of Liberty are words supposedly uttered by our patroness:

> Give me your tired, your poor,
> Your huddled masses yearning to breathe free
> The wretched refuse of your teeming shore,
> Send these, the homeless, tempest-tossed to me . . .

And the rest of the world did just that. We became the world's greatest experiment in landfill. America is built on an awesome amount of wretched refuse. But if we are trashy, at least we are trashy in that grand and gloriously anarchistic-qua-democratic manner that no other part of the world has ever been able to develop or enjoy, and it is because of this characteristic that the gun industrialists find us such suckers for their merchandise. They know the right social nerves to touch, the right patriotic ligaments to twang, the right slogans to keep repeating, "God made man, but Colonel Colt made him equal." It's a cheap, flip, simplistic, wahoo, strutty way to view life. It's the kind of sloganeering that has made us the most violent major nation in the history of the modern world.

If we assume that Robert Sherrill is correct about this country being violent and liking it that way, what can be done? Should we throw in the towel and order bulletproof vests? I do not believe that we need view violence as our kismet. I do feel that psychiatrists have some answers, even though there are not enough of them around to do the total job. There are people whose criminality and violence is predictable. Police have been doing it for years and crisis intervention centers have had to develop the type of knowledge in which you can feel the violence potential like the measle sniffers among the older physicians who would enter a house and could smell the disease.

Why have we not utilized what we do know? The answer is that we have trouble in coming to terms with our priorities. In 1965 one billion dollars was spent on prisons (Goldfarb and Singer 1973) but less than 10 percent of that amount was spent on rehabilitation within the walls of those prisons. It will cost a great deal of money to implement detection, to understand the dynamics and causes, to locate the means of control. We must decide whether we need better armament and weapons systems or better protection from our own breeding grounds of violence—a force which stands to be our most powerful enemy.

In prison, we need to make privacy for prisoners possible. Better standards of human care in terms of simple things such as toilet paper, showers, home visits, and working conditions are necessary to assist people in feeling they have a life of dignity and a future even though in prison. We need to train psychiatrists and parapsychiatric personnel and allow them to function outside the bureaucratic and power structure of the prison. Personal material should be removed from general prison records and treatment should be conducted with confidentiality so that inmates can develop trust for the mental health therapist. Personal relations between staff and inmates should be permitted so that role rigidity is minimized and isolation abated. Overcrowding must be eliminated and racism must be corrected by an equitable distribution of races on the staffs of prisons. Psychiatrists and other mental health experts can offer advice about how to diminish the air of suspicion which pervades the prison atmosphere. Greater independence and self-sufficiency when responsibility is demonstrated must be a standard part of the penal setting from the standpoint of rehabilitation.

Correctional staff must be updated and oriented toward a feeling of professionalism. They need to learn how to deal with typical problems among inmates. We have to give them the insights available from psychiatry, and the recognition they deserve for dealing with the criminal and violent person. Few psychiatrists would be able to work with such persons without having them handcuffed to the wall during a therapy session. Yet the corrections staff and the police are often downgraded and considered killers until trouble arises and they are called upon for help.

Psychiatry must consider the experience and knowledge of the police officers and corrections staff. The psychiatrist must develop flexibility in dealing with innovative approaches to the violent patient and must learn more about this type of behavior in general.

Rehabilitation of the violent person can be geared to extinguish certain behaviors and teach new ones which are socially acceptable. Eliminating criminal behavior is essential to successful retraining. Treatment should be voluntary for inmates. In fact, if we were able to remove insanity as an issue in the area of criminal responsibility, the psychiatrist could then assist the court in recommending for treatment those who could profit from therapy. He could also help to evaluate those, like Mickey, who do not have the personality resources or motivation for treatment so that they could be placed in mental institution or prison. In this manner, efficient use would be made of the knowledge and facilities currently available as well as providing opportunities for study.

In order to implement this approach it will require a shift from the use of 90 percent of the current funds for security and housekeeping in prisons, and medications and "quick Bandaid" measures in state hospitals. We need better screening, treatment, and educational programs for those suffering from minimal cerebral or brain dysfunction, as this group represents a potential violence-prone group which also commonly falls into the social loser category. We need to build such programs on a foundation of social values which expresses the conviction that violence is not beautiful even though fights may be thrilling. We must teach that life is meaningful and important, and that suicide and violence are antithetical to these values. Only then can progress be made toward a safer, more peaceful society.

REFERENCES

Blake, J. 1971. *The Joint.* New York: Doubleday.
Cohen, S. B. 1968. "Psychiatrists Look at Capital Punishment." *Psychiatric Digest* (February).
Danto, B. L. 1973. *Jail House Blues—Studies of Suicidal Behavior in Jail and Prison.* Detroit: Epic.

Goldfarb, R. L. and L. R. Singer. 1973. *After Conviction: A Review of the American Correction System.* New York: Simon and Schuster.

Hefferman, E. 1972. *Making It in Prison: The Square, the Cool and the Life.* New York: Wiley-Interscience.

Holmes, O. W. 1970. "Medical Limits of Criminality." *Annals of Internal Medicine* 73:849–51, November.

Menninger, K. 1969. *The Crime of Punishment.* New York: Viking Press.

Ohlin, L. E. (ed.). 1973. *Prisoners in America.* Englewood Cliffs, N.J.: Prentice-Hall.

Sherrill, R. 1973. *The Saturday Night Special.* New York: Charterhouse.

INDEX

CONTRIBUTORS

◇

Nancy H. Allen, M.P.H., Health Education Specialist, Neuropsychiatric Institute, University of California at Los Angeles, Los Angeles, California

Elissa P. Benedek, M.D., Director of Research and Training, Center for Forensic Psychiatry, and Clinical Professor of Psychiatry, University of Michigan Medical Center, Ann Arbor, Michigan

John Bruhns, Policy Academy Coordinator and Assistant Project Director, Macomb Criminal Justice Training Center; Consultant and State of Michigan Certified Instructor on Police Techniques and Procedures; Detective Lieutenant (retired), Detroit Police Department, Detroit, Michigan

Harold J. Bynum, M.A., Psychologist, Detroit, Michigan

Stephen Cain, Journalist, *Detroit News*, Detroit, Michigan

H. H. A. Cooper, M.A., LL.B., LL.M., President, Nuevevidas International, Inc., Dallas, Texas

Leah L. Curtin, M.S., M.A., R.N., Editor, *Nursing Management*, Cincinnati, Ohio

Bruce L. Danto, M.S.W., M.D., Clinical Associate Professor, Department of Psychiatry, Wayne State University School of Medicine, Detroit, Michigan

Peter E. Deegan, LL.D., former Prosecuting Attorney, St. Clair County; Judge, St. Clair County Circuit Court, Port Huron, Michigan

Neil H. Fink, J.D., Attorney-at-Law, Detroit, Michigan

Irwin S. Finkelstein, M.D., Forensic Psychiatry; Associate Clinical Professor of Psychiatry, Michigan State University, East Lansing,

Michigan; formerly, Co-Director, Inpatient Unit, Detroit Psychiatric Institute, Detroit, Michigan

Herbert Goldenberg, Ph.D., Professor of Psychology, California State University, Los Angeles, California

Irene Goldenberg, Ed.D., Associate Professor of Medical Psychology, Neuropsychiatric Institute, University of California at Los Angeles, Los Angeles, California

Alton R. Kirk, Ph.D, Associate Professor, Counseling Center and Department of Psychology, Michigan State University, East Lansing, Michigan

Dr. Austin H. Kutscher, President, The Foundation of Thanatology; Associate Professor, Columbia-Presbyterian Medical Center, New York, New York

Lillian G. Kutscher, Publications Editor, The Foundation of Thanatology, New York, New York

Henry Krystal, M.D., Professor of Psychiatry, Michigan State University, East Lansing, Michigan

Cynthia R. Pfeffer, M.D., Assistant Professor of Psychiatry, Cornell University Medical College; Chief, Child Psychiatry In-Patient Unit, New York Hospital-Westchester Division, White Plains, New York

Jonas R. Rappeport, M.D., Chief Medical Officer, Supreme Bench of Baltimore; Clinical Professor of Psychiatry, University of Maryland School of Medicine; Associate Professor of Psychiatry, Johns Hopkins University School of Medicine, Baltimore, Maryland

Justin C. Ravitz, Judge, Recorders Court for the City of Detroit, Michigan

Joseph Richman, Ph.D., Associate Professor, Department of Psychiatry, Albert Einstein College of Medicine, Bronx, New York

Robert L. Sadoff, M.D., Clinical Professor of Psychiatry, University of Pennsylvania School of Medicine, Philadelphia, Pennsylvania; Lecturer in Law, Villanova University School of Law, Philadelphia, Pennsylvania

Columbia University Press / Foundation of Thanatology Series

Teaching Psychosocial Aspects of Patient Care
Bernard Schoenberg, Helen F. Pettit, and Arthur C. Carr, editors

Loss and Grief: Psychological Management in Medical Practice
Bernard Schoenberg, Arthur C. Carr, David Peretz, and Austin H. Kutscher, editors

Psychosocial Aspects of Terminal Care
Bernard Schoenberg, Arthur C. Carr, David Peretz, and Austin H. Kutscher, editors

Psychosocial Aspects of Cystic Fibrosis: A Model for Chronic Lung Disease
Paul R. Patterson, Carolyn R. Denning, and Austin H. Kutscher, editors

The Terminal Patient: Oral Care
Austin H. Kutscher, Bernard Schoenberg, and Arthur C. Carr, editors

Psychopharmacologic Agents for the Terminally Ill and Bereaved
Ivan K. Goldberg, Sidney Malitz, and Austin H. Kutscher, editors

Anticipatory Grief
Bernard Schoenberg, Arthur C. Carr, Austin H. Kutscher, David Peretz, and Ivan K. Goldberg, editors

Bereavement: Its Psychosocial Aspects
Bernard Schoenberg, Irwin Gerber, Alfred Wiener, Austin H. Kutscher, David Peretz, and Arthur C. Carr, editors

The Nurse as Caregiver for the Terminal Patient and His Family
Ann M. Earle, Nina T. Argondizzo, and Austin H. Kutscher, editors

Social Work with the Dying Patient and the Family
Elizabeth R. Prichard, Jean Collard, Ben A. Orcutt, Austin H. Kutscher, Irene Seeland, and Nathan Lefkowitz, editors

Home Care: Living with Dying
Elizabeth R. Prichard, Jean Collard, Janet Starr, Josephine A. Lockwood, Austin H. Kutscher, and Irene B. Seeland, editors

Psychosocial Aspects of Cardiovascular Disease: The Life-Threatened Patient, the Family, and the Staff.
James Reiffel, Robert DeBellis, Lester C. Mark, Austin H. Kutscher, Paul R. Patterson, and Bernard Schoenberg, editors

Acute Grief: Counseling the Bereaved
Otto S. Margolis, Howard C. Raether, Austin H. Kutscher, J. Bruce Powers, Irene B. Seeland, Robert DeBellis, and Daniel J. Cherico, editors

The Human Side of Homicide
Bruce L. Danto, John Bruhns, and Austin H. Kutscher, editors